Daffs, Chimps & Giant Dogs

Pamela M. Sumner

BALLYPHELAN Press
GWYNEDD

Daffs, Chimps & Giant Dogs

I have tried to recreate events, locales and conversations from my memories of them. In order to maintain their anonymity in some instances I have changed the names of individuals and places, I may also have changed some identifying characteristics and details such as physical properties, occupations and places of residence.

ISBN: 978-1-5272-7923-0

Editing, Cover Design, Interior Design and Layout by Christopher J. Sumner

Front Cover: The Author, with Jeannie the Chimp, Chester Zoo, 1962
Back Cover: The Author, with Wolfhouse Kennels, forest walk, Denmark, 2014

Photographs by P.M. Sumner, J.E. Sumner and E. Kirkland
(Except where otherwise indicated)
E.Kirkland's photographs reproduced from unpublished & privately owned original prints.

DAFFS, CHIMPS & GIANT DOGS

For all my family and friends, who for years have been telling me to write a book. Well, here it is. You can stop nagging me now...

Also to my eldest son, Christopher, for all his hard work in turning my scribblings and pictures into a real book.

Introduction

I have many clear memories of events starting from when I was quite small. So after years of regaling family and friends with tales of my childhood, school, work, married life and children, they kept saying to me, "You must write a book!"

I don't profess to be a writer, but with their encouragement I thought I would give it a go. So here it is.

As a small child I was besotted with animals – the more exotic the better. I was born in the industrial town of St Helens, in Lancashire, so the nearest I got to anything exotic was a moth-eaten stuffed Tiger in the small museum in Victoria Park near my home.

When I was a little older, I realized that my dream of striding through the jungle in jodhpurs and a pith helmet, tracking wild beasts, was just a fantasy. So I decided that the next best thing would be to get a job as a keeper at Chester Zoo when I left school.

I never wavered from this decision and bored my family and friends senseless talking about it.

I no longer work at Chester Zoo, but I now have a "Zoo" of my very own.

I

Roots & Branches

1: FAMILY

In 1942 my parents, my sister Patricia—'Pat'—and my brother Richard—'Dick'—moved to St Helens from the little village of Sychdyn in North Wales. Although Father had obtained a better paid job, I don't think they had really taken into account that everything would now have to be bought and paid for.

They had been so used to the bounty of the countryside; but now there was no orchard, kitchen garden, poultry, eggs or pig in the sty.

It was wartime. Food and commodities in towns were scarce and mundane, so it must have been a culinary and financial shock for Mother.

Sychdyn (pronounced *'Suck-dun'*) was—and mostly still is—surrounded by farmland and woodland. My brother and sister were typical Welsh bilingual country children. They roamed the woods and fields, fished in the streams, worked in the vegetable garden and helped with the hens and pigs. They also helped in the fields at haymaking and harvest time.

Pat told me that they loved to ride the cart horses back down to the farm when work for the day was finished. As a small boy, during the school holidays, Dick would sometimes be allowed to go off for the day with his special friend Dai Jones, the Coalman.

Mother would pack sandwiches, and with a billycan of cold tea and dressed in his oldest clothes, Dick would be lifted into the coal lorry by 'Dai Coal' and off they would go around the villages.

He told me that he loved his day out, as he was frequently plied with all kinds of cakes and goodies at the houses they delivered coal to. Mother said Dick would come home looking like a chimney sweep, happily uttering all the swear words he had learned after his day with Dai Coal.

Dick was a handsome little boy, and the older ladies in the village used to make a fuss of him—especially Miss Pugh. If Dick saw her coming down the lane he would turn tail and run. Though if Pat was with him, she would drag him along to meet her.

Miss Pugh, seizing him by the head, would say, 'Oh! Little Ritty! Let me kiss those golden locks.'

Dick said that it wasn't worth the sixpence she would give him to be slobbered on this way.

Pat would say, 'Oh, yes it was!'

Pat and Dick had a free and happy childhood in Wales and they loved to tell stories about it—both to me, and to their own children when they came along.

Dick was eleven, and Pat was thirteen when they moved. They told me that they were so shocked when they saw the small terraced house in a cobbled street that they both burst into tears. It was devoid of even a blade of grass.

Evidently the move was Father's idea. One day when we were reminiscing, I asked Mother why she had agreed. She told me that it was her Christian duty to follow Father.

Very strong on 'duty' was Mother.

So my stoic, resourceful Mother just rolled up her sleeves and got on with a very different life in St Helens.

I came along in 1943, when Mother was 42 and Father was 48. So she had another shock, and now an extra mouth to feed.

Whilst still in Wales, Pat and Dick had been attending the Alun Grammar School in Mold. After the move they attended the excellent Cowley Grammar Schools, which were near to where we lived.

My sister enjoyed school and was extremely bright, excelling in mathematics. She was also very sporty, and at age fourteen was already a member of the school hockey team.

It broke her heart when Mother made her leave school at the age of fifteen to get a job. No amount of pleading would make Mother change her mind. Pat told me that Mother had said that "sitting on her backside in a classroom" or "running around a field hitting a ball with a stick" didn't put food on the table. Mother could be very hard and single minded at times, and when Pat married aged eighteen, and went to live in London I don't think that was quite what Mother expected.

Dick also left school when he was fifteen. At the age of fifteen and a half, and with Fathers written permission, he joined the Royal Navy and went down to *H.M.S. Ganges*, the Naval Training Base in Shotley, Suffolk.

His joining the navy upset Mother terribly, as again this wasn't what she had in mind when she had also made him leave school.

Dick had left Cowley Boys Grammar School without qualifications, so he finished his education courtesy of the Royal Navy, specializing in communications.

In 1947, aged seventeen, Dick was out in the Far East aboard HMS London. He was in Japanese waters where the Royal Navy were on manoeuvers. He told me how shocked and troubled he was on seeing the appalling conditions and abject poverty that the ordinary Japanese people were living in after the war.

In 1948, during the first Vietnam War, he was in Indo-China. He said that the French had recruited German ex-soldiers—including ex-SS —to fight in the mountains and jungles, and to go up to the front to spy.

These soldiers would buy young Vietnamese girls to do their washing and share their beds. They would then sell these poor girls to brothels in Saigon when they came back to base. Although the British sailors were no angels, they detested this practice and the German soldiers, as the girls were little more than children.

Next, serving as Leading Telegraphist, in 1952 Dick was aboard the Aircraft Carrier *H.M.S. Indomitable* in the Mediterranean. The Indomitable was one of the ships that escorted the Egyptian Royal Yacht taking ex-King Farouk of Egypt to Italy, when he went into exile.

Dick said that the escort was to make sure that there were no political incidents, and that Farouk landed where he was supposed to. That's actually the polite and diluted version of Dick's comments about Farouk.

During exercises off Malta, in February 1953, the Indomitable caught fire due to careless loading of fuel. Nine sailors were killed outright or burnt to death, and many more injured. Of course we knew nothing about the fire until Dick came home on leave. Which was just as well, as had she known Mother would have been frantic with worry.

It was very exciting having a brother in the Royal Navy. I loved the letters, postcards and presents Dick sent me from countries all over the world—Borneo, Malaya, Ceylon, China, Hong Kong, the Philippines, Japan and the Mediterranean countries to name but a few. I remember for my fourth birthday he sent me a blue silk dress from Ceylon, with flowers embroidered around the hem. Even as a small child I wasn't really keen on dresses as I preferred shorts, but I liked this one. Much to Mothers relief.

When I was seven I came into the possession of a large tattered map of the world that was being thrown away at school. I had asked my teacher Miss Wild if I could have it, so she helped me repair the tears in it with gummed tape. Mother stuck it onto my bedroom wall with flour paste (plain flour and water mixed together). I then plotted Dick's voyages with pins and black cotton, as I didn't want to spoil my precious map by drawing lines on it.

At the age of twenty-five Dick transferred to the Royal Canadian Navy. Then his letters and cards came from Sweden, Norway, Iceland, Greenland, The Artic, West Indies, Costa Rica, Panama and many more countries. When on NATO exercises in Atlantic, Artic and Scandinavian waters, he said that their ships would be followed by Russian spy ships disguised as fishing vessels. Both sides were up to all kinds of tricks trying to outwit the other. He married and lived in Nova Scotia for the rest of his life, and retired with the rank of Chief Petty Officer 1st Class. His combined service totalled thirty nine years, for which he received a medal, presented to him by the Prime Minister of Canada.

In May, 2014, I had an urgent message from my niece Linda to say her Dad was terminally ill, and could I come quickly. I was in Demark at the time visiting the *Wolfhouse Kennel*, but was due home the next day. I flew out to Nova Scotia two days later.

Dick had Lymphoma and only had weeks to live. Although desperately ill, he was absolutely delighted to see me. Linda would drive me to the hospital every morning and stay for a while. I would stay all morning, and she would come to pick me up at lunch time. We would visit again in the evenings. Dick talked for hours about his childhood and his navel career. He told me he was involved in top secret communications during the Cuban Missile Crisis, but I will not risk giving details in case I get arrested!

I stayed for two weeks, and Dick died a few days after I returned home. Linda said she thought he had hung on until I went home.

As Pat and Dick had left home, from the age of three I was, to all intents and purposes, an only child. Though I definitely was not spoiled. Mother was a typical Welsh Mam—loving, religious and very strict.

As well as I loved animals, I also loved books. Here I was lucky, as there were lots of them in our house. Mother, Father, Pat and Dick were all avid readers. I realized, when I was a little older, that very few of my friends owned any books at all—I thought that very strange.

As a tiny-tot, I especially loved a book of Polish Fairy Tales belonging to my sister, as it had the most wonderful colour plates. In this day and age, in the wrong hands I believe the plates would have been taken out and sold separately as pictures. This wonderful book had been given to Pat, when a little girl, by the owner of Clawdd Offa[1] Farm where Mother had worked part time. Mother had read the stories to me so many times, that at three years old she said I had learned to recognize and point out many of the characters names.

1 *Clawdd Offa is Welsh for Offa's Dyke*

2: SCHOOL AT LAST

I had been longing to go to school and in September 1946, aged three-and-a-bit, I started in the nursery at Windle Church of England School, situated at the end of our street. I can clearly remember the big nursery cupboard full of toys and games. I particularly liked the jigsaw puzzles.

There was a big coal fire at the far end of the room, surrounded by a huge fireguard. Very often the room was filled with the smell of wet wool and rubber from jumpers and canvas pumps, steaming merrily away as they dried on the fireguard. These soggy items belonged to children who had walked to school in the rain without coats or wellingtons.

Every day after lunch, little folding beds were put out for our afternoon nap. Each bed had a little blanket, and a felt mat on which to place our shoes. The teachers used to come around and pull the blanket up around us. I hated the feel and smell of the horrible, itchy thing and would push it away from my face.

Each bed, mat and blanket had a matching picture on it so you knew which items were yours. Mine had a picture of a house on it, but I really coveted Kevin Winstanley's as he had a picture of a dog on his. I don't believe for a minute that the blankets were ever washed from one year to the next.

In the New Year, because I was thought bright, I was grateful to be moved into Miss Cotter's class. Thankfully, there were no more naps. Now I didn't have to suffer the torture of the itchy blanket anymore, although I never slept anyway.

I didn't like Miss Cotter very much. Once she gave me a telling off because I had not told her that the boy sitting next to me, Gordon Bellard, had wet his pants. I couldn't understand why it was that I should have to tell her, or why she was cross with me and not with him. I never forgot the injustice of this telling off. I was very happy when, at the age of four-and-a-half, I went up into Miss Marley's class.

Miss Marley had the most well behaved class in the school. Any boy that had the courage to misbehave would have the blackboard duster thrown at him. More often than not, this boy would be Billy Parr.

Billy was a big boy for his age, but sucked his left thumb. He continued to do so all the way through junior school. I was always fascinated by this one stunted, clean, bright-pink digit compared to the other normal-sized, dirty ones. None of us would have dared comment or make fun of the thumb sucking, as even at the age of five, Billy was built like a night club bouncer.

Any boy that did happen to get hit with the duster would shout 'Ow!'—as it was a big block of wood with a thick piece of felt stuck onto it. There is no doubt it would have hurt enough to make them cry, but they would pretend to be brave in front of their friends. I am sure if any of my class mates had complained to their parents, they would have been told 'Serve you right!'—then got another whack for misbehaving Nowadays, Miss Marley would be sacked and prosecuted for child abuse, but back then we just accepted the discipline as normal.

If you were willing to learn, Miss Marley would take the time to explain things to you. I loved her. Knowing how desperate I was to learn to read, she taught me phonics. The penny dropped almost immediately. Any words I couldn't spell out phonetically, I could remember. My comprehension was good, so after once being told what the words were, within a few weeks I was zooming along.

Every week, Miss Marley would bring down two different books from the junior school and let me take them home for the week. I read and re-read them over the week, and still remember some of my favourites: *Orlando the Marmalade Cat*, *Rupert the Bear*, *Wolf Story*, *Adventure Stories for Little Children*, *The Moomins and the Great Flood*, *When We Were Very Young* and *Now We Are Six* by A. A. Milne, *The Daffodil Book of Poetry for Little Children*, *The Faraway Tree* stories by Enid Blyton and many more.

I would curl up in Mothers big chair after tea and just lose myself in the stories. I became a real pain to family and friends when out and about, as now everything had to be read—shop names, street signs, adverts, names on vans; even the writing stamped on the grids in the gutter. Every now and then, Father would buy cheap second-hand books for me and some were a little 'tatty' to say the least. Mother was not too happy about Fathers acquisitions, as she thought I would catch some dreaded disease from them.

At break time each morning, Miss Marley would go into the tiny kitchen just off from the classroom and make Horlicks for the whole class. It was only made with water and was totally revolting. I would pass my full mug to my friend Leslie, who thought it was delicious. Good old Les! He came up trumps for me all the way through junior school in many different situations. He lived next door to us and was like a brother. I loved him dearly.

Once a week the nursery and infant children would form a queue. Each child in turn was given a dessert-spoon of cod liver oil, followed by a spoonful of concentrated orange juice. More than often than not, I would be standing behind a child that smelled of pee. I would try to hold my breath, which wasn't a good idea, for when I finally had to breathe I sucked in twice as much of the aroma. In between each child, the communal spoon was just swished about in a jug of cold water. I shudder to think how many germs were on that spoon; it was like a scene from *Oliver Twist*. I was violently sick after my one and only time of tasting the foul stuff. I very rarely told Mother about anything that happened at school, but this was just too terrible to bear without complaining. How the other children could take Cod Liver Oil without retching is unbelievable.

Mother–God bless her!–went up to the school to tell Miss Cotter that I didn't need the Cod Liver Oil, as my diet was perfectly adequate. She was a wonderful and inventive cook with the limited ingredients available at the time. Although we were luckier than most. Periodically, fresh vegetables, fruit, eggs and the occasional chicken, rabbit or lump of ham would come our way from the Uncles and Aunts in Wales.

When I was about three years old, we were shopping in town one day when Mother heard that the Co-op butcher had rabbits for sale. As she was registered with the Co-op, she joined the extremely long queue outside the shop. We queued for what seemed like hours, and had almost reached the front, when Mother realized I had disappeared. Looking around she saw me across the road, staring into the toyshop window. I must have become bored standing and waiting—people must have spent half their lives queuing in the '40s.

Mother had to leave the queue to come to get me. It was one of the few occasions when I received a good smacking. She really made me dance, as she whacked me on the backs of my legs. Poor Mother! She must have been frantic. After standing for hours, not only had she missed the chance of purchasing some decent, and much needed meat—but I had crossed an extremely busy road and was lucky not to have been knocked down.

Mother was very generous with the bounty we received from the Uncles and Aunts, and would share it with the neighbours. Her 'Christian duty' wasn't just talk, but a real and positive part of her life. She was respected by the neighbours, but there was always a little reserve on her part. Everyone in the street called each other by their first names, but Mother was always Mrs. Logan, even to her friends from church.

Mother also pickled, preserved and jammed any surplus and our pantry shelves were full of very colourful bottles and jars. I especially loved her rhubarb and ginger jam. Spread thickly on the crust of a freshly baked loaf it was heavenly. If I had a cold, or a sore throat, a tablespoon of her black currant jam dissolved in a glass of hot water cured all ills. After I had drunk it, I would eat all the black bits left at the bottom of the glass with a spoon.

At school, just before lunch time every day, Miss Marley would hand me a small black shopping bag and a little purse containing a shilling. I would go on my errand to Tarran's Off-Licence, opposite the school. Inside, after handing over the purse to Mrs Tarran, I would ask for a bottle of ginger beer. Then with the change safely in the purse, I would take bag, purse and ginger beer back to school. Miss Marley would drink it with her lunch. One day I told her that Mother made ginger beer, so she gave me a little sip of hers to compare.

I said, 'Mother's tastes much nicer.'

She replied, 'I don't doubt for a minute that it does.'

When the little ones in the nursery woke from their nap in the afternoons, Miss Marley would send through those of us who knew how to tie shoe laces to help them on with their shoes. Quite a lot of the children wore canvas pumps during both Summer and Winter, very often without socks. Some of the children just had a piece of elastic tied through the last two eyelets, so they could just slip their pumps on and off. Many of these so called 'little ones' were the same age as me, and in the case of the Kellys and the Parrs, twice my size. They certainly didn't look undernourished, unlike the poor Wardle twins, Pauline and Tommy.

Shortly after I joined Miss Marley's Class, Mother had obtained a job as one of the school's 'dinner ladies'. Windle School was too small to have its own canteen, so all the children had to walk the half mile or so to St Mary's Secondary School dinner hall. Like me, I suppose many of the other children were receiving free meals. Unlike me though, for many it would probably be their only hot meal of the day.

At lunch time, Mother and other dinner ladies would lead a crocodilian line of children past our house, on the way to the dinner hall. On some days, Mother would make the children stop and wait while she dashed across the street into our house. There she would pick up the ointment and strips of clean cotton sheeting she had left standing ready. These were for Pauline and Tommy Wardle's poor feet and toes, as they often wore old, badly fitting shoes without socks. The constant slipping up and down caused broken skin and blisters.

Mother would quickly apply some of her special homemade Marigold ointment to their heels and toes, then bandage them with the strips of clean cotton sheet. The crocodile of children would then continue on to St Mary's. I know Mother worried desperately about these two poor little souls. Years later she told me that she had mentioned her concern about the twins to the teachers, but was told there wasn't much the school could do other than sending them to the school clinic.

The Wardle twins always had *Gentian Violet* around their mouths for their Impetigo, and Pauline always wore a head-scarf, as their heads were kept shaved because of head lice. They were just like two little waifs from a Dickens' novel. I remember one day Pauline threw her arms around Mother's neck and kissed her face as her feet were being bandaged, and Mother hugged her in return. No one else wanted to touch them or sit next to them—including me, I am ashamed to say. Mother could be a tartar at times, but she was very gentle and caring to anyone in need. I have often wondered how the twins fared in the world when they left junior school.

On arrival at the dinner hall, we sometimes had to wait outside for a while if the pupils from St Mary's Secondary School hadn't finished eating. If it was raining, or very cold, we would be allowed inside but had to stand in a line against the wall. I hated having to do this, as the Secondary pupils seemed large and intimidating. I expect they were annoyed that they had to gulp down their dinners and vacate the canteen early just for us.

I can still remember the smell of that dining hall and the ghastly food that was served. Although it was post-war and there were still food shortages, there was no excuse for it being so badly cooked. Our potatoes and vegetables were boiled to death, until they were practically transparent. We were served mutton mince that smelled of rancid old ram, slopped all over mashed potato that resembled *Gloy Glue*. The fish was so dry and over cooked, it was hard to swallow. Our gravy, poured from a huge, chipped enamel jug, used to set solid as soon as it hit our plates. When having sliced Spam, it was warmed up for so long that all the edges were hard and curled up. We got horrible liver and onions, with liver so tough it was like shoe leather. The steak and kidney pie was a joke—it was 1% steak and 99% kidney. Even today, I still detest the smell of kidney.

Then there were the puddings—apple pie with soggy pastry, bullet sago with jam, rice pudding with jam, semolina with jam. Jelly so stiff you could hardly get your spoon into it, and when you did manage it, the lump you had excavated had to be chewed. Sponge pudding so dry that it had to be washed down with water. Lumpy custard with skin. The rice pudding at least was eatable, and I could tolerate the custard if there wasn't any skin in my portion. Last, but not least, was the blancmange, which came in two colours—beige and dirty pink.

The few of us who were used to good wholesome cooking at home would pick at our food, then slide our plates down to Billy Parr and Dennis Kelly at the end of the table. They would devour with gusto any left overs that were put before them—even the bits of un-chewable, gristly meat that had actually been in our mouths and left on the side of our plates. Thanks to Billy and Dennis, our table always had the cleanest plates in the dining hall.

I stopped having school dinners when I was about eight. Instead, Mother would drop me off at home as the lunch-time 'crocodile' went past, then she would pick me up on the way back from the dinner hall. At home I would find sandwiches and a flask of cocoa she had made for me before she went to work. If the weather was cold there was always a good fire in the kitchen range, banked up with 'slack'.[1] A couple of large shovelfuls on top of a good fire would form a hard crust. This made the fire underneath last for ages. When I came home, I'd give this a good rattle around with the poker. This would break the crusted top, and the fire would blaze away again.

We had a big fireguard that fitted right around the range, and with

1 *Tiny pieces of coal and coal dust, dampened with water*

the fire revived, I would sit on a cushion with my back against it, eating my sandwiches and reading my latest book. I loved being on my own at dinner time. The hour seemed to go so quickly that I was always surprised when Mother knocked on the door for me to go back to school.

On the rare occasion that I was poorly enough to stay off school, I would be tucked into Mother's big chair in front of the fire. She would leave sandwiches and a slice of fruit cake for my lunch, and cocoa or milk to drink. In the chair, I would sleep, read or do a jigsaw puzzle. I had a board that Father had made, that fitted across and over the arms of the chair. He had cut a half-moon shape into the edge where my chest was, and had put a raised edge all the way around so my puzzle pieces couldn't fall off. It was marvellous and I loved it. The board was very stable and it left plenty of room for me to sit comfortably in the chair. I had strict instructions to only get out of the chair if I needed to go to the toilet. These instructions were followed to the letter, as it never occurred to me to do otherwise. Mother must have been so worried about leaving me while she was out working—Father had died just before I was seven, and she had to work so very hard now to keep us.

3: MOTHER

My Grandpa had a Market Garden at The Green in Northop, North Wales. It was here in September 1901 that my mother, Marjorie Rose Oldcorn, was born—the eighth of ten children. She attended the little village school and hated it. Being left handed, she was forced to write with her right hand. She frequently received a rap across the knuckles from a large wooden ruler if her teacher Miss Price saw she had reverted to using her left hand. Sometimes Miss Price would tie mothers left hand behind her back, as there are only so many times you can hit a little girl across the knuckles without crippling her. Miss Price had a speech impediment and talked through her nose: 'Nyou shnupid nlittle girl Nmarjorie', she would shout.

Mother would tell me tales of her time at Northop School and make me laugh when she talked like Miss Price. She was so brutalized at school, I really think it affected her view on education.

There was only one earth lavatory for all the children and at lunch time some of the mothers would bring a chamber pot for their children to use, shouting through the gate, 'Mammy's brought the piss pot!'

One of the Mothers would shout, 'Roger come and get your titty!'

Roger was still being breast fed at the age of five. Mother said he lived at one of the big farms and was a pampered only child. Infant sons of wealthier families were 'frocked' until the age of five, meaning they wore frocks instead of trousers. They weren't 'breeched' until after this age, or sometimes a little older. I wonder at what age Roger's doting mother let the poor little soul start to wear trousers?

Mother and her siblings had a very hard, but mainly happy childhood—all things considered—as Granny was a darling and very loving. Even from being quite small, they all had to help with the gardens, pigs, hens and geese. When Grandpa had a big order for poultry, they had to also help pluck and dress the birds.

Some days they barely had enough to eat. Every day the younger ones would wait with a piece of bread to wipe round Grandpas plate, after he had finished his always substantial breakfast and dinner. The children lived on porridge, potatoes, bread, milk and the occasional egg during the week, but on Sundays they had potatoes and vegetables with bacon or a small portion of chicken.

Although there was an abundance of fruit and vegetables, Grandpa wasn't over-generous with the produce he brought from the gardens into the house. What he did bring in would be the marked or bruised items he couldn't sell. In those days the man of the house expected to be well fed, regardless of wife and children, and his word was law. The children would 'scrump' the fallen fruit that was lying in the grass, praying they would not be caught. They would take it to their 'den' to eat. The den was in a huge holly bush and they would have to wriggle on their tummies to get into the hollow part in the middle.

Mother was quite frightened of Grandpa, because if he thought any of the children had been naughty he would shut them in the cupboard under the stairs. It was no wonder that for the rest her life, Mother hated enclosed spaces and would never use a lift.

Every morning before they went to school Mother, and her sister 'Bloss', would have to thread sewing needles with white and black thread, then put them in the pin cushion that was fastened on the arm of their mother's rocking chair. My Granny was long sighted and couldn't see to thread the needles herself. Having the girls do this for her meant that when breast feeding baby Rupert, who would be securely wrapped in her shawl, she could also do some sewing and mending.

There were six girls: Mary ('Polly'), Winifred ('Win'), Audrey ('Dede'), Kathleen ('Bloss'), my mother Marjorie and Milly. All of them went into service when they left school.

There also four boys: William, who was deaf and dumb worked with Grandpa. James was a valet for the Bishop of Bath and Wells and was killed in World War I, at the Battle of Cambrai. Henry ('Harry') joined the army, then worked at Courtaulds[1] for many years. He had a wonderful garden with greenhouses full of produce and plants. Rupert was head gardener on an estate in Devon, then later on an estate on the Wirral. As adults, all of them were keen gardeners, even if some of them had very little space to grow anything. Aunty Polly's two sons, Michael and William, became head gardeners on the Royal Estates (At Sandringham and Windsor respectively I believe).

I loved to visit Aunty Win and Uncle Vern, who then lived in a large first floor flat in Aquinas Street in London S.E.1. Though if the truth were told, it was the huge wooden box of lead farmyard figures I was

1 *Courtaulds ran a number of textile and yarn processing factories and mills in Flintshire.*

really interested in.

I could hardly wait for Aunty Win to say, 'Would you like to play with the farm animals Pammy?'

The balcony, and every step of the fire escape down to the ground floor, would be completely festooned with boxes and pots full of lovely plants and flowers. You could just about get down the steps to the tiny back garden, and I can remember as a small child looking up at the fire escape. As young as I was, I realized that the display was something very special.

Mother missed her lovely garden when she moved from Wales to the terraced house in St Helens. The only outdoor space it had was a brick paved back yard. She dug up some of the bricks to make a narrow border the length of the yard.

Once, when I was a small child, Uncle Harry sent Mother a dozen Gladioli corms to plant in the yard. Poor Mother had to practically breast feed them to get them to grow, as the soil was so poor. But she persevered and won. After they flowered, I presented her with a picked bunch of her precious gladioli. She burst into tears. I couldn't understand why she was upset. She made me promise not to pick anymore flowers as she told me she liked them growing in the garden best.

There were no 'Garden Centres' in those days, but she wouldn't have been able to afford compost even if there had been. Only Marigolds, Asters and Nasturtiums grew well in the poor soil. One day she acquired some wood and panes of glass from somewhere—she probably bartered something for them. She asked a neighbour to build a veranda onto the back of the house. Over the years she filled this with many different varieties of her beloved Fuchsias. Any cuttings she took and planted grew like billy-o.

As adults, we children would buy her Hyacinth and Narcissi bulbs, or Fuchsia varieties that she didn't have, as birthday presents.

Before her lunch time 'dinner lady' job, Mother had a cleaning job. For three days a week she worked from nine until eleven at different houses, all within walking distance from home. I remember most of the people she cleaned for, because during the school holidays when I was small I had to go with her. Of all Mother's employers, Miss March was one of my favourites.

Miss Marsh was a tall, regal lady who lived in a lovely big Victorian house on Cowley Hill Lane. It was absolutely full of antiques and display cabinets containing beautiful china. I liked to sit and watch while the china was dusted, and occasionally washed. Sometimes Miss Marsh would come and sit by me and tell me all about the china. I especially loved the little Meissen figures, and would hold my breath in case Mother dropped them. Many of the facts Miss Marsh related to me were absorbed by my receptive little brain and stored in the 'General Knowledge' compartment.

Miss Marsh once let me borrow a lovely silver chamber stick, when at the age of ten I played the young Queen Victoria in a history pageant at school. On performance day, dressed in my very best nightie, with my hair loose down my back, I held the candlestick aloft. In my best Lancashire accent, that had just a tinge of Welsh, I delivered the line 'Ma-ma, Ma-ma, they have come to tell me that I am Queen!'

For a while, Mother also cleaned for a school teacher and his family twice a week and I recall going with her once or twice. They had every gadget that was available to buy at the time, including a Television, which I thought was amazing. The house looked like a rubbish tip and the kitchen was just left to fester between Mother's visits, so she did not work for them very long! She said that they might have all the latest gadgets but they lived like pigs. Mother so rarely made derogatory comments about anyone that I knew she must have found them truly disgusting.

On two evenings a week, Mother cleaned at the Refuge Assurance Offices in the town centre and also at an Architects premises in the same building. I would go with her on Friday evenings as there was no school the next day. I liked the swivel chair in the manager's office at the Refuge and would wind it up as far as it would go, then jump on to get it spinning. It would slowly wind down to the floor again if I kept pushing with my feet against the leg of the desk. I would empty the ash trays and collect the cups and wash them. The kitchen was always left dirty and untidy, so Mother was permanently disgusted with the state the place was left in.

In the Architects' offices I loved looking at the models of the projects they were working on. To help I would empty the waste paper baskets. Very often I would find stubs of coloured pencils that had been thrown away, which I wanted to take home. My totally honest Mother would not let me have them until she had asked permission, so she left a little note on one of the desks. On her next visit, a reply had been left to say she could have anything that was thrown away. From that point on, the pencil stubs miraculously started to get longer. After a while I had a wonderful collection of top quality pencils!

Sometimes architectural plans were thrown away too. Most of them were on linen and had been treated with something to make the material stiff. Mother would take these home and boil them until they were soft and clean. Now she had material to work with, she would make pillow cases or pram sheets, stitching them on her hand operated *Singer* sewing machine. The machine was her engagement present from Father—she had asked for it instead of a ring. From being tiny, I could thread the machine and fill the bobbins with cotton for her and from the age of five or so I was taught to use it properly.

There were other cleaning ladies in the office building who would gather for a natter when they had a tea break. One day, Mother gave one of the ladies a jar of goose grease for her bad chest. A while later she told Mother it hadn't done her any good and that it tasted horrible. Mother pointed out that the reason it tasted horrible was because it had camphorated oil in it, and that she was supposed to rub it on her chest not swallow it. I found this extremely funny. It took one of Mothers special withering looks to turn my laughter into the pretence of a coughing fit.

Every year, for a few weeks before Christmas, any spare hours Mother had would be spent plucking poultry, sitting at the back of Fishwick's Grocers Shop in North Road. It was freezing cold in the back room and all she had to take the chill out of the air was an old paraffin heater. Her thumbs and fore fingers would be raw from the cold and constant plucking, her feet frozen from the chill of the concrete floor. It is a wonder she survived the cold and the paraffin fumes. All of this she did just to make a little extra money for Christmas.

Every Wednesday afternoon, from three until four, was Mother's bible class at the church hall. After school I would slip into the meeting to sit on the vacant chair that had been left for me between Mother and her friend, Mrs. Smith. Mrs. Smith was very fond of quoting proverbs but always got them muddled up:

'Better never late, Pam. Better never late!'

'A bird in the tree is better than in the hand.'

'A sow's ear is not a silk purse.'

'Want no waste, Pam. Want no waste!'

When I was old enough to know the correct sayings I found it very difficult to keep a straight face. There were many more of course—some of the longer ones were hilarious—but I cannot recall them now. Mrs. Smith always put on a very serious expression when imparting her wisdom, bless her heart. Along with many other silly sayings we have picked up over the years, Mrs. Smith's mutilated proverbs are now family favourites.

On Thursday afternoons, Mother cleaned for the Miss Mills who had a newsagents and sweet shop quite near to school. I would go to the shop after school to wait for her, and would receive a glass of milk and chocolate biscuit, which were always there waiting for me. The Miss Mills would put a tall stool behind the shop counter for me, where I could sit and watch the customers whilst waiting for Mother to finish her work. When I was older I was allowed to take money from the customers and put it into the till. It was wonderful to play 'real shop' instead of 'pretend shop'. At Christmas I was always given a Liquorice selection box, which I loved. Sweets were still rationed, so this was a real treat. Mother always received a box of *Yardley's* Lavender Soap and Talcum Powder. I still love Lavender as it reminds me of Mother, and my sister's children also say the smell reminds them of their Nan. The Miss Mills were two old dears who were very kind to Mother and me.

Cooper St, were we lived, was a very long street with eight other streets running vertically across it. On almost every corner was a grocers, pub, newsagents or chip shop. Some were a little 'grotty' to say the least, so Mother did her shopping at Hawkins a few streets away, which was always spotlessly clean and consequently up to Mother's exacting standards. One time, Mr. Hawkins sent his son John up to our house to kindly let Mother know that he had acquired a small amount of pudding rice and wouldn't put it out on display just yet, as he knew she would like to buy some. She was out of the door like a shot to get to the shop.

Mr. Hawkins was very good to Mother, always letting her know if he managed to obtain something special. Without fail, she paid for her items when received, not at the end of the week when the little tally books most customers had were totted up.

I was sworn to secrecy about the rice, as Mother wanted to surprise

Father. She produced a wonderful rice pudding at teatime the next day. Father was delighted – it was his favourite – and he danced Mother all around the table. It was the first time I had ever tasted a rice pudding and it was wonderful. It had been cooked slowly in the smaller oven in the range and was so creamy, with a lovely thick skin on top which I liked. Unlike custard skin, which I hated, perverse child that I was. Father scraped all around the edge of the empty dish to remove the last vestiges of the delicious skin for me, which I ate with great relish. I am amazed that I can recollect these events so clearly, as evidently Father was still working at this time so I must have been about four years old.

The little corner shops would all happily sell very small quantities of almost anything. A single cigarette from a whole packet – usually Woodbines – or a single Oxo cube. I have heard women ask, 'Can I 'ave a small tin o' corned beef, a carrot, an onion, a big spud and an Oxo cube? 'E wants 'ash fer 'is tea.'

Some of the shops were not the cleanest of establishments. One of them near our house was top of the league in this department. This particular shop used to sell winkles that had been boiled in a filthy old pan, on a *Primus* stove that stood on the counter. My friend Rita would buy them and they were sold in a cone of newspaper. I would watch fascinated as she took a winkle shell out of the bag, and with a safety pin flick the little hard black scab from the end of the shell onto the floor. Then she would push the pin into the shell and pull out the winkle—which in all ways that really matter, is a fishy snail—and eat it with relish. It's a miracle that no one got food poisoning. Evidently everyone who partook of these delicacies must have been immune to all bacteria known to man.

In the same shop, there was always a large wooden tray containing what could only loosely be described as 'fresh' cream cakes—sitting there uncovered on the counter, right next to the boiling winkles. On the floor, at the end of the counter, was a paraffin drum which had a little tap at the front. Underneath this, a floral china chamber pot had been placed to catch any drips of oil. I wonder if it was used for its intended purpose at night time. I do know for a fact that Miss Hitchmoore's hands were never washed between paraffin, cream cake and winkle transactions. The aroma of boiling winkles and paraffin coming from this shop was enough to clear the most congested of chests. It was a little like Arkwright's shop in the TV comedy *Open All Hours*, only with added filth. I was forbidden to eat anything from this shop, but Mother needn't have worried. You couldn't have paid me to partake of anything from this establishment.

Once I was out of the nursery, Mother did not need to take me to Windle School anymore. Although it was across a busy road, there were always older children to take your hand and see you across North Road. All the little ones waited at the curb to be seen safely across by the older boys and girls. Though on some mornings I would walk with Mrs. Price—she always took her son Ronald to school, even up until he left at age eleven. He was a very odd boy. From the age of nine I sat next to him for a while in Miss Horton's class. He would write 'RUSSIA' over and over again, inside and outside the covers of his exercise books. I was quite frightened of him and when he started to pinch me very hard on my leg I told my friend Leslie. It never entered my head to tell Miss Horton, but telling Les probably got the best result. Ronald never pinched me again. Now he would sit as far away from me as he possibly could without falling off the end of the bench. My hero Les came to the rescue once again!

Harry Pritchard was another boy I sat next to for a while. He had a permanently runny nose that he used to wipe on his sleeves. As he always wore a green blazer, it showed up very nicely when the streaks of mucus dried. Consequently he was known to us all as 'Harry Snail Trail'. Why it always seemed to be my privilege to sit next to the strange boys I shall never know. Perhaps it was me that was strange in noticing their little peccadillos.

On the 2nd June, 1953, we all had the day off school for the Coronation of Queen Elizabeth II. Mr. Prescott, our Headmaster, hired two Television sets so we children could come and watch the BBC coverage of the event. The TV's were placed in the school hall. On a table nearby, there was a bottle of orange juice and a commemorative tin box containing chocolates for each of us. It was wonderful to sit eating the sandwiches we had brought from home as we watched the spectacle, as no one had a TV in those days—except of course the teacher Mother had worked for, and Mrs Dagnall, who kept the drapers shop opposite our house. The TV screens were so tiny, with the picture in black and white of course, but a real treat for us children who had been born during WWII, and then lived through those austere years afterwards.

A little later that year, Mr. Prescott and some of the teachers also took the eight, nine and ten year olds to the cinema to watch Edmund Hilary and Sherpa Tensing's ascent of Everest. I would love to know where Mr. Prescott acquired the money from to fund these treats for us, but acquire it he did from somewhere or someone. He always managed to think of some special treat for us, especially at Christmas time. They were very tame treats, compared with what today's children have or expect, but in those days we didn't expect anything. Consequently we were very happy and grateful to receive anything at all out of the ordinary. He was a strict headmaster and ran a very tight ship—the bigger boys were very often punished with the cane, and there was usually a queue of naughty boys outside his office. But he was liked and respected by us all, and I still think of him with fondness.

I remember the whole school being gathered in the hall to watch Mr Prescott caning Brian Wilson, who had been stealing money from his Mother's purse. His Mother was at her wits end and after several unheeded warnings from Mr. Prescott, Brian was given the choice of the humiliation of a caning in front of the school, or being reported to the police. He chose the cane. Now, I had taken a penny from Mother's purse a little while before thinking she wouldn't notice, I knew I shouldn't have done it and felt very guilty. But I still took it. Actually seeing Brian receiving six of the best and witnessing his humiliation in front of us all put the fear of God into me. I never stole anything ever again. I do not know if Brian ever mended his ways, but I know that it had a great effect on me—and many more like me.

After this incident, and as soon as I had earned a few coppers from running an errand for a neighbour, I put the threepenny bit I was given straight into Mothers purse. Now I felt a little less guilty.

The next day Mother opened her purse and gave me two pennies saying, 'I think these belong to you'.

Clearly, she had known all along that I had taken the penny. I just burst into tears. After giving me one of her withering looks, she gave me a hug.

'I will not hide my purse from you Pam.' She said, holding me. 'I trust you not to steal anything ever again.'

I felt absolutely wretched for days. I think I would have preferred a good smacking, but Mother was a wise woman and an expert at psychological warfare. Of course I realise now that money was so tight whilst I was a child that even one penny would be missed.

At the age of ten I developed a very painful left leg and could hardly bear any weight on it. I was also feeling tired all the time. To get to and from School, my friend Les would push me there and back again in an old pushchair Mother had acquired for the purpose. He was a lovable rogue of a boy. On the journey I would shut my eyes, holding my breath as he ran as fast as he could, charging at every lamp post then just swerving aside at the last minute. I was a nervous wreck by the time we got to school.

I was eventually diagnosed with Osteomyelitis and spent three miserable unhappy weeks in a Catholic hospital. Although most of the nuns and nurses were kind, there was one, Sister Imelda, who was a sadist. We all dreaded her being on duty because instead of giving injections into your bottom, she would inject into your thigh instead. That was much more painful, which I am sure was the point. As I was having penicillin injections every four hours, it was torture.

During ward walks, Sister Imelda would come around with the *Flit* Fly Spray in a large metal spray pump. If we children ducked under the bedclothes to avoid getting DDT in our faces, she would just smile then give an extra pump over us, making sure there would be some residue left for us to inhale when we came up for air. How we weren't poisoned is a mystery.

Sometimes we were given mutton mince for a meal, which just like my school dinners smelled and tasted of old goat. Sister Imelda would stand over me and make me eat it. Every time she forced me to eat it, I would be sick. Then she would shout at me—which was clearly the object of the exercise. She took great pleasure in making me miserable. I should have just refused to eat it, but I didn't have the courage to disobey.

In the cot next to me was a toddler, who would wet the bed during the night. Imelda would then shake and shout at her until the poor little mite was sobbing.

On the other side of me was an older girl called Cecilia. She was Imelda's pet and bullied me verbally for practically my whole stay. That is until Johnny Walker, a boy from my class at school, was admitted. He was put in the bed opposite me. I don't know why he was in hospital, but he never seemed to be in bed for more than two minutes at a time. I was so happy to see him that I cheered up immediately. When he heard Cecilia saying nasty things to me, he marched over to her bed.

'Do you see this?' he said, shaking his fist at her. 'Well this is for you if you don't leave Pam alone!'

Cecilia said that she was going to tell Imelda, so Johnny then shook his other fist at her.

'See this other one?' he said. 'That's for you as well, if you dare tell!'

To my amazement she did not tell. For a small boy of ten Johnny had great wisdom. He said that I ought to start sticking up for myself, otherwise I would get walked on. Which was very true. He was a friend of Leslie's and came from a large and loving family—and it showed. He would bring a chair to sit by my bed, then chat to me and play 'Peep-O' with the little girl in the cot to make her laugh. The nuns and nurses didn't faze him in the slightest. When they used to tell him to get back into bed he would say, 'No thanks Sister, I'm not tired yet'. His sunny personality rubbed off on the nuns, as even at just ten years old he was so cheerful and confident. He said to me just out of the blue one day, 'My Mam's very beautiful you know'. When Mother came to visit me he told her not to worry because he was keeping an eye on me. Mother knew him well, as he was one of her school dinner time children, and she solemnly thanked him and shook his hand while trying not to laugh. He was a real diamond of a boy.

A lot of children were in the hospital to have their tonsils out. After surgery, they would come back from the operating theatre on a trolley, lying on a thick red rubber sheet which always seemed to be awash with blood. For a child with a vivid imagination like me it was very frightening. I would cover my face with the bed clothes as they passed.

For the three weeks of my stay, I never got out of bed except once to shuffle across onto a trolley to go down to the X-Ray Department. On the last day of my stay, a doctor got me out of bed to watch me walk down the ward. I was very wobbly and in a lot of pain, as my legs and feet—with a cage over them and hardly any room to move—had been in almost the same position for all of the three weeks. I was so desperate to get out of there and go home, that I gritted my teeth and walked slowly down the ward.

When Mother came at visiting time I was allowed to go home with a prescription for penicillin tablets, which were to be taken for another week. Mother and I walked the mile or so back to our house. I was trying to walk with my feet and ankles straight without crying, but I had to stop frequently to sit down. I sat on a wall, shop step, a tea chest full of books outside the second hand shop—anything I could. It seemed to take forever to get home. Although the Osteomyelitis was gone, I was in more pain than when I had gone into hospital, but I didn't tell Mother in case she took me back.

When I got home I crawled underneath the kitchen table, which was covered by a large chenille cloth, and stayed there until bedtime. That was a sign of a traumatised child, if ever there was one. Mother popped food and drinks under the cloth for me. At bedtime she was shocked when she realized just how much pain I was in. I started crying and was begging her not to send me back to hospital. Then I told her, at last, everything about my stay. She was absolutely furious about the way I had been treated and I suppose was also feeling guilty that she hadn't picked up on the signs. She wrote a scathing letter to the hospital, but I don't know if anything came of it. Poor Mother! She was always dashing from one job to another and yet she had always managed to be on time for visiting at 2pm to 2-30pm. She had to walk everywhere so must surely have been worn out.

Mother massaged my twisted ankles and feet using warm glycerine and rose water, as the skin on my legs and feet was very sore. She promised me that I would never, ever again have to cross the threshold of the children's ward at Providence Hospital, no matter how poorly I was. Gradually, with Mother's care and attention, my feet and ankles straightened. I stopped walking like a duck, the pain finally receded and with her good wholesome food I gained the weight I had lost.

I am sure if I had had Johnny's personality, I would have fared much better. However, apart from the occasional little burst of naughtiness, I was a repressed, quiet, bookish child who thought I should be seen and not heard. Johnny was back at school before me and when I did return, both he and Les welcomed me back with big grins and lots of pats on the back. Johnny even made me an honorary member of his gang in the playground. The girls and boys were kept separate at playtimes, so I couldn't join in their play. Even so, Johnny and Les would shout and wave to me as they zoomed around their yard. It was certainly not the 'done thing' to be friends with a girl, but Johnny made his own rules.

Such was his popularity, his gang members simply followed suit—if they wanted to stay in the gang that is. This little act of kindness boosted my confidence no end, so I started to become a little more daring and a little less of a wimp. I was also given a nick-name, just like the rest of the gang. From then on I was known as 'Logie' when out in the playground.

Back in Cooper Street, my friend Doreen and I would act out the Famous Five stories, each of us playing multiple parts and arguing who was going to play tomboy Georgina. One day, Doreen decided she was going to be Superman instead. So, tying her coat around her neck by the sleeves to make a cloak, she climbed up onto the alley wall. Spreading out her arms, she launched herself into the air. She landed with an almighty wallop on the cobblestones below, breaking her jaw and smashing her left elbow. She spent most of the summer holidays that year in hospital having multiple operations.

I had another friend called Rita, who lived in the street behind mine. Her house was next to St Mary's Lowe House RC Boys Boxing Club and Gymnasium. If we saw Father Kelly coming to open up the club, Rita would run to ask him if we could go inside.

'Can I come and swing on the ropes for a few minutes Father?' She would say. 'And can my friend come in as well, even though she is a Protestant?'

Father Kelly would look at me with great sadness, pat me on the head, then say in a broad Irish accent, 'A Protestant is it? Poor child, poor child.'

He was a nice man. All the children would run to him and hold his hand as he walked along the street.

Both Rita and Doreen always had comics to read, so I liked going to their homes to get my fill of *The Eagle*, *Girl's Crystal*, *School Friend*, *Topper*, *The Beano*, *The Dandy* and many more—including Cowboy comics, which I liked best of all.

Eunice Jones, a girl from school, would ask to borrow my wellies if she was going potato picking. So I would swop the loan of my wellies for a loan of her cowboy comics. I had to hide the comics and hope Mother didn't notice my wellies were missing. She did not approve of comics or the loaning of my wellies. The Lord knows why, but it was just one of her many little foibles. I would have loved to have gone potato picking with my friends and their Mams, but of course I was not allowed too.

In the evenings I always had to be home by 6-30pm. After supper and a wash, I would be in bed by 7-00pm and would read until 8-30pm. In the summer my friends would still be outside playing. Sometimes, if I knew Mother was busy downstairs, I would get dressed again and go back out and join them. This was the new much bolder me and it entailed climbing out of my little back bedroom window, lowering myself onto the shed roof, walking along the wall between our house and the neighbours then lowering myself down the back wall into the alley.

When it was time for my friends to go home they would give me a leg-up onto our back wall. It was much trickier getting back in through the bedroom window, as I could only just reach over the window sill and had to haul myself in. I had to be sure to be back in bed before 8-30pm, because Mother always brought me a drink of Ovaltine at that time to settle me down for the night.

After going through this performance a few times, the soles of my pumps were leaving black marks on the bricks where I had scrabbled to get back in. I prayed that Mother wouldn't notice, as she was an expert at putting two and two together. She very rarely smacked me though, because one of her looks alone was enough to crack concrete.

4: AUGHTON

Aunty Mill, my Mother's youngest sister, was Cook-Housekeeper for Mr. and Mrs. Parker, at a country house near Ormskirk. She would visit us on her day off, which was most Tuesdays. She would always bring a cream bun for me and peanut brittle for Mother. If there had been a dinner party the evening before one of Aunty Mills visits then there might be some left over goodies for us in her bag. Game Chips for example. I loved these and I am positive she made extra just so she could bring some for me. Of course she could only bring the left overs that wouldn't go off so I never got to taste the more exotic dishes, especially anything with seafood. She brought Pheasant for me to taste once, but quite frankly I could never understand why people made such a fuss about it. Of course I liked all the 'cakey' things like Macaroons, Petite Fours, and slices of all kinds of delicious cake.

Just thinking about Aunty Mill's Raspberry Roulade makes my mouth water. Very often she would be given boxes of chocolates by Mr. and Mrs. Parker, in appreciation of her wonderful food and messages would come through to the kitchen from the dinner guests to thank her for her amazing cooking. As Aunty Mill only liked chocolates with hard centres she would press her finger into them to find them, (much quicker than looking at the pictures on the leaflet) so the boxes would only contain squashed ones, but I didn't care as all chocolates were gratefully received.

About every six months or so Mother and I would go and visit her for the day. We would start out very early and the bus journey to Ormskirk, then out to Aughton, seemed to take forever when I was small. Once I could read however, I passed the time with my nose in my latest book. We usually arrived mid-morning and after a snack and a drink I was allowed the run of the grounds. I would roam all over the place dreamily pretending I lived there. The owner's pure white toy poodle 'Clicquot' would very often keep me company on my rambles— more often than not he was a dark shade of grey by the time we went back in. He spent most of his time in the kitchen with Aunty Mill and she adored him.

There was one area called 'The Ride' that I especially loved. It must have been about a quarter of a mile long and was banked on either side by dozens of varieties of Rhododendrons with deep moss underfoot. It was just like walking on a cushion. I would gallop up and down on my imaginary horse slapping my thigh with a stick and whinnying at the top of my voice.

If we were visiting when the 'Rhodies' were in full bloom Mr. Becket, the head gardener, would come up to the house and take Mother down to see them. If I met Mr. Becket on my travels he would smile and tip his hat to me. He didn't mind my wanderings and I was allowed to walk through the greenhouses, as long as I remembered to close the doors behind me. If it was raining I would play in the huge glass covered yard at the back of the house just off the kitchen. In the yard was the laundry room, the log store, the coal store, the boiler room, the rack room—where washing was hung to dry—two small stables for ponies and also a locked door to the corridor that led to the gun room. There was a store room which was full of all kinds of very interesting rubbish, including an old tricycle that I was allowed to take out and ride. There were some old tennis racquets and a big bucket full of tennis balls. I would take a racquet, then hanging the bucket on the trike's handle bars I would push it to the tennis courts—I couldn't peddle the trike as my knee banged on the bucket. I spent many a happy hour lobbing balls over the saggy old net by bouncing them on the floor first before whacking them, then changing sides and lobbing them back again. I had to hold the racquet with both hands, as my little thin arms soon got tired. Mr. Becket came one day with the handle that wound the net up. He thought he was being kind, but actually it was much harder to lob the balls over once it was straight and tight and I was much too polite to tell him. Clicquot would run up and down barking and chasing the balls until he was worn out. By now my arms would be aching, and as we were also very thirsty it would be time to go. I would put him in the basket on the back of the trike and he would sit in it quite happily on our way back to the yard. We would then dash into the kitchen, both of us begging Aunty Mill for a drink of water.

Mr. and Mrs. Parker the owners of the house would come through to the kitchen to say hello if they were at home but mostly we just saw Miss Susan[1], their daughter. One day, when I was about eight, I was curled up reading in the window seat in the corridor by Aunty Mill's private sitting room, when Miss Susan came and sat beside me. 'Milly tells me you love

1 *If I remember correctly, I think Miss Susan was a solicitor.*

books, Pamela.' She said, 'Come with me, I have something to show you'.

I followed her through parts of the house that were out of bounds to me, until we stopped outside one of the doors in a large hallway.

'Give me your hand and close your eyes.' She led me into the room. 'Now open your eyes', she said.

I found myself standing in a library. Every wall had books up to the ceiling. I could hardly get my breath. We had stopped in front of the section containing children's books. Sumptuous volumes of fairy tales, leather bound copies of Dickens, *The Iliad*, Greek Tales, Stories of Ancient Britain, and tales from Wagner. Animal story books by Ernest Thompson Seaton, A.J. Dawson, Lady Kitty Ritson and many, many, more.

'These are my books,' she said. "And the leather bound ones are school prizes of Father's. Every time you visit, you may come in here and read if you wish—as long as you promise to only use the books from this section. I know I don't need to tell you to make sure your hands are clean.'

I was so overwhelmed that when I tried to say 'Thank you' I just burst into tears. So on subsequent visits to Aughton I would disappear into the library after lunch.

Probert, the butler, would appear around mid-afternoon with a glass of milk and a plate of very fancy biscuits on a silver tray, with a starched white napkin, a scented flannel and a towel for my hands—prepared of course by Aunty Mill. Placing the tray on the table in the bay window Probert would look down his nose at me and say, in a voice that would curdle milk, 'Your afternoon refreshment, Miss.' Although he was a large man, he had such tiny feet that he looked as if he was tip-toeing everywhere. His tiny little shoes creaked as he walked and there was always a strong aroma of mothballs emanating from his person. Years later, Aunty Mill told me that Miss Susan had left instructions with her to send refreshments through for me when I was visiting. Poor Probert. It was quite beneath his dignity to serve a common child like me. Quite frankly, I would rather have gone without refreshments—he gave me the creeps.

A few years later Miss Susan sent me all her Father's school prizes, and also all her animal books. They arrived by Railway lorry, packed in a tea chest—included in the collection was my favourite book *Finn the*

Wolfhound by A.J. Dawson. Who would have guessed then that Irish Wolfhounds were to become such an important part of my life!

Just before Aunty Mill retired, she was the only member of the household staff left. Probert had long gone and so had Doris, the maid, and the cleaning ladies. Mr. Becket had also gone and the grounds were looking sad and neglected. The area around the estate had been sold for building land and I presume this is what happened to the grounds. I looked on Google a little while ago and the house is still there but I expect it will now have been turned into apartments.

It is so sad, but times change and the expense of maintaining such a large place must have been crippling. It was such a memorable part of my youth and childhood and I think of it often.

5: BOOKS & SWEETS

My Aunty Win in London, and Aunty Dede in Surrey, would send me books for Christmas, usually the *Daily Mail* and *Daily Express* Annuals. They were wonderful and full of stories, facts and puzzles.

Aunty Mill always bought me wonderful wildlife books for Christmas and birthdays. When my brother Dick came home on leave he would buy me story books that I especially wanted—usually *The Famous Five* and the *...Of Adventure* series by Enid Blyton. So I was a very lucky child and probably a very strange one, as I floated along in a dream world most of the time. I just loved the feel and smell of new books and still do.

My story book collection was kept in our front sitting room, on the shelves above the gas meter cupboard. Consequently they always had a slight whiff of bad eggs about them. My wildlife books were kept in the bottom half of the big bookcase. The top half contained my brother's books and was kept locked.

Dick had a subscription with the *Reprint Society* and would receive a book of their choice every month, unless you requested another title. I looked forward to the books arriving as I had chosen them! When the society letter arrived addressed to him, Mother would just screw it up and throw it in the bin. I would retrieve it, choose the book I liked best from reading the synopses, tick the box on the list and post it back in the prepaid envelope. As Dick was away at sea most of the time his collection consisted of—unbeknownst to Mother—mostly my choices.

Mother kept the top of the bookcase locked, as she considered them unsuitable for a child to read. However, I knew where the key was and by the age of thirteen I had read most of them by sneaking them up to my bedroom. There were books by Ian Fleming, Laurens Van Der Post, Francoise Sagan, Ernest Hemingway, and Marjorie Rawlings. There was *Seven Years in Tibet*, *The Yearling*, *Appointment with Venus*, *Venture to the Interior*, *The Lost World of the Kalahari*, *Elephant Bill*, *Casino Royale*, *Moon Raker*, *Live and Let Die*, *From Russia with Love*, Gerald Durrell's *The Bafut Beagles*, David Attenborough's *Zoo Quest to Guiana* and more. All wonderful and interesting.

Sometimes I made a mistake in choosing a book—*The Bulls of Paral* for example. I didn't finish that as it was a little too brutal for an animal loving child of thirteen. But mostly I got it right.

I had to guard my books with my life, as Mother was very adept at passing them on if she thought I had outgrown them. The most dangerous times were when there was a jumble sale or bring-and-buy sale at church. Mother had very firm ideas on what was suitable reading matter for me. She nearly had a fit one day when, aged about ten, I arrived home from the Children's Library with a copy of *Anna and the King of Siam*. I had to return it immediately, with a note informing the Librarian that it was totally unsuitable reading for a child. Of course I didn't want to show the note to the Librarian, so I pushed it down a grid in the gutter outside. I realized later that Mother must have assumed Anna Leonowens was living in sin with the King, and I shouldn't know about such things.

Oh Mother, Mother! If only you had known what I did know and what your sneaky, conniving little daughter was reading behind your back!

By the time I was twelve or so I had a wonderful—if motley—collection of books that had been given to me, or bought from jumble sales and second-hand shops. Mother wasn't happy about some of my acquisitions in case they carried disease, but as I had already had all the usual childhood ailments, I doubt there was much risk.

Sometimes she could afford to give me a few pennies to spend and sometimes I could earn a few by running errands or walking dogs for the neighbours. So most Saturday mornings, when I had a few coppers to spend, would find me rooting in the tea chests full of books outside Sara Ann Taylor's second-hand shop not far from where I lived. The shop did house clearances, so very often there was a fresh intake of books to root through. I especially liked tales of adventure and derring-do and obtained books with lovely embossed fronts and spines with pages full of black and white engravings, mostly published in the late 1890's or early 1900's. They had titles like *Amazon Adventure*, *Tales from the Congo*, *Down the Orinoco in a Canoe*. The stories were total rubbish, but I loved them.

Occasionally, among the jumble of books, I would find a lovely nature book with gorgeous colour plates; some of which I still have. Sometimes I was spoilt for choice and it was so hard putting back books that I really wanted. Most books were tuppence or thruppence, so if I really wanted more than I could afford, I would just take them to the counter anyway—wearing the best, sad, 'I'm half an orphan' expression I could muster. Very often it worked and I got two for thruppence. My deviousness knew no bounds where books were concerned. I can still remember the smell in the shop of damp musty furniture, piddled mattresses, sweaty second-hand clothes and the ever pervading smell of mothballs. But it was worth running the gauntlet of the smells to get to the counter with my treasures. Sometimes I would have a penny or two left over for sweets.

I think I was about ten when sweet rationing ended and we could then buy as many as we liked. As children we were spoilt for choice for sweetshops, but if we wanted our money to go a long way we always went to Mrs. Cathcart's. The 'shop' was actually just the front parlour of her house, with the sweets displayed in the window in the full sun. She would move the boxes around until the melted ones set hard again, then they would then go back to the front. We would peer in the window to watch the progress of the melted toffees, so we would know exactly when they were misshapen and grotty enough to be sold off cheaply. We would then go in and ask for two ounces of squashed toffees.

'Toffees' in St Helen's dialect meant any and all varieties of sweets—what most people meant by 'toffee' we called Caramel. Sometimes it was difficult to get the paper off the melted sweets, but if you sucked them for a while and then took them out of your mouth, you could then pick the bits of soggy paper off. Disgusting little brats that we were.

If you wanted to buy *Everton Mints* or *Uncle Joe's Mint Balls* out of the big jars, Mrs. Cathcart would attack the congealed lumps with a large, long screwdriver kept especially for the purpose—all perfectly normal behaviour as far as we were concerned!

One of the few sweets kept inside the shop on the little counter—as well as chocolate—was liquorice. This was my favourite. In St Helens it was called 'Spanish' and was one penny a stick. So we would ask for 'a penny Spanish'. We could also buy 'Spanish Root'[1] which was a halfpenny and just like a twig. When you had chewed and sucked it for a while, the strands of the root would get stuck between your teeth. Mother never knew about any of this, as I certainly wouldn't have been

1 *Spanish Root was the raw unprocessed root of the liquorice plant.*

allowed to buy sweets from there.

Mrs. Cathcart was a real character. One day our lodger, Eric, gave me a shilling and told me to go and buy twelve penny Spanish's—four each for me, him and his wife Joan. When I asked Mrs. Cathcart for the Liquorice she refused to serve me.

'Nay Lass, I'm not serving thee all them! Tha'll never be off t'lavvie!'[2]

Eric had to come back to the shop with me to explain that they weren't all for me.

2 *"...you will never be off the lavatory".*

6: FATHER

Father had died just before I was seven years old, from a form of Motor Neurone disease. He had been ill for about three years and totally bedridden for over a year. He just wasted away. When he first became ill I used to sit on his bed and he would read to me. Then when he lost the use of his arms, and couldn't hold a book anymore, I would read to him. But before he was bedridden, and while he still had the use of his arms, he taught me semaphore and I drove my friends mad, demonstrating and showing off my newly acquired skill.

Mother nearly had a fit one day when she found me reading all the salacious stories from *The News of the World* newspaper to him. She needn't have worried. Although my comprehension was good, it wasn't up to understanding smutty news reports. Father laughed when Mother made a fuss. When the muscles eventually wasted on his face he couldn't even smile at me anymore. For my sixth birthday he gave me a little book of poems for children and wrote inside, 'Happy Birthday Pammy, with love from Father, June 1949'. His lovely copperplate handwriting was very wobbly, and it must have taken great effort to write this dedication. It is now my most treasured possession.

Every Saturday I would go St Mark's vicarage for the day to play with the Vicar's children—Joy, Gilly and Richard Carver. One Saturday at the beginning of May, 1950, Mr. Carver called me into his study. I can remember it as if was yesterday. He was sitting at his desk, and when I approached he took my hands in his, kissed me on my forehead, and told me Father had died. I didn't really feel anything except terror that I would have to go home and Father's dead body would be in the front room. Then I asked Mr. Carver if it meant I was half an orphan now. God! I was such a weird child, as my imagination was constantly in overdrive.

Poor Father had suffered with bouts of stress and depression all his adult life after his experiences in World War One. I suppose it would be called PTSD these days. When he was feeling anxious and stressed he would go off on his own and walk for miles until he was exhausted and his feet were raw. I remember one time he was away all day. Mother was frantic as he was already ill with Motor Neurone disease, and had to wear a caliper brace on his right leg. He was in a terrible state when he finally came home. She had to cut him out of his trousers, as they were ripped and soaked in blood where the caliper had cut into his groin and his knee.

I can see Mother now, kneeling down in front of Father, bathing his feet in a bowl of water, washing and tending to his broken skin, with tears rolling down her face. Father was holding her face in his hands, telling her how good she was to him and how much he loved her. I was crying because they were crying. Poor, poor man to suffer such mental torment. To then have this horrible disease and die at fifty-five was so cruel. I didn't really understand what the matter was at the time, but I do now and often think of how brave they were and how much they loved each other.

It must have been extremely wearying for Mother, both mentally and physically, as she worked so hard to care for Father and me, to keep us fed and a roof over our heads. What a fantastic job she did of it. As Father could no longer work, and as she didn't get much financial help from anywhere, she was the only breadwinner. She was such an indomitable woman. After Father died she decided to take in lodgers so she could give up a few of her cleaning jobs.

When I was a child I didn't appreciate that our house was always spotlessly clean. We always had clean beds, clean clothes, good nourishing food—and plenty of it—and a good fire. Washing day was once a week, and was done by hand in the big metal Dolly Tub out on the veranda. There was a grid under the kitchen window, so the water in the Dolly Tub could be tipped down the drain when the washing was finished, or sometimes it would be tipped onto the yard and I would scrub the bricks clean with a yard brush. The water was heated in buckets on the range, which of course had to be lifted on and off.

Once the sheets and clothes had been swirled and pummeled—to Mothers satisfaction—with the dolly stick[1], the smaller items of washing were lifted out of the hot water, item by item, with a pair of wooden tongs. A clean stick was placed across the top of the Dolly tub, so that the heavy items could be draped over it and then the stick was lifted and the item flopped into the tin bath. If I was at home when she washed, I would turn the handle of the large old mangle as she fed the items

1 *This looked like a three-legged stool with a long handle sticking up out of the middle of it, with two shorter handles across the top. This was twisted and turned in the dolly tub to agitate the water.*

through. The washing then had to be rinsed, but at least she could fill the Dolly tub up from a hosepipe on the kitchen tap. Then of course it had to be mangled again. This was hard work and took hours so Mother always started early morning on washing day.

When the weather was fine the washing was pegged out on the line. Or if it was raining, it was put on the ceiling rack over the kitchen fire—I loved to help pulling the rack up and down. On the rare occasion that the washing was bone dry when brought in, we would dip our fingers in a bowl of water and flick drops over the items. They were then rolled up tightly ready for ironing—there were no steam irons in those days. When I was about eleven, a Launderette opened a few streets away and we could wash and dry everything for a few shillings. Mother said that if she ever met the man who invented them, she would kiss his feet.

The women in the street would 'Donkey Stone' their steps every morning. This was a hard block of a chalk-like substance that was dipped into the mop bucket and rubbed on the step to whiten it. Some of the women whitened right across the pavement down to the edge of the kerb. Anyone who did not do this was considered lazy, which was hilarious—most of the houses behind the gleaming white steps were mucky to say the least. Mother didn't Donkey Stone anything. As she said in Welsh, "Dim amser am lol!"[2]

Not one of the neighbours would have dared comment within Mothers hearing about the un-whitened step, as I am sure she would have floored them with one of her very best withering looks.

What a complex person she was. Clever, kind, loving, resourceful, inventive, strict, controlling, religious, honest, hardworking, interfering, tea-total and very strong willed. She also had a great fear of debt, and consequently never owed a penny to anyone in her life. She was—like I have already said—an indomitable woman.

2 *"No time for nonsense"*

7: LODGERS

Our first lodger was Uncle Bert, who had just retired from his job as a game keeper on an estate near Malpas, in Cheshire. His wife Polly, my Mother's eldest sister, had died in 1949—so Mother said he could come and live with us.

After a while Bert started to court Aunty Mill, and they wanted to get married. Mother was scandalized and she must have persuaded Mill that it wasn't the thing to marry your brother-in-law. It was absolutely none of Mother's business of course, but Uncle Bert had to go.

Next to come were Paddy and Mikey, two Irish brothers. They were lovely to me, and fine from Monday to Friday—but at the weekends they would get roaring drunk. We only had an outside loo and sometimes on coming home from the pub they would forget, go upstairs and—unable to find the loo—would pee on the landing. So they had to go.

Then Nicolai came. He was a Romanian who had walked across Europe to get to England after the war. I liked him most of the time except first thing in the morning—when I was eating my breakfast he would come past, holding his night time chamber pot aloft, saying 'Good Mornink, Good Mornink' as he passed. He had a piano accordion and would sit and play to us, but as he only knew two tunes the novelty wore off quite quickly. The first bone of contention between him and Mother were the dozens of sugar paste Easter eggs he insisted on displaying all over his bedroom. They were still wrapped in cellophane, and had little windows in the side with religious scenes inside. He would put them out on display and Mother would put them away in the chest of drawers. This palaver went on day after day. 'Dust gatherers' Mother called them.

When Aunty Mill came to visit us on her days off, she started going to the cinema with Nicolai. Mother did not approve at all. Nic and Mill were both in their late forties, and again it was none of Mothers business, but it caused endless arguments. As they ignored Mother's disapproval, Nic had to go. I asked Mother years later why she had interfered, and she said that Milly was making a fool of herself. Poor Milly. Perhaps she was making a fool of herself, but good grief! She was old enough to make her own decisions and she deserved a little romance and spice in her life.

Mother put another advert in the paper and this time it produced the best lodgers anyone could wish for—Joan and Eric, a newly married couple. They had the front bedroom and the sitting room and the use of the kitchen. They stayed with us for nearly two years while they saved for a deposit on a house. They both worked, but I can't remember where. Eric was also a trombonist in one of the local brass bands and we loved to listen to him when he practiced. I remember one piece he used to play called *The Acrobat*. I liked to watch him take his trombone apart to clean it, thinking how clever he was to know how to put all the various bits back together again.

Each Thursday evening he would go to band practice and Joan would come through and sit with Mother and me. They would usually sit knitting, as there were never any idle hands in our house. I was allowed to stay up until Eric came in, then Mother would make supper for us all. Occasionally Eric would bring fish and chips for supper which was a real treat. They were lovely people and Mother was very fond of them. It must have been an easier time for her as she didn't have to cook, wash or clean for them; they looked after themselves.

I missed them terribly when they bought their own house, but for years I would cycle the few miles on my ancient old bike to visit them every few weeks or so until I left school.

One evening, just after I had gone to bed, I heard a knock at the door and the sounds of Mother showing someone into the sitting room. I had been moved out of my little back bedroom into the front one for a while, so my room was now directly above the sitting room.[1]

I really wanted to know who Mother was talking to, and as I wouldn't have dared to go downstairs I got out of bed and put my ear to the floor. The voices were just a mumble. So being a nosey little madam, I thought of a cunning plan. I decided that if I pretended to fall out of bed Mother would come upstairs, then I could ask her who it was. I stamped on the floor and waited. Nothing happened. So I stood on the bed and jumped off and this had the desired effect, as up the stairs she came. However, I could tell by her footsteps that I was in trouble. Mother came over to the bed, pulled back the covers flipped me over onto my front and whacked me across the backside. Then she said, 'I heard you the first time and I

1 *Mother wanted to paint the window frame and window ledge as, to her surprise, the paint was looking a little worn, and the wood outside had little nicks and splinters out of it. The discovery of the scratched worn paint had me very worried for a while in case Mother put two and two together about my illicit excursions out of the window.*

am not, I repeat *not*, going to tell you who is downstairs!'

I didn't very often get one over on her.

The next day the mystery visitor moved in. It was Miss Rogers, the new lady worker from our church, St Mark's. I think she dealt with the social problems in the parish, for she was certainly nosey and interfering enough.

I didn't like her and she stank of body odour. As Mother was always very strict about personal hygiene, I wondered why she didn't tell her to have a wash. Miss Rogers had the downstairs front room as a bedsit, and Mother would go in to put her clothes on hangers by the open window—probably hoping that she would take the hint that they smelled. If I was helping with the housework, I hated having to go into the front room to dust, or clean out the grate and set the fire ready to light. I would try to hold my breath—for as long as I could—before dashing into the passage way to take a lungful of clean air. As all Miss Roger's meals were cooked for her, and more often than not she ate with us, I asked Mother if I could have mine a little earlier as I hated sitting at the table with her.

Miss Rogers was always telling me what to do. If I was reading she would rudely take my book off me, examine it and then pass comments on whether she considered it suitable, or suggest books I should be reading instead. If I was drawing or painting she would come and tell me how to do it another way. I also liked making models, and she would pick them up before they were dry and very often wreck them. She nearly drove me mad, and I avoided her as much as possible. I was too polite to say anything to her, but for once I complained to Mother. I think she did tell Miss Rogers to mind her own business, in a roundabout way. However, I believe the Vicar had asked Mother to let her lodge with us, so Mother was a little more reticent in laying down the law than usual. Consequently, Miss Rogers got away with an awful lot.

It finally came to a head one evening. I would always read for a while after I went to bed, then after Mother had brought my usual drink of Ovaltine up at half-past eight, I would settle down and sing myself to sleep. I sang everything from school songs and hymns, to songs from the radio. I had always done this, from being really tiny. Miss Rogers came up the stairs knocked very loudly on my bedroom door and told me to be quiet as it was time I was asleep. I then heard Mother coming up the stairs and could tell by her footsteps that she was angry. She told Miss

Rogers in no uncertain terms that she had no business being upstairs, and how dare she tell me to stop singing. Mother gave her a fortnight's notice there and then. I wickedly did a quiet little victory dance behind the door. So she went, thank goodness! Poor Miss Rogers. With hindsight I believe she was probably a very lonely person, as she certainly didn't endear herself to anyone.

Early every morning, while I was still using the front bedroom, I would hear the work men passing by in the street on their way to Pilkington's Glass works. In the early 'fifties in St Helens, the majority of the men—and some of the older women—still wore clogs. These had leather uppers and a wooden sole, with metal clog irons nailed onto them. They made quite a clatter on the cobbles as the men passed by.

One of these men would stop every morning by our front room window, then hawk phlegm from his throat and spit onto the metal cover of the stop tap in the pavement. He would then hold his nose and snort its contents down the wall. Mother was furious having to clean the mess up every day, so one morning she stood behind the front door with the yard brush, and a mop bucket full of soapy water. When she heard him stop and spit, she shot out of the door threw the bucket of water over the wall and pavement—and over his clogs—and called him a 'Mochyn gwarthus!'[2] Then, with a look that would crack concrete, she handed him the brush and told him to brush his disgusting mess away. Many of the men from the surrounding streets were pretty rough and tough but he said, 'Sorry Missus!' Then did as Mother told him. You didn't argue with Mother.

The next day at school I got thumped by the man's son, and he called Mother 'A bloody Welsh Witch!'—evidently repeating his Father's words. I was frightened, but stood my ground with fists raised ready to defend my Mother's honour. My friend Leslie came to my aid before I got flattened. He defused the situation by making fun of the bully, and shaming him for hitting a girl.

Our next lodger was Eileen—a clean, quietly spoken, very pleasant Irish Lady. Mother cooked her meals, but Eileen cleaned her own room and did her own laundry. She stayed with us for a year or so before going back home to Ireland to live with her sister.

Then Stanley and Ernie came. They had been in lodgings elsewhere, but the food had been awful and they were delighted when Mother said

2 *"Disgusting Pig"*

she would take them. She asked if they would share a double room, but Stanley said they really would prefer separate ones. So Stanley had the upstairs front and Ernie the sitting room. It only took one night before we realized why Stanley needed a separate room—Ernie snored. Oh my word, did he snore! The house practically shook when he was at full throttle. We couldn't sleep for the noise, and even the neighbours could hear him. His family lived in Bolton, so he would go home on Fridays and come back early Monday mornings. So we looked forward to three nights of undisturbed sleep. He was such a nice man, and poor Mother was desperately trying to pluck up the courage to give him notice when, thankfully, he announced that he had got a job nearer to home and would have to give Mother a week's notice.

So that just left Stanley. He was a nice enough man I suppose. He was in his mid-twenties, and very pale and thin. Mother would pile the food on his plate as she thought he needed fattening up. He had five older sisters who would visit him occasionally, and he would then revert to pampered, baby boy mode and act very silly. I had left school by now and thought he was an utter twit.

Mother used to mutter under her breath, 'Beth babi mawr!'[3]

He was no trouble for Mother, except when he was mooning about the house—like an actor in a Victorian melodrama—over the latest girl he had a crush on. Then Mother would pull her face at me and mutter, 'Llawer o lol!'[4] Stanley stayed for about three years I think.

After Stanley left, Mother got a job as Head Cook in the staff canteen at the large Woolworths store in town. I think her hours were nine-o-clock to half-past-three. She said she needed eyes in her backside to try to stop the daft and unhygienic things some of the kitchen staff would do. These are some I can remember her telling me about.

One girl, when she was asked to take a large tray of roast potatoes out of the oven, attempted to do so without wearing oven gloves. Consequently there were multiple burnt fingers and many potatoes all over the floor, and to the annoyance of the shop staff there were no 'roasties' with their lunch.

Another girl would lick the butter knife before sticking it back into the butter—and yet another girl would carry two full plates of dinner, one on top of the other, instead of one in each hand.

3 *"What a big baby!"*

4 *"Lots of nonsense!"*

After being shown how to crimp the edge on an apple pie, Mother was horrified to see a trainee girl licking her fingers between crimps. Mother said that she also had a running battle, with some of the girls, about not washing their hands after they had been to the toilet.

One new kitchen girl asked Mother if she could have a cloth and some disinfectant. When Mother asked her why, she said that she had to wipe the toilet seat before sitting on it as she didn't want to get pregnant.

Another girl, on finding out Mother was Welsh, said that she had been to Wales once and that it was boring—as there was nothing but 'sodding trees and scenery.'

The little lady that did the dishes told Mother that she and her husband were moving from their council house into a one bedroom flat. 'It means I have got to be in with him again,' she said. 'But I have told him there's not going to be any of that bloody honeymoon business!'

Mother's last lodger was Mr. New and he stayed for about twelve years. He would get up very early in the morning, make his own breakfast, go to work, come home, have a wash, eat his evening meal and go to bed about 6:30 P.M. At the weekend he would sit and read the paper, go out before lunch, then come back home for his evening meal and then go to bed.

One day three men came to the door saying they were Mr. New's brothers and that they had been trying to trace him for years. Evidently when their Father had died, Mr. New had sold the house and contents, then pocketed the money and disappeared. When Mother told him his brothers had called he didn't comment, but the next day he didn't come home from work. When Mother looked in his wardrobe, all his clothes had gone—but hanging there, on a hook inside, was an envelope with two weeks bed and board in it. There was no note—just the money. So he had disappeared and avoided his brothers once again. He never caused Mother any problems, but he was a very strange man.

As Mother was now in her seventies she decided not to have any more lodgers and to just manage on her pension.

8: MAKE DO AND MEND

Times were tough during and just after the war, and food was boring and hard to obtain—unless you had an inventive Mother like mine. I have mentioned that we were lucky, because now and then extra food reached us from two of Mother's brothers in North Wales. She would share this bounty with friends and neighbours and would also barter for extra sugar to make jam. Fresh eggs were preserved in Water Glass[1] and I can remember as a small child stirring the water in a large glazed terracotta pot, as Mother added the powder. The eggs were then carefully placed, one by one, into the gloop then the pot lid put back on. After a while, they could be taken out, washed then used as wanted. They had a funny taste when boiled or scrambled, but were fine in cakes and puddings. They were still a lot more appetizing than tinned powdered egg.

If Mother was baking, my friend Les would miraculously appear. He would shout over the wall, 'Are you making cake Mrs. Logan?'

'Climb over and come see!' Mother would shout back.

If Les' brothers were there, then she would give them all a taste. One day she gave all three of them a thick slice of homemade bread, generously covered with damson jam. Les took his swiftly, then—holding it in his teeth—shinned up the drainpipe onto the back bedroom roof, up onto the main house roof and sat there holding on to the chimney while he ate his slice. This was the only place his older brothers couldn't reach him, as they would have taken it off him. He did the same thing when Mother gave them half an orange each—Dick had come home on leave from Gibraltar, and brought back a box of oranges. They were absolute treasure to us. We turned the peel inside out and scraped off every last morsel of flesh with our teeth.

Leslie's brothers used to thump him a lot, and we would often hear the sound of him crying through the living room wall. Mr. and Mrs. Stocks weren't often home in the evenings and would be across the street in the pub. I used to get terribly upset when I heard Les being set upon. Mother would bang on the wall with the handle of the poker to make them stop. There were little round indentations all over the wallpaper

---

1 Sodium Silicate dissolved in water

were Mother had hammered on the wall. When Les was a little boy, he would come in to play and he would have mock battles with my big teddy bear 'Old Ted'. Mother would be in stitches from laughter, as he battled Ted around the room, then on and off the settee—falling over the back and off the arms as he wrestled the ferocious, growling bear. Then finally, when he was triumphant, he would sit on our old stool with his back against the fireguard, eating a scone or a piece of cake, or whatever Mother had given him as his victory prize.

Les and his wife, Lorraine, and their children have lived in Australia for over fifty years now. I was so sad to see them go, as it was like losing a brother. I am in touch with them now through Facebook, and I was telling Lorraine all the stories about Les that I was putting in this book. She told me one that I didn't know, about when Les and I were toddlers, that Les's Mum had told her.

Apparently on Saturday evenings, Mother would knock on the living room wall with the poker to let Mrs. Stocks know that she was about to bath me. Les would be lifted over the garden wall wrapped in a towel, and he would join me in the big tin bath in front of the fire. When bathed and dried, Mother would knock on the living room wall again and he would be passed back over the garden wall—all ready for bed. Of course, the water would have had to have been heated in buckets on the range—so once the bath was full, it was just as easy to bath two toddlers as one. This was a typically kind and neighbourly gesture from Mother.

At Christmas time, Mother and I would make cards and calendars. Some of my school friends would be invited to come and make a calendar and card too. She would save pictures from magazines—usually the *Picture Post*—and the Miss Mills would give her adverts with nice pictures, and clean cardboard boxes for the backing. Sometimes Aunty Mill would bring the pictures off the boxes of luxury chocolates from the Parkers at Aughton. These were usually lovely scenic views, or displays of flowers. Calendar tabs, and little rolls of narrow red and green gummed tape, were bought from Woolworths. These were then cut and folded length-ways to finish off the edges of the calendars. A loop of ribbon was stuck on for a hanger, and two little pieces were used to hang the tab from. Then, 'hey presto', my friends had a present to take home for their Mams. The gummed tape was measured meticulously, as it was so precious—even the little snippets from the mitred corners were saved to make patterns on the cards.

The old adage of 'Waste not, want not' is still embedded in my brain—or as Mrs. Smith would say, "Want no waste Pam, want no waste!"

Taught at Mother's knee to cook, bake, sew, knit, darn and peg rugs I always had a project to be worked on—if Mother could drag my nose out of my latest book. She would buy second hand clothes, which would be washed, then we would cut them up into strips to make rag rugs. I liked sorting out the different colours and designing the patterns. Old washed potato sacks were used for the backing, and because the weave was open and straight, they were easy to peg into. We would each start at opposite ends, with the sacking draped across the big wooden stool that Les liked to sit on. When the rugs were finished they were thick, warm and very bright and colourful. Mother would sell them to make a little extra money and I remember her swopping one for a pair of old step ladders with a friend of Father's—both happily thinking they had got a bargain.

Sometimes Mother would acquire good quality woollen coats. These she would unpick at the seams, turn the material inside out, then cut and remake into coats and skirts for me. When finished with a different lining they looked as good as new.

When I was about seven or eight, Mother made me a cream woollen coat, with a red velvet collar and red velvet piping on the pockets, which was only worn on Sundays. Unfortunately, she also made a hat like a beret to go with it. I hated the damned thing, and on my way to Sunday school I would take it off and kick it up the street. As I passed a neighbour's house one day, Mrs. Bromilow saw me through the window and came out and told me off. I knew she would tell Mother, and I waited for a few days for the hammer to fall. Actually it hardly came down at all—surprisingly Mother told me I didn't have to wear it if I disliked it so much. Perhaps she was cross about Mrs. Bromilow telling tales on me.

Once, Mother acquired a big blue woollen dressing gown from somewhere. From this she made me a lovely dressing gown with pockets, and embroidered my initials on the breast pocket. I thought it was wonderful, as it was just like the dressing gowns Enid Blyton's *Famous Five* wore.

I always had good leather shoes on my feet, and sometimes Aunty

Win would send, from London, my cousin Sheila's outgrown, 'almost new' school shoes for me.

Father was creative as well. He made me a lovely big doll's house, which opened in the middle at the front and had a little catch to secure it. Our big tabby cat Darby would flick the catch with his paw, pull one side open, climb inside one of the bedrooms, then go to sleep with his head hanging out of the back window. Father had made cellophane window panes, but they hadn't stood up to Darby pushing at them with his head and paws. He was such a sweet tempered cat, and would allow me to dress him up in my dolls clothes. More often than not he would be walking around in a matching outfit of a blue or pink knitted dress and cardigan. He would allow me to put a bonnet on him, but then rub against the sides of the arm chairs to remove it. Poor thing! I must have been the bane of his life.

I also had a doll's pram that Father had made for me. He had managed to obtain an old pram chassis, some small pram wheels and some oiled cloth for the hood from goodness knows where. He made the body of the pram from plywood and when finished and painted it was really rather splendid. Mother made the sheets and pillow and my doll—'Crossed Eyed Jane'—was very comfy in it.

Father also made small wooden toys, from off cuts of wood from the saw mill. These would be sold at Christmas time to make a little extra money. He couldn't work anymore as he had to wear a big, heavy caliper brace on his leg, so the extra money was needed. When he arrived home with a sack of wood bits on his back, I could hardly wait for him to tip them out onto the shed floor. I loved the smell of the wood, and would have great fun sorting the bits out into shapes and sizes, so he could decide what to make with them. The glue he used looked like flakes of hard toffee, which would be melted down in an ancient metal glue pot on the kitchen range. It absolutely stank, as it was made from horse and cattle hooves. Much to my and Mother's relief, he eventually acquired an old *Primus* stove from somewhere—so was able to melt his glue in the shed from then on.

Father also mended our shoes and I liked to sit and watch him. He would put the tacks, which he nailed the new soles on with, between his lips. If he tried to talk to me, I would vigorously shake my head shouting, 'Don't talk, don't talk!' I wanted to stop him speaking, just in case he swallowed the tacks by mistake.

I remember him kneeling by my bedside one morning, when I was poorly, before he went to work. I think I had mumps, as he said he would bring me a present to make me feel better when he came home. The present was a set of miniature metal traffic signs, all beautifully painted in a lovely wooden box with a sliding lid. There were twelve of them. I absolutely loved them and kept them for many years. I don't know where he bought them from, or who they were made by, but they looked expensive. He must have bought them second hand from somewhere. Unfortunately, they didn't stand up to the bashings my nephews would later inflict upon them on one of their visits, and must have eventually been thrown away.

I think back to my little box bedroom, with the two wooden steps that went down into it from the middle bedroom. It had just enough room for a single bed on one side, and a small chest of drawers and a half size wardrobe on the other. The narrow space in between was covered by a long rag rug, with a pattern of autumn leaves, made by Mother and myself. I had drawn the leaves on the sack backing, and we had worked these first. We had then filled in the background with random shades of green. It was lovely and I had it for donkey's years, as I took it with me when I eventually left home.

My brother had bought the bedroom furniture for me, when he had been home on leave from his stint of duty in the Mediterranean. As there wasn't any room for a bookcase, Mother asked a neighbour to make a book shelf for me as a birthday present. Although my brother had said he would make it, Mother erred on the side of caution and said 'No thank you'. He was to DIY what an Elephant would be to brain surgery—Poor Dick. The family creative gene had totally passed him by.

I couldn't wait to get home from school the day the shelf went up. It was even better than I expected as it ran the whole length of the wall, over the side of my bed, and was wide enough to even take my wildlife books. My map of the world was moved to the wall over the window. The joy of having my books in my room, and being able to lie in bed and look at the long row of them was indescribable. It may seem such a tame present, compared to what most children receive nowadays, but I think it was one of my best ever.

My sister Pat was also very creative. I can picture her now sitting on the chair in her living room, with her legs tucked up beneath her, busily knitting or sewing—totally oblivious to the chaos and noise around her as the children played and argued, with Robert practicing his euphonium and David his violin. It was a good thing she could switch off like this, as it was the only way to keep her sanity. When the children were older, she became an avid quilter and everyone in the family owns one of her lovely quilts. Each new grandchild was presented with a specially themed quilt for their beds. She was addicted to material, and her idea of a day out was to trawl around haberdashery shops buying yet more. The cupboards in her work room, and elsewhere in the house, were just bulging with projects and material of every type, pattern and hue. My niece Margaret, her youngest daughter, would now and then be able to persuade her to have a clear out before the cupboards collapsed.

Pat also loved crosswords and would finish the *Daily Telegraph* cryptic crossword in the time it would have taken me to guess just one clue. In June, 2008, all her children and grandchildren, myself and my children and our brother from Canada—and all the spouse's—gathered together to celebrate her eightieth birthday. She had a wonderful day and sat in the sunshine, with a glass of Baileys in hand, like a Queen on her throne as we all told her how much we loved her, and presented her with her presents. It was a very special day. Sadly the next time we all got together, a few years later, was to say our final goodbye.

9: SCHOOL HOLIDAYS

In the school holidays when I was small, I would have to go with Mother to her many cleaning jobs. But from the age of nine I was allowed to stay home on my own. I had a key to the front door, which I kept in a secret pocket in my brown corduroy shorts. This was a little pouch sewn inside the waist band at the front. The shorts were the nearest thing to a pair of boy's trousers you could have found. I loved them.

As most of my friends parents were out at work all day, it was normal for all of us to fend for ourselves, but there would always be at least one of Mam's friends we could go to if needed. Sometimes a few of my friends had to look after their younger siblings, so a gang of us would go up to the park with prams and pushchairs in tow. There would never be any question about them looking after their younger brothers and sisters if told to. Even the big rough boys didn't dare answer back or give cheek to their parents.

As most of us had roller skates, a trip up to Victoria Park was a must, as the pathways were very smooth and just perfect for skates. We would have to watch out for the Park Keepers, as they would chase us and make us leave if they saw us roller skating. I don't know why—we weren't doing any harm. They would shake their sticks at us as we skated to the gate, the miserable old devils. I had saved and saved every penny of birthday and Christmas money, for over two years, to buy a good quality pair of roller skates. They were priced at thirty seven shillings and sixpence, which was a small fortune to me. When at last I had enough money saved, I dashed to the bicycle shop in Duke St. I proudly counted out my money onto the counter, only to be told by the assistant that after two years they now cost thirty nine shillings and sixpence. It was such a shock that I was near to tears. I blurted out that was all I had, and had been saving up for such a long time. He looked at my face, patted my hand, put my money in the till then wrapped up the box of skates and gave them to me. Bless his heart. It was such a kind thing to do for a little girl who, for a moment, thought the world had come to an end. When I got home with my precious parcel, I told Mother what had happened. The following Saturday she handed me an envelope containing a note and two shillings, and told me to take it to the bicycle shop. I was to be sure I gave it to the same man who served me, and to say thank you once again. As I have mentioned before, Mother made sure we never owed a penny to anyone.

In the holidays, my friends and I mostly stayed around home and played in the streets. We played games like *Tick*, *Tin Can Bung Off*, *Duck Stone*, *What Time Is It Mr Wolf*, *Statues*[1], *Double Ball*, cricket, marbles, skipping or football.

If any of us had a packet of chalks, we shared them and would go to a place in Hailfield St. The paving stones were lovely and smooth, and just perfect for drawing on. As they were not in front of anyone's house, no-one bothered us.

I had an old bicycle, and I would let my friends take it in turns to ride around the block of streets that was our territory—which usually took about five minutes. I lent it to Les one morning, and I didn't see him again until the next day. He had decided to go to Southport, which was an all round trip of about fifty miles. As my bike was ancient, and he was only ten, it was quite a feat. No one had a clue where he had disappeared to, and Mother and I were more worried than his own family. He came around to our house later the next day with my bike, even more battered and with two flat tyres. He had to do a lot of grovelling to Mother. When he saw the expression on her face, he asked if this meant there would be no more cake in future. She couldn't keep up the cross face and burst out laughing, gave him a hug and said to come back in a week. One of his cheeky smiles could have charmed the birds out of the trees, and they always worked on Mother. She asked his brothers to mend the punctures, which they weren't happy about, but you didn't argue with Mother. He probably received a thumping from them—which he deserved this time—the naughty boy.

I loved going to Southport as a child. Very often Mother and I would go on a coach direct from our street, organized by a neighbour—or we would go by bus. All I ever wanted to do when we got there, was to visit and stroke the St Bernard dog which was kept in a little enclosure in the children's fun fair. The kennel inside the enclosure was just like a miniature Swiss chalet. I knew it was a Swiss chalet as I had read about Switzerland in the encyclopaedia that Aunty Mill had bought me. I wasn't

1 *The little ones could join in with these*

the slightest bit interested in the fun fair. There was a booth nearby, in a garden area, were you could purchase a large pot of tea—so Mother was quite happy to sit there in the fresh air and sunshine with her knitting, while I stroked the dog and dreamed of being able to take him home with me.

On most days during the holidays, Mother would have made sandwiches for my lunch—but sometimes she left me sixpence for chips. You could take your own plate to the chip shop, tell them what you wanted, then the plate would be put in the rack. At most lunch times women from around the area would converge on the shop with their plates, then hang around nattering waiting for the chips to be cooked. There was one very fat old lady who lived near our house who would clatter down the street in her clogs, plates held against her ample bosom with one hand and a large enamel jug in the other. The jug was left at the Pub opposite the Chip Shop to be filled with beer. Then she would cross the street to the Chippy, spitting on the plates as she clattered along, then wiping them on her mucky apron before she got to the door. She was known as 'Nellie Belly' and my friends and I would wait until someone else's plate was next to hers in the rack before we took ours in—you seemed to get more chips for you money on a plate. I thought the ladies in the shop were amazing—not only did they know who the plates belonged to, but remembered each order without writing it down. I would sit with my friends on the pavement outside to eat them, then wipe my hands on my shorts. I was supposed to go home with my chips on the plate, sit at the table and eat them with a knife and fork, then wash my hands, plate and cutlery when I had finished—like a well brought up child. But there wasn't much fun in that!

I remember one day during the holidays just roaming around with Doreen. We decided to go into the telephone box opposite Mr Hawkins shop a few streets away. We had just picked up the receiver when the door opened and a very large policeman yanked us out by the backs of our cardigans. We both nearly wet ourselves, as he said that he knew where we lived and would be telling our parents. I managed to stutter out that I only had one parent, and that she would be very cross and we would never do it again. He said that he would let us off this time but would be watching us. Oh my word! I have never been so frightened in my life. I didn't budge out of the house for days afterwards.

One Saturday morning, Doreen and I were walking along the street when we saw a cat stuck in the cellar grating at the chip shop. The poor thing was hanging by the neck from the gap between the grating and the wall. Doreen lay on her tummy on the pavement and managed to scruff it by the back of the neck. I got hold of the slats in the metal grating and just had enough strength to lift it a little and pull it forward. As it slid forward Doreen pulled the cat free and it ran off. Unfortunately I lost my balance, tipped forward and fell down into the cellar and couldn't get out. Doreen ran to get the chip shop lady to open up to let me out. As I had put my arms out as I fell, they took the brunt of the fall and I could tell they were both broken by the pain and their wobbly shape.

After a trip to the Casualty Department—where an X-Ray showed I had greenstick fractures—I came home with both arms in plaster. A couple of days later I was back outside playing, proudly displaying my plaster casts and relating to anyone who would listen how brave I was. The story of the cat rescue became a little more embellished each time it was told. Mother insisted I wore old socks over my arms to keep the plaster casts clean, but once outside I would remove them and stuff them into my pocket—the tatty old socks rather spoiled the image of the intrepid rescuer. I could have broken my neck when I fell. It was a long way down onto the concrete cellar floor. I did some daft things as a child, but most times managed to come out pretty much unscathed.

Another daft incident, though not a serious one, happened one night after I had just gone to bed. I decided to push my right arm down the opposite sleeve of my nightie from the neck downwards. Then I could just about push my left arm up the right sleeve. I haven't a clue why I did it. It must have seemed a good idea at the time. When I tried to take them out I realized I was well and truly stuck. I sat for a while trying to pluck up the courage to shout for Mother. When my arms started to go numb I panicked, and was crying by now, so I sat on the side of my bed and drummed on the floor with my heels. Mother came dashing upstairs and was saying, 'What's the matter? I'm coming I'm coming!' When she saw my predicament she burst out laughing but then when she realized she would have to cut me out of—and ruin—a perfectly good nightie she was not best pleased. She had a hard job cutting it off as there was no room to get the scissors between my skin and the material. She was saying 'Plentyn ffôl!'[2] over and over again. Finally when the offending garment

2 *"Foolish child!"*

lay in tatters on the floor, and she had rubbed the feeling back into my arms—and I had a fresh nightie on—then she really was angry with me. I cried myself to sleep, but in the morning I found a *Jungle Doctor* story book that was on my Christmas list on my pillow. It was Mother's way of saying I was forgiven and that she wasn't cross with me anymore.

After Father died, Mother and I would go to London to stay with Aunty Win and her husband, Uncle Vern, for a week in the summer holidays. We would visit my sister and her growing family, and also another of Mother's sisters, Aunty Dede—and husband Uncle Jack—in Surrey. We would travel up to London by coach. Uncle Vern would meet us at Victoria Coach Station. The coaches in the 'fifties were rickety old things, and very often without heating. This was just about bearable in the summer, but if we went up to my sister's for Christmas—as we often did—we were frozen by the time we got to London. On one journey, I was so cold a very kind man in the opposite seat took off his jumper and gave it to Mother, so she could put my legs into the sleeves to keep warm. The journey used to take nine hours and I hated it. The coach always smelled so badly of petrol fumes and cigarette smoke that I would be sick. Feeling a retch coming on, I would say to Mother, 'My mouth's going square!' At least it did give her a warning of the event to come.

It was lovely to see my sister Pat, and the children, at Christmas. But Mother and Dennis—my sister's husband—did not get along together. After a few days, the atmosphere was thick with ill feeling. Being a perceptive little madam, I had sensed this mutual dislike from a very early age.

My sister had twelve children and the eldest, Peter, was only three years younger than me. Over the years, Pat and the children would come to stay, but from when I was about eleven years old they would come on their own to stay with Mother—for the whole of their summer holidays. The eldest five came first—until they got too big—then the middle ones, and finally the younger ones. I had left home by the time it was the youngest ones' turn. I can picture Mother now, standing at the end of the tea table, with a large loaf tucked in the crook of her arm. The bread would be buttered and spread with jam before she cut perfectly even slices from it with a huge bread knife. A loaf was always held and cut this way. There would be lots of eager little hands waiting but anyone who dared to take a piece, before there was enough cut for all, would be given what the children called the 'Logan Look'. For very naughty, greedy little boys with snatching hands, there was a long thin cane that would be used to give a quick little whack across the knuckles—typically Robert's.

When the middle children—Stephen, David, Barbara, Christopher, Ruth and Margaret—visited, I was working at Chester Zoo. I would give Mother the money for the bus fare for a zoo visit. Also I would take them on a shopping trip, togging each of them out in a new outfit. I would let Mrs Wall—in the zoo entrance kiosk—know the day they were visiting and she would just wave them through. When John and I were courting, we would take them on days out to Southport fun fair. One summer, Pat and Richard—the youngest child—visited as well. John and I were married by then and he took us all in his transit van to visit Grandpa and Granny's old house in Northop. We borrowed two wooden benches from St Mark's Church Sunday School, which we put in the back of the van for the children to sit on. The only concession to safety we made, was that John tied rope around the bench legs and secured them to the stanchions inside the van.

It was a lovely day. Mother had cooked two legs of lamb, and with fresh salad, homemade bread and chocolate sponge cakes to follow, it was a real feast. We boiled a kettle for tea on the old Primus stove we had in the back of the van, and the children had pop. My eldest child, Christopher, was about six months old and was given a fresh peach. He ate every scrap, making contented little humming noises which made the children laugh. We had our picnic in Grandpa's old garden. It was just a wonderful day, and my nieces and nephews still remember it with great fondness. The old house had been pulled down, and a modern one built in its place. Mother and Pat were upset at first, to find the old place gone, and the Market Garden derelict. But they were happy to find out that the new house was now owned by one of Pat's childhood friends from Sychdyn.

One summer, when the children were coming to stay, Mother realized she was a little short of dinner plates. So she decided to go St Helens Market, to see if she could get a bargain. There was always a man or two who would sell crockery from the back of a van, and always sold by a falling auction. They would hold up various assortments of crockery, state the price, then keep reducing it until the first customer to put up their hand bought the items. Mother acquired six nice, white plates quite cheaply and was pleased with her bargain. When she got home and unwrapped them, she found they were not the ones she had been shown. They must have been swapped. Every plate had lumps of dis-coloured glaze on the rims. None of the children wanted to eat off them. They were known from then on as 'Nanny's Snot Plates'. I can assure you that was a very accurate description.

All of my nieces and nephews made friends with the local children, and these friendships were renewed every year. One year Richard—the youngest—had been given a dressing up costume for his fifth birthday, and wore it every day for a week. A little boy knocked on the door one day, and made Mother laugh when he said, 'Is the Red Indian that lives in your house coming out to play?'

If the weather was fine they all spent a lot of time in Victoria Park nearby, but all had to do their chores before they went out to play. Mother must have been worn out washing, cooking and looking after up to seven children at a time. My nieces and nephews are all grandparents now, but still talk about their Nan and—even though she was very strict—how much they loved her.

10: WALES

I must have been about five years old the first time I remember visiting my Uncles and Aunts. As we crossed the old iron bridge across the River Dee at Queensferry, Mother told me that we were now in Wales. I was so excited, but when we got off the bus in Mold, the excitement turned to disappointment, as the people looked exactly the same as us. No national costume and no dancing in the street. My imagination had been running riot as usual.

We caught another bus to Sychdyn, where Uncle Harry and Aunty Greta lived. Their house was called 'Springfield' and I always thought it was a lovely name. When we approached the house, I noticed the big side gate into the garden had a little iron wheel on the bottom. So a little while later I opened it wide, then stood on it as it swung shut—with the wheel making a lovely crunching noise over the gravel. The only thing I didn't like about Spring Field was the old well outside the back kitchen door. Although this was coved over with a big iron grating, I was terrified of falling into it. Extensions had been added to the back of the house over the years, bringing the house nearer and nearer to the well until it was directly outside the back door. To get past it, I would flatten myself against the door jamb and the wall. By placing my feet sideways there was just enough room to shuffle past without standing on the grating. My fear was made worse by Uncle Harry.

'Off out again are you? Mind you don't fall down the well!'

I am sure if he had known how terrified I was he would not have said it. Stupid child that I was, it never entered my head to tell them. Being brought up by a Mother who always coped in awkward situations, I did the same—and still do.

While Mother, Harry and Greta were catching up on all the news, I wandered about the garden and up and down the road, as there was hardly any traffic in those days. On this very first visit I met old Mr. William Williams. He was known locally as 'Billy Twicey', for obvious reasons— the Welsh are so good at nick names. He was peddling up the road on the biggest tricycle I had ever seen. I couldn't believe a grown up would own and ride a trike. He stopped to talk to me and asked who I was, and I was so pleased when I told him as he knew Mother well. I wasn't at all shy with him—as I usually was with strangers—and I asked him about his bike. He told me he oiled it with rum and milk and that's why it had grown so big. I believed him of course.

In late afternoon, Mother and I walked over to Northop to visit Aunty Charlotte—who was known as 'Nanty'—and Uncle Jim. Nanty was Mother's dearest friend and not related to us. She was one of the few people outside the family who used my Mother's Christian name. I came to love her dearly and had some wonderful holidays with her, usually when Mother had gone to London to look after Pat's brood, when a new baby was on the scene. Uncle Jim always had a couple of pigs in the sty, and it wasn't until a few years later that I made the connection between them and the hams and sides of bacon hanging in the back pantry.

Mother and Nanty had a wonderful time talking about their childhood. Mother was reminiscing about my Grandpa Oldcorn's market garden and about how—once or twice a week—he would take the produce around the neighbouring villages in his pony and trap. If Polly the pony didn't want to be harnessed, she would go and stand in the middle of the duck pond. Mother said that Grandpa had a very short temper and would be shouting and jumping up and down in a rage at the edge of the pond. When it got to the point where he took off his hat and stamped on it, then that was the time for all the children to disappear. Sometimes he would drive to Chester in the trap to buy seed potatoes, and vegetable and flower seeds, from Burgess's the seed merchants. He would usually take one of children with him and it was a real treat to be chosen. It would take all day to drive to Chester and back, and Polly was always kept in the stable overnight just in case, as they always had to make an early start. Mother said that Aunty Mill had gone with him on his village rounds one day, and when she returned home told Granny, 'Dada kissed Miss Price by the privy!' As you can imagine, none of them ever went with him again—the naughty man.

Mother and I stayed at Nanty Bateman's overnight. The next day we caught the bus to Cerrigydrudion, to visit Mother's youngest brother Uncle Rupert, his wife Aunty Flo, my cousin Russell and Granny Oldcorn. Granny had lived in Sychdyn with Mother and Father until the family moved to St Helens, then she went to live with Uncle Rupert who was the youngest of her brood of ten. Uncle Rupe had a small-holding and also bred rabbits for the table. Until he bought the small holding he had been a head gardener on different estates, one down in Devon and one on the Wirral. He was also an avid cultivator of carnations.

I was so excited about seeing Granny. She was bedridden by now, so I went up to her bedroom and climbed onto the bed to give her a kiss on her lovely, soft skinned Irish face. My Grandmother, Alice Campbell, was born in County Tyrone in 1864 and her surname was the anglicized translation of Mac Cathmhaoil. In her white nightie and knitted bed jacket, I thought she looked just like the Granny from the tale of *Red Riding Hood*. I proudly told her I could read and she was very pleased, as she had always been an avid reader herself. Picking up her bible from the bedside table she asked me to read Psalm 121 as that was her favourite—'I will lift up mine eyes unto the hills, from whence cometh my help.' I managed to get through it without too many mistakes, and I was so happy when she praised me. We stayed overnight, so when it was my bedtime I went to say goodnight and sang *Away in a Manger* for her. I didn't see her the next morning, as we left for home early and she was still asleep.

Mother said that she was an educated woman, and when they were children the Vicar and local Roman Catholic priest would come up to the house and have long discussions with her about politics and religion. Also when the Gypsies came and camped at Northop every year, if they needed any letters writing they would come up to the house to see Granny. She even went to court as a character witness for one of the Gypsy men, when he was arrested for threatening to harm his son. He told Granny that his son had let the horses wander off when he was supposed to be watching them, and that he was angry with him and had threatened to cut his 'bloody ears off'. Someone overheard him and reported him to the police. Granny convinced the Magistrate that it was just a figure of speech, and that the father was an honest, hard working man. He was released with a caution. I would have loved to have known her for longer than I did, as she must have been a very interesting woman. I know my brother and sister adored her and Grandpa—as both he, and his temper, had mellowed with age.

In this day and age we can pop into a car and visit anywhere at any time, but our journey to Wales entailed getting a bus to Liverpool from St Helens, walking down to the Pier Head, crossing to Birkenhead on the ferry, catching a bus to Mold, then another bus to Sychdyn. It seemed to take forever. When I was a little older, Mother and I would manage to do the visit in one day and just visit one Uncle and Aunt at a time. On the journey home we were always laden with produce from the garden.

One of the Greenhouses at Uncle Harry's was always full of beautiful potted plants, and Mother would have her eye on the one she wanted.

'Not that one Madge,' Uncle Harry would say, winking at me. 'That's for exhibition. You had better pick another one.'

He would tease her until just before we left for home, then present her with the one she really wanted already wrapped up. I could just about manage to carry the huge bunch of flowers Uncle Harry had also cut—and Mother would struggle with the bags of produce, not wanting to leave anything behind.

As I got older I realized that Mother and Aunty Greta didn't really like each other much. They would be politely catty to each other.

'That's a nice dress Madge. So well designed, that the sleeves disguise the plumper arm.'

'The colour suits you Greta, although at your age I thought you would prefer the hem a little lower', says Mother. 'Your dress is nice Greta, it is so well tailored it flatters the fuller figure.'

So it went on. I stored all these little snippets in my retentive, nosey little brain in the compartment labelled 'family quips'.

I loved Aunty Greta. She was big, kind and jolly and very Irish. Pat and Dick loved her too. I tasted Cadbury's *Mini Rolls* for the first time at Uncle Harry's, but Mother said I was only allowed one. After tea when I went back out into the garden, Uncle Harry sneaked another one for me and said it was our secret. My delight was rather spoiled by my fear that Mother would find out and be cross, but I stuffed it down anyway. I think Mother thought Greta was a little lazy—a deadly sin as far as she was concerned. Harry and Greta had one son named Roy, and evidently he had practically lived at Mother's when he was a boy, as he loved her cooking. Mother commented that Greta didn't exert herself in the kitchen department.

It's strange that Uncle Harry, Uncle Rupert and Roy all had Irish wives.

A few days after Father died, I was packed off to stay with Aunty Bloss and Uncle Joe in Buckley until after the funeral. I can't remember how I got there—perhaps my cousin Bobby came to fetch me. Bloss was an older sister of Mother's and very small, thin and fierce. Uncle Joe was just the opposite— he was plump with big red rosy cheeks, and a real darling. I adored him.

Auntie's name was really Kathleen, but she had been called 'Little Blossom' as a child and it had stuck. They looked after me very well and took me on lovely days out. Aunty was kind in her own way, but I was still a little frightened of her.

They had a bathroom, which was very posh compared to our outside loo and tin bath. I was told not to touch anything except what I needed to. Standing in the bathroom on my first day looking at the two cords hanging from the ceiling, and wondering what they were for, I couldn't resist giving the one by the loo a tug. When the extractor fan came on I nearly died of shock and didn't know how to switch it off, never thinking that pulling it again would do the trick. I was afraid to go and tell what I had done, so I climbed onto the loo seat, then onto the small cupboard at the side—then tried to push the cord back up into the ceiling. It was only when I wobbled a little and jerked the cord that I realized how it worked. I nearly cried with relief. I am sure Aunty wasn't that fierce—it was just me being a wimp.

The next hurdle to overcome was the small glass of Epsom salts I was presented with each morning. I am sorry to say that, after the first morning, the potted palm in the corner of the dining room drank it instead. I don't know if the poor thing survived, as it wasn't there on subsequent visits and I certainly didn't enquire after its health. After Aunty had placed my glass on the table, she would go and hunt down Uncle Joe to give him his dose—he always disappeared at Epsom salts time. If she found him he would refuse to drink it and tell her to drink it herself. I always thought he was so brave refusing to do what she told him.

One morning, I was sitting in the doorway of his shed with him while he smoked his pipe, and I told him about the bathroom cord 'episode'. He patted me on the hand and told me I could always go to him if I had a problem, as he was very good at keeping secrets. So I told him about the Epsom salts and the Palm plant. He laughed and said that he wished he had thought of that.

Uncle Joe was twenty two years older than Aunty Bloss. Before he married he was, for many years, personal Valet to Lord Cholmondeley—

who was known as a 'gentleman's gentleman'—and had travelled all over the world with him. Uncle Joe and Aunty Bloss met while working at Cholmondeley Castle, when Bloss was a ladies' maid there. Mother said that his fate was sealed once Aunty Bloss got her hooks into him. Joe told Mother that Lord Cholmondeley had once asked him if he really wanted to marry, and that he had said 'Not really.' But he wouldn't go back on his word. So William Joseph Titcombe married Kathleen Georgina Oldcorn in Ffestiniog in 1922.

After they were married, they worked as Butler and Cook for the Greaves family at Wern Manor, near Criccieth.[1]

Mother told me that Aunty Bloss ruled all the kitchen staff with a rod of iron, even opening any personal letters that the kitchen maids received. Mother was scandalised by this, and felt so sorry for the kitchen maids. She told Bloss that she had no right to open the girls' letters. But in those days the Cook's word was law, so Bloss took not a jot of notice of Mothers disdain—she just carried on being the ruler of all the staff 'below stairs'. Before the war—and up until they moved to St Helens—Pat and Dick would spend part of their summer holidays at Wern. They had the run of the grounds and would swim in the lily pond. They were pretty much left to their own devices in the day time, as Uncle and Aunty were busy working in the big house. On most days they would walk over the mountain to Black Rock Sands at Porthmadog, taking sandwiches and an enamel billycan full of cold tea. They would stay all day playing on the beach, then walk home in time for their evening meal—which they usually had in the kitchen of the big house.

Aunty and Uncle had their own cottage in the big yard at the back of the house. When my brother visited us from Canada about twenty years ago, we went to Wern and he told us so many stories about his childhood holidays there. At the time of our visit, Wern had become a Care Home and the manager kindly took us on a tour of the house. Dick was delighted to see that the motto 'Waste not, want not' was still painted on the wall in the kitchen and the sign 'Butlers House' was still on the door of the old cottage.

After Joe and Bloss retired they bought a house in Buckley, then after a few years moved to the village of Fawnog into a bungalow, with a much bigger garden and a small orchard. I had some nice holidays with them, and as I was now a little older coped much better with Aunty B's rules

1 *The Greaves were the owners of the Llechwedd slate quarry in Blaenau Ffestiniog.*

and regulations. Amazingly I was allowed to walk across the fields on my own —to Sychdyn or Northop—to visit my Uncles and Aunts.

Uncle Joe was not allowed to smoke in the house so would sit in the doorway of his shed, happily puffing away on his pipe. My cousin Bobby had part of the shed as his workshop. He was a keen builder of petrol powered model aircraft and I loved to watch him make and fly them. Uncle Joe was very slightly deaf, but used to pretend he couldn't hear anything at all when Aunty B was nagging. He would cup his hand around his ear, wink at me, and say, 'What, what? Do speak up Kathleen!' When the apple, pear and plum trees were fruiting, I was only allowed to pick up the fallen fruit. But Uncle Joe would hook the handle of his walking stick around a branch and give it a shake and say, 'There you are dear child, lots for you to choose from!'

When Aunty Bloss had to call tradesmen to the house, she called them just by their surnames. Mother used to get cross and embarrassed at this. She used to say that she didn't know where Bloss got her 'airs and graces' from, as she had been at school with most of them and had gone barefoot like everyone else. It must have been from when she was in service as the Cook Housekeeper and had ruled the roost—according to Mother, 'rule the roost' she most certainly did. Although Mother also ruled with a rod of iron, she was but a pussy cat compared to Aunty Bloss.

Joe and Bloss would often visit—and sometimes stay—with us in St Helens. Aunty would still have a mission to hunt down Joe every morning, glass of Epsom salts in hand. I don't know why she continued with this nonsense. It was totally unnecessary. Joe would never drink the damned stuff anyway. The performance was very amusing though, as although now Uncle Joe used a walking stick, he certainly could move at speed when chased.

Uncle Joe died in the summer of 1964, aged ninety. For the last few weeks of his life, Mother went to help Aunty Bloss look after him. Mother said Bloss hadn't much patience and didn't like washing him, or carrying out any of the other tasks that went with looking after a dying old man. She told me that she was so glad she could show him a little love and affection, and help him keep his dignity in his last few weeks. I was working at Chester Zoo by then, so I managed to visit him a few times in those last weeks. On the day of the funeral—when the

Undertaker brought the coffin back to the house—I went and picked one flower each from the many different varieties in Joe's beloved garden. Mother and I placed them all around him in the coffin. Aunty Bloss was quite touched by this and when Mother placed his favourite pipe in his hand, Bloss at last had a little weep.

I had loved this kind, dignified gentleman with all my heart. As Mother said, he was a darling man.

11: RIVINGTON SCHOOL

I didn't pass the eleven plus, as my Maths let me down. I had sat the exam just before I was diagnosed with Osteomyelitis, and Les had pushed me in the push chair to the school where the exam was held. The old bat who was the adjudicator refused to let Les push me up the aisle to my allotted desk—God alone knows why—and I had to hop almost to the back of the room. When the exam was over and I got up to start hopping down to the front, Les came zooming up the aisle with my pushchair, making a noise like a racing car. I sat in it, then he zoomed back down the aisle shouting, 'Make way for the invalid!' He was so quick the old bat didn't have time to stop him. She just stood with her mouth opening and shutting like a goldfish. He was such a clown of a boy and everyone was laughing at him. My kind, cheeky friend. How I loved him!

When the exam results were announced at Windle School I was disappointed, but had expected that I would fail. Mr Eaton, my teacher, told me that I was 'border line' in Maths and that I would have a chance later in the year to re-sit. In the meantime I had to decide which school I wanted to attend, as there was a choice of three. Most of my friends were going to Rivington. Mr Eaton had told me that, as it was the best of the three, to get my name down for it quickly. I told Mother what Mr Eaton had said. Thank goodness she did go and put my name down promptly.

Mother couldn't afford a new school blazer for me. I had a hand me down from my cousin Sheila in London—it was grey with royal blue and silver piping. As the Rivington Girls uniform was brown, cream and gold, Mother had to dye it. Thankfully it took the dye well, as I would have had to wear it no matter what. Luckily it turned out fine, and with a new badge on the pocket it was really very smart. There was no spare money for a real leather school satchel, so Mother made me a canvas book bag. However, at Christmas time I received a parcel from Aunty Dede and Uncle Jack, who were now living in Durban, South Africa. In the parcel was a splendid leather school satchel full of pens, pencils and lots of school paraphernalia—including a very 'swish' wooden pencil case that had my name on top. I was thrilled with everything and just loved my satchel, as it was all stiff and shiny and smelled wonderful.

On the first morning of term Doreen and I set off, meeting and picking up other friends on the way. It was the furthest distance from home of the three schools, but the best academically. I settled in quite quickly and I loved all my lessons—except the dreaded Maths of course. I was in the A-Stream and only had two friends from Windle in my class, but I made a new best friend, who had the wonderful name of Patricia Jane Wedgewood Briscoe. We had some inspirational teachers, but also some not so inspirational. And some, in fact, quite odd.

Kind Mrs Moss taught me History, and she nurtured my already deep love of the subject. Tiny Mrs Freeman, our English teacher, made every lesson so interesting. Dear old Miss Hall was my Music teacher, and she introduced me to—and fostered—my love of classical music. I remember listening to the old 78's she would play on the music room's wind up gramophone. At the age of twelve I listened to the beautiful *Adagio* from Bruch's Violin Concerto with tears rolling down my face. She introduced me to Mozart, Beethoven, Ralph Vaughn Williams, Verdi, Puccini, and many, many more. When I heard the Duet from Bizet's *The Pearl Fishers*, sung by Jussi Björling and Robert Merrill, I was once again reduced to tears. This is my favourite performance of the many I have heard over the years. I just love Jussi Björling's voice. Miss Hall once taught the class Strauss's *Radetzky March,* and I still remember the words to Schubert's *Hark, Hark the Lark!* Later in life, I would sing this to Matthew—my youngest child—as a tiny boy while watching and listening to the larks in the field next to our house. I don't think it's an exaggeration to say Miss Hall changed and enriched my life.

Miss Wroe, my Geography teacher, took the class on wonderful field trips. Miss Roe was the Art mistress, who I didn't like much, but I did enjoy her Art classes. Mrs Howard, the Maths and Combined Science's mistress, tried her hardest to help me enjoy Maths. Miss Yates—my much loved R.E. and English Lit teacher—was in charge of the school library. We had the most wonderful discussions about books I had read, and books she suggested I should read. Miss White, the 4th form English mistress, was not very likable but a good teacher, though she liked to remind us constantly that she was Deputy Head Mistress—as if we cared a stuff.

Mrs Bagnall—we nicknamed her 'Baggy Aggie'—later replaced Mrs Freeman. Aggie was big, loud and terrifying. Her motto was 'When in doubt, give a clout!' This she would shout at us while whacking the desk with a ruler. The only girl she had no effect on was Norah Bishop, as she was tough and intelligent and didn't take any notice of Aggie's threats. We all wished we had her courage. I have no clue why Aggie thought it necessary to shout and bawl at us.

Miss Greenall was the quintessential Gym mistress with her muscular thighs, big teeth and great enthusiasm in lessons—rather like one of Joyce Grenfell's characters but much larger. With my big feet and skinny, uncoordinated legs I was useless at Gym—Miss Greenhall would just sigh, shake her head and say that I needed to try a little harder.

With Miss Millington, the Domestic Science teacher, there was a mutual feeling of dislike between us from the word go. There was a lot of theory and very little practical teaching in most of her lessons in the first year. The majority of girls in my class—including me—could already make tea and toast and boil, scramble and poach eggs with our eyes closed. The majority of the class knew the names of the different sizes of spoons and could also tell the difference between the salt and pepper pots. We were eleven years old for God's sake, not three! There was always a charge of one shilling and sixpence for ingredients, but we didn't do much cooking in the first year as it was mostly the boring theory. Mother always managed to give me the money but a class mate, Ava Gill, never had the money to pay as she was from a large family—there just was not any to money to spare. We always felt sorry for her, as Miss Millington would make such a fuss and Ava would be in tears. It just made me hate the nasty cow even more. I disliked Domestic Science and all the 'faff' that went with it. All utensils had to be laid out in straight rows, all ingredients were to be weighed and put into separate bowls before we started cooking, and pastry to be measured as it was being rolled out.

I got into trouble for leaving my apple pie in the oven longer than I was supposed to. Miss Millington liked the pastry pale, but I was used to Mother's superb baking and said that we liked our pastry cooked. I wasn't being rude, just stating a fact. But I received my one and only demerit mark in my whole time at school for this remark. Mother and I could have baked enough food for an army in the time it took to make one apple pie at school.

After my second term, I was told that I could re-sit the Eleven Plus. Mother actually asked me if wanted to take the exam—which was a minor miracle—but I said no. I didn't want to change schools. I had been top in all of my subjects except Maths in the Christmas exams. I loved school and sailed through my four years at Rivington, coming top of the class every year. In my last year I was made Head Girl. I went home so full of my exciting news. When I told Mother she looked at me and said, 'Well the title fits your head. It's certainly looking much bigger than it did this morning.' Good old Mother. One of her cutting comments always deflated my ego, and this brought me crashing back down to earth. I was hoping for just a little 'Well done Pam, that's fantastic', but never mind.

Every Friday afternoon, after break, one of my tasks as Head Girl was to collect all the merit books from the form teachers, then make the house charts to determine who had won the house cup that week. There were four houses, Windsor was red, Buckingham was blue, Sandringham was yellow and Balmoral green. I was in Balmoral and, much to my shame and annoyance, we were—more often than not—bottom of the chart each week. However, I would happily sit in the Prefects room with a cup of tea totting up the points, and drawing and colouring the charts. It was a lovely way to while away the last double lesson as—joy of joys!—I was usually missing Domestic Science.

As the time came nearer to leaving school, my thoughts turned to getting a job. I had written to Chester Zoo and they had replied, informing me that as I would have to live away from home they wouldn't take me until I was eighteen—and to apply again in a few years. How strange and old fashioned that sounds now. Although I was disappointed that I would have to wait a while, it was really a good thing. At just fifteen I definitely wasn't mature enough to leave home and live in lodgings. In fact I was a bit of a twit and not at all worldly wise.

The school Careers Officer nearly had a fit when I told him what I intended to do.

'What a waste of a brain.' He said.

He told me that I should get a job in an office. I told the ignorant man that it took more brains to be a Zoo Keeper than it did to work in an office, and the idea of being shut inside all day was my worst nightmare. Even Baggy Aggie gave me the third degree, but seeing the mutinous look on my face she did eventually stop her constant nagging. Even to this day, most people think that working with animals requires little to no intelligence.

12: TURNER'S FLORISTS

I did think about working in a boarding kennels, but the only decent one I could find had no vacancies. As I wanted to work outdoors I asked at Turner's Florists, in the middle of the town, if there were any vacancies at their market garden. Mr Turner said that there would be a vacancy after Christmas, and that in the meantime I could have a job in the shop. Mother was pleased with my choice, and so began my wonderful three years working for the Turners, who became my second family. Most of the employees in the shop were real family members. Mr Turner was known as 'Daddy Joe' and I was told to call him this as well. It was funny to see the expression on customers faces when all six female assistants called him Dad—they must have thought, 'Poor man, with all those daughters to keep!'

I learned such a lot in my time at the shop, but of course I got all the worst jobs at first, due to being the youngest. By far the worst job was lacing up Aunt Moll's corsets after she had been to the loo. She was an old Aunt of Daddy Joe's and a real character. The shop had a huge cellar, where the flower stock was kept, either in large buckets or in the walk-in fridge—which was for blooms that had to be held back a little in their development. Around the walls were huge cupboards, where the wreaths and bouquets were placed in the dark, after they had been dampened down, until they were ready to go out to the customers the next day. Also in the cellar was the loo. If I was working down there, my heart would sink if I heard Moll's footsteps on the stairs. If I was upstairs in the shop after she had been to the loo, she would stand at the bottom of the stairs and shout, 'JOE, JOE? I HAVE FINISHED, SEND HER DOWN!'

She never used my name. It was always 'her' or 'you, what's yer name.' Maris used to grin when she heard Moll shouting, as she had been the youngest until I arrived. Can you imagine any employee being willing to carry out this task nowadays! Moll was in her late seventies, but was still very quick when making wreaths, and it would take two of us to 'wire' for her. 'Wiring' was taking one or more flowers and wrapping a wire around the shortened stem, leaving a piece long enough to be pushed into the straw and moss wreath base. Roses were wired through the base of the flower with very fine wire first, then the thicker wire could be twisted around the stem with no fear of the head dropping off. Margaret and Lucy always made the wedding bouquets, and it was a while before I was skilled enough to wire for them, as the flowers were very delicate and often very expensive.

Daddy Joe's son-in-law—also called Joe but known to everyone as 'Huttie'—made the wreath bases. It looked much simpler than it was, and involved taking a handful of straw and moss then moulding it and tying it to a wire base, until the shape was finished. The wreath bases came in different shapes—rings, small crosses, large crosses, rectangle's and coffin lids. Sometimes there would be a request for a special shape, so Huttie would cut and reform wire bases to the required shape. Customers would order the shape, and sometimes the type and colour of flowers they wanted. Very often the requests would be completely over the top, and the colours just ghastly. When making them we would be muttering about people's bad taste. Funerals were huge affairs in the 'fifties, and even the poorest of families would go into debt giving their loved one a good send off.

Huttie was also the delivery van driver, and sometimes I would be sent with him if he had a really big load. He had a bad leg and found it difficult to keep getting in and out of the back of the van—but I could nip in and out quickly. On one memorable occasion, when delivering a large amount of wreaths to a small terraced house, we were asked by the owner to leave them on the pavement outside—there wasn't enough room for them in the house. When they were all in place, the neighbours emerged from their houses to look at them, wearing suitably sad faces and remarking on the display.

The house owner said to us, 'Come in and have a drink with our Mam!'

I thought 'How kind! I would love a cup of tea.' We stepped into the tiny living room to find that 'Our Mam' was lying in an open coffin on the table, surrounded by dirty breakfast plates, empty glasses and port and whiskey bottles. Oh my God. I couldn't believe it!

'Come and raise a glass to Mam,' he said, nudging me nearer. 'Doesn't she look lovely?' He said, nudging me even nearer.

'Our Mam's' face had so much make up on it was grotesque. I had never seen a dead body before, and by now was feeling a little faint. Huttie was smiling at me—the devil!—as he had known full well what to expect. Whereas I, at fifteen, was as thick as a brick and had not a clue. Still smiling, he said he would have a small whiskey. A used glass was wiped out with the corner of a none-too-clean apron and a very large 'small' whisky was pushed into his hand by—I presume—the daughter-in-law of 'Our Mam'. Smiling through gritted teeth I politely refused a drink. By now I was feeling a tad queasy and just wanted to get out of there. When we got back to the shop, Huttie told the tale and we all had a good laugh about it. The teasing and the banter at my expense continued for a few days. The novelty of going on deliveries waned after this experience so after that, if I did have to go, I stayed in the van—while Huttie alone had the pleasure of raising a glass to the corpse.

So under the Turner family's tuition, my journey into how things fared in the 'big wide world' began. Aunt Moll didn't approve of me going out on deliveries, because she thought I wasn't earning my wages—not that it was any of her business. I remarked that I should be getting paid double for working with Huttie. He laughed at this, and putting his arm around me said that he was proud of me for coming along nicely in the 'learning not to be so thick' department. Maris wasn't keen on me going out on deliveries either, as that meant she was on corset duty when I wasn't there. So I would grin and wave cheerily to her whenever I left the shop.

Aunt Moll was a bit of a kleptomaniac. At most lunch times, while we were all busy eating, she would toddle off to the market around the corner to see what bargains could be had—helping herself out of the shop till as she passed. We always knew when she was approaching the till, because she would sing the 23rd Psalm very loudly. The strains of 'The Lord is my shepherd, I shall not want', followed by the loud ding of the bell on the till drawer rather gave the game away. After she returned from her shopping trip, we would wait a few minutes, then all the stall holders who she had pinched things from would come to reclaim their goods. They were different things every day, and could range from a ball of wool, and lumps of cheese to jewellery—and nearly always a cabbage. Moll was very fond of a nice fat cabbage. The person on counter duty at lunch time would go into Moll's big black bag under the counter, and hand all the goods back to the owners. She was a real pest, but everyone knew her and never challenged her. They just came in quietly and asked for their goods back—bless their hearts.

Once a year, the Dutch bulb merchants that Turner's dealt with would come to the shop. Daddy Joe would order the required amounts and varieties of daffodil, hyacinths, tulips, lily bulbs and iris corms for the Nurseries for the following year. The Dutch men always brought an enormous box of chocolates for the staff to share, and would present it to dear old white haired, apple cheeked Moll. She would smile sweetly at them, then toddle off and put the box in her big black bag under the counter—so we never even caught a glimpse of a chocolate let alone got to taste one. This performance had been going on for years. When Moll passed away a few years later, dozens of boxes of chocolate were found stashed, and going mouldy, under her bed.

The hours at the shop were nine to six. We were supposed to have an hour for dinner, but we never did. If there was a large wedding or funeral order, we would work over time and start at eight and sometimes work until seven. This happened quite often and we were paid two shillings and sixpence for this extra hour. As I was only earning one pound ten shillings a week—which I gave to Mother—this was treasure indeed. Some weeks I could double my wages. We all had an overtime pot in which we saved our money, only counting it up at the end of the month. The pots were kept high up on a shelf—just in case Moll's sticky little fingers wandered.

One of the biggest weddings we catered for was when Margaret—who worked in the shop—married Young Joe, Daddy Joe's son. It was a lovely wedding and Margaret looked so happy. She was such a nice person and was loved by everyone who knew her, including me. She had taken me under her wing when I first started working at the shop, and patiently taught me so much about the florist trade. Margaret and Joe were Godparents to my children when they came along. We kept in touch until she died tragically in her early sixties. I was bereft when Joe rang to give me the sad news. St James' Church, Eccleston Park, was packed both inside and out with hundreds of people for her funeral service. It was a token of how much she was loved, not just by family and friends but also people in the wider community, of all races and creeds. She was such a happy person and a committed Christian and was a shining example of her faith.

As Christmas approached, I kept nagging Daddy Joe about keeping his promise of the job at Nutgrove Nurseries, because he wanted me to stay and work in the shop. When he finally said I could start there in the New Year I was so relieved. I asked Huttie if he would be guarantor for the new bicycle I needed—I would have to buy it on Hire Purchase. He said that of course he would. Huttie seemed to know just about everybody in St Helens, and he took me to a bike shop owned by a friend of his. I had been saving my overtime money so I could put down a decent deposit, and as Huttie had wrangled with his friend to give me a good discount, I could actually afford a better quality model than I expected. So I became the owner of a rather splendid Raleigh ladies' bike. Mother was horrified when I told her it was bought on HP, as her mantra was 'If you can't afford it, you do without'. I pointed out that I would save a fortune in bus fares and it would be paid off in six months. She could see the wisdom in this, but her fear of debt was so ingrained in her psyche that it was difficult for her.

On Christmas Eve, as a surprise, the girls at the shop presented me with a copy of David Attenborough's latest book—*Zoo Quest for a Dragon*. Earlier in December, I had told them that I was hoping Mother might buy it for me for Christmas. Evidently Margaret had met Mother in town and told her not to buy it, as they had already bought it for me as a surprise. It was such a lovely thing to do and—I very much suspect—instigated by Margaret, bless her. At the beginning of January—on my last day at the shop—the girls, Huttie and Daddy Joe gave me a splendid penknife to use at the nurseries.

13: NUTGROVE NURSERIES

The long awaited day had finally arrived, and I set off early on my shiny new bicycle. I had been to the nurseries a few times, on my half days off on Thursdays, so I already knew everybody. Daddy Joe's two brothers worked there. Uncle Bill was the boss and lived in the nursery house with his wife Mabel and their family. Uncle Eric—the youngest brother—was the sweet pea and cucumber expert. Also working there were Young Joe, David—one of Bill and Mabel's sons—and Little Chris, who was Uncle Eric's son and the same age as me. The other employees were not family members, and they all had their names prefixed by the word 'Owd'—which means 'old' in St Helens dialect. There was Owd June, Owd Geoff, Owd Bessie, Owd Winnie and last but not least Owd Donald. None of them were actually old—it was just Uncle Bill's wicked sense of humour. Oh boy, did he have a sense of humour! I soon learned not to let slip any snippet of information that he could pounce on and turn into the amusement of the day. It was hilarious if you were not the victim.

Owd Donald didn't mind being teased by Uncle Bill, as he worshiped both him and Aunty Mabel, but he would not take it off anyone else. He was a big man and very strange, with a violent, unpredictable temper. Smelling like a midden, he would most certainly not have been employable anywhere else.

The first job I worked on was bringing in the daffodil boxes from the field. The bulbs had been planted out in the field the previous autumn, and the boxes covered in soil. Now it was time to bring them in to be 'forced' in the warmth of the greenhouses. The men carefully dug the boxes out of the frozen ground, then the girls tipped them onto their sides and poked between the shoots with a piece of bamboo cane to remove the soil. This had to be done quickly but carefully. Anyone who broke the shoots got a whack from Uncle Bill's trilby. It was only a token whack, and didn't hurt much—he saved the more powerful whacks for Owd Donald. We never thought anything of it though, and accepted any discipline as normal. When the shoots in the boxes were clear of the top soil, they were loaded onto the tractor trailer. Some of us would go down on the trailer and some would stay in the field, so there was always another load waiting when the tractor came back. We took it in turns going down with a load, as it was a chance to warm up a little. The daffs were brought in from the field in stages, so that there would be flowers to sell in the shop and take to Liverpool flower market up until Easter.

The girls showed me how to put hay in my wellies to keep my feet warm, and we wore thick rubber gloves over our woolly ones. We also had sacks tied above our waists with string. These kept our fronts clean and also acted as padding, as constantly lifting heavy boxes up against our fronts, to put them on the trailer, made our stomachs sore. It was hard work but I was young and strong, and soon very fit as well.

At break time and lunch time we all piled on the trailer to go down to the blessed warmth of the conservatory, singing and laughing on the journey back to the yard, and even though I was half frozen I had never felt so happy in my life.

Hyacinths were always planted three to a bowl outside in 'clamps' in late summer—some of these were brought in earlier than the daffs, as they were needed for the Christmas trade. The lifting and placing on to the greenhouse benches had to be done very carefully, so as not to crack the terracotta bowls—this was a job for the girls. They were 'brought on' until the flower spikes were just appearing through the leaves and were then ready to be sold. Others were allowed to grow on into full flower, and then used in funeral wreaths. The sight and smell of thousands of hyacinths in full bloom was glorious. Hyacinth pollen didn't affect me much, but Uncle Bill used to get a dreadful rash on his hands from handling hyacinth and tulip bulbs—the skin between his fingers would crack. We would dress the tops of the bowls with moss before they went to the shop and flower market.

The little moss man would arrive in the autumn in an ancient little van, which seemed to be held together with string and prayer. He was tiny and thin, with a thick thatch of white hair, tinged with green. I don't think it had seen shampoo for years. He wore an old brown mac down to his ankles, tied around his middle with string. His Yorkshire accent was so thick that we almost needed an interpreter. Surprisingly, he was very strong and would swing the long giant sacks of moss around with ease. Uncle Bill said he had been coming for donkey's years, and had sold moss to them when Grandad Turner was alive—so he must have been at least eighty.

Although the hyacinth pollen didn't bother me too much, the daffodil pollen affected us all. The girls showed me how to tie a scarf 'turban style' around my head to cover all of my scalp and ears. The pollen made your skin itch, and once you started scratching you would get a horrible rash. We would plaster our faces and necks with *Nivea* cream. Antihistamine cream was expensive, so we just used that on our lips, around our eyes and especially our nostrils—as the pollen could cause nose bleeds. After all this palaver, and once we had our sleeves tucked into our long rubber gloves, we were ready to start cutting.

In spite of the pollen, I loved cutting and bunching daffs and soon got the hang of keeping the flower heads all facing the same way—slipping a rubber band halfway up the stem, then twisting another twice over the bottom of the bunch.

The boys would carry the finished bunches in their arms into the packing shed. They wore long thick rubber aprons and rubber gloves, as by now the sap would be copiously oozing from the bottom of the stems. Without the protection of the aprons, it would have run down their fronts, soaked through their clothes and made their nether regions absolutely raw.

Sometimes Uncle Bill would take on an extra boy for the week before Easter, due to the extra demand for daffs. I remember one lad looking at the rubber apron he was handed, shaking his head and refusing to wear it—saying that he wouldn't be seen dead in it.

'Tha'll wish thee were, if tha don't!' replied Uncle Bill.

So, while waiting to go to Chester Zoo, I happily settled into working at Nutgrove. It was a great place to work but very much like taking part in a *Carry On…* film most days. I had got used to plenty of banter and teasing at the shop, but this was in a different league at Nutgrove—especially when you included the swear words that interspersed every conversation. I never told Mother anything about what went on of course, as I knew what her reaction would be.

The employees were a motley crew, and Uncle Bill was a soft touch when it came to taking on staff—Aunty Mabel would be tearing her hair out some mornings, when she saw the characters that turned up for work. The majority didn't last long. This was the case with Janet, who turned out to be another of Uncle Bill's lame ducks—quite frankly, we would have probably got more work out of a duck. Oh boy, she was a corker and drove us all to exasperation. Like me, she had left school the year before and was the same age, but had never had a job. Her Mother had begged Uncle Bill to give her a job and—much against Aunty Mabel's wishes—he said she could come on a week's trial. She had been indulged by her elderly parents, who waited on her hand and foot and pandered to her every whim.

On her first morning she turned up half an hour late, and when Uncle Bill brought her into the greenhouse—where we were cutting daffs—we all turned to look at her. She took one look at the strange be-turbaned, white faced creatures then screamed and ran out of the greenhouse and up the path. Uncle Bill had to chase her and bring her back. We were all laughing, but Aunty Mabel was shaking her head, muttering that she knew Janet was going to be useless. She was assigned to work with June, but after a day even kind, patient June was tearing her hair out. Janet didn't take instructions from anyone—when shown how to do a job she would say, 'I will do it my own way, thank you.'

The second day her job was easy enough—it was just carrying daffs up to the packing shed. Uncle Bill said that she would be fine doing that. She refused to wear an apron at first, but finally June managed to persuade her. She was shown how to lay the bunches carefully across one arm, and hold them steady with the other, but she was so rough that she kinked the stems and the broken heads were all hanging down.

'Oh my God!' Aunty Mabel said. 'That's today's profit gone!'

Day after day, Uncle Bill tried to find an easy job for her to do. He put her to watering the tulips—in the big greenhouse we called 'The Steps'—showing her how to hold the hosepipe low, so as not to splash the flowers. He stayed with her for a while, and said she seemed to have understood his instructions. So he left her—the foolish man—to go and do something else.

Instead of making her way slowly up the greenhouse, Janet stood in the same place for over an hour until all the bulbs were washed out of the soil, and the water was running down the greenhouse steps onto the main path. Winnie noticed what was happening and rushed to turn off the tap. Aunty Mabel was furious, with both Janet and Uncle Bill, and said that she would find her a job that even the village idiot would find easy. So Janet was given a metal kitchen spoon, then put to removing the little bit of moss that was growing along the bottom of the nursery house wall. Aunty Mabel said that it was impossible to make a mess of this job. She was wrong, however. Not only did Janet remove the moss, but chunks of the render, leaving exposed brick. How on earth she managed this, with just a small spoon, was amazing. We practically had to sit on Aunty Mabel to stop her committing murder. At last we realized that Janet wasn't stupid, but actually a cunning little madam. She was making a mess of every job on purpose, showing no remorse at the damage she caused, because she just didn't care less. She wouldn't even take a turn at making tea for everyone at break times, as she genuinely didn't know how. When Aunty Mabel tried to show her, she had no intention of learning and just stood looking bored. On the last day of her week's trial, Uncle Bill couldn't be bothered to find her a job, so she just sat on a box in the greenhouse watching us work. Now and then she would give a big, dramatic sigh. We all ignored her, but really felt like giving her a good slap—something her parents should have done years before.

At the end of her final day—when Uncle Bill told her she hadn't got the job, and handed her a small wage packet—she didn't even say thank you, but gave a sly little smile and went up to the yard to wait for her parents to pick her up. She didn't live far away, and could have walked home quite easily. We all rushed up to the yard to see her off. We were so glad to see the back of her. When Janet's parents arrived we had a demonstration of how she treated them— or rather, how they allowed her to treat them. We watched her walk around to the front passenger door, where she stood with hands on hips, tapping her foot, until her Mother got out of the front seat and got into the back.

I thought, 'I'd love to send you to live with my Mother, you little madam! She would soon knock you into shape!'

Aunty Mabel said, 'Well that's an example of spare t'rod and spoil t'child, if ever there was one!' Then she turned and gave Uncle Bill a withering look.

'Now Mother, don't start scolding!' He said, feeling chagrined.

Though I liked cutting and bunching daffs, I liked pulling and bunching tulips even more. The specimen bulbs had been planted directly into soil, in the Steps greenhouse on the main path. We would go along the rows, put a foot against the bottom of the stem over the bulb, then pull and cut the white ends off the stem and band the blooms into bunches of six. We all had our own penknives—I was really proud of the one Daddy Joe, Huttie and the girls had bought me. We grew two varieties of specimen tulips—*Oriole*, a pale orange bloom with gold edging and *Elmus*, a dark pink with cream edging, and tall with strong stems and long lasting. Shorter stemmed, mixed varieties were also grown in boxes for using in the funeral wreaths.

As soon as the tulips were finished, the soil was rotavated then raked—to get rid of the old spent bulbs—then the soil would be sterilized with steam. Owd Geoff was in charge of the portable steam boiler, and the water pipe that fed it from the storage tank. He kept all things mechanical working on the nursery, including the temperamental old coke boilers that heated the greenhouses. He was an indispensable young man.

The steam pipes had rows of holes in them. These were laid in trenches—mostly dug by Owd Donald, with help from Uncle Bill—and then covered with soil. Steam was then pumped into them. The whole area of this large greenhouse was sterilized in this way, yard by yard. It was very hard work and took days to complete. Owd Donald was always happy to work on his own with Uncle Bill—certainly no one else was eager to do the job, as the smell from the sterilizing soil wasn't pleasant. When combined with the smell of a hot, sweaty Donald, it was truly horrendous—personal hygiene wasn't Donald's forte. If Uncle Bill was needed elsewhere, we would wave at him from the door, or throw a stone to attract his attention over the noise from the steam boiler. None of us would want to venture into the fug, but Uncle Bill always seemed to be immune to the smell emanating from Owd Donald.

Owd Geoff started work very early in the morning, and finished well into the evening. He lived with his Mother, in a house whose garden backed onto the nurseries, up by the Big Two greenhouses. He had put a gate into the back fence and it opened straight onto the path by Big Two. These greenhouses were used for growing Sweet Peas, and he worked with Uncle Eric, Joe, David and Owd Donald when the house's needed preparing for planting. Deep trenches were dug, manured and watered well, then filled in.

All the girls worked on pushing the strong 9ft cane supports well into the soil, then the tops were tied to wires that ran across the greenhouse.

We all stood on stacked tomato crates to reach the wires and frequently fell off, but just got back up and carried on. We were probably breaking every modern health and safety rule, but we never came to any serious harm—just the odd graze or bruise. String was crossed between the canes to make a trellis, then small canes were placed beside each plant for support, until they were strong enough to be tied to the trellis.

The crop that was produced was amazing for its quality, quantity and colour—and the smell was heavenly. We all loved cutting and bunching sweet peas. It was the best job ever. Sometimes we would work overtime and cut them in the cool of the evening, so they were fresh and ready for Young Joe to take to Liverpool Flower Market for 5am. We would have a meal break, but Geoff was such a workaholic that he would just carry on. We knew his tea would be ready and waiting at home, so we would wait for his Mum to come marching along the path shouting, 'Geoff-ree! Geoff-ree! Your tea is on the table, and if you don't come right now, it's going in the bin!'

Owd Geoff would hide in the sweet peas, and we would let his Mum march past and just keep her talking—he could then sneak home, eat his meal and get back without her seeing him. We loved a little subterfuge—it brought an extra sparkle to our day.

June's boyfriend, Brian, came one day to take some Cine film of us all working in the sweet peas. There was to be an evening event—at June's church—of cine films taken by parishioners. There would be a small charge and refreshments afterwards. We all bought tickets—except Owd Donald of course—and looked forward to seeing ourselves on the screen. On the evening of the event, we all arrived at the church hall and took our places. The programme showed our film was to be about halfway through. Most of the other clips were the usual boring holiday films, and some only in black and white. So when Brian's film came on in full colour, there were lots of 'ooh's' and 'ah's' from the audience. The greenhouses full of sweet peas looked amazing, with us all looking very happy and waving at the camera. Suddenly Owd Donald's face appeared, full screen, leering at the camera.

There was a loud scream from the back of the hall. 'That's him! That's him!' A woman shouted. 'That's the man that exposed himself to me in Taylor Park!'

Uncle Bill just put his head in his hands and said, 'I'm going to kill 'im!'

The outraged woman from the back row bore down on us. She announced that now she knew where the pervert worked, she was going to go to the police. There was a lot of muttering in the room, and we were all getting dirty looks from the woman's family. So that was the end of the evening for us. We made a hasty exit, looking longingly at all the lovely refreshments on the table as we passed—muttering that we wanted to kill Owd Donald as well.

The following afternoon we were on the nursery yard, loading boxes of tomatoes onto the lorry, when we heard a police siren coming from the main road. Then we realized the noise was getting nearer, and coming down the nursery path. We all looked at Owd Donald—even under all the grime, we could tell he had gone pale. He dropped the box of tomatoes he was carrying and ran. He just made it across the yard, and into the girl's loo, as the police car swung around the corner of the house and screeched to a halt. Uncle Bill went to speak to the policemen and then they went and hammered on the loo door—but Owd Donald wouldn't come out. On hearing the siren, Aunty Mabel had come out of the house, and seeing what was afoot, asked the policemen to let her try to persuade him to come out. So she got down, on her hands and knees, to talk to him under the gap at the bottom of the loo door. 'Come on out Donald and talk t'the nice policemen! It's better if you give tha self up.' But he still wouldn't budge. Eventually he did come out—because Uncle Bill shouted, 'If a'aff t'brek doower down, cost'll come out yer bloody wages!'[1]

We all thought the pantomime was hilarious, and even the policemen were trying not to smile—evidently Owd Donald was a regular 'customer' at St Helens' Police Station. So he was bundled into the police car, and we didn't see him for a week. Presumably he was placed in custody. Bill and Mabel would have known, but nothing was said to us.

When he did come back to work, I think he had another good drubbing from Uncle Bill, as he was very subdued for a few days. We all kept well out if his way, as he was at his most volatile and dangerous when he was in this kind of mood.

Dear God above! When I think back how we just simply accepted that Owd Donald was as mad as a box of frogs, it doesn't seem possible. I didn't relay these events to Mother of course. She certainly would have

1 *"If I have to break the door down, the cost will come out of your bloody wages!"*

been shocked, and wouldn't have approved of me working anywhere near him. She needn't have worried though, as after nearly three years working with the *Carry On…* crew, I was more than capable of looking after myself.

I met some other real 'characters' while working at Nutgrove. There was the little tally man, who sold second-hand work clothes, wellies, boots and shoes. I bought a few things off him over the years, including two pairs of nearly-new, good quality jodhpurs—ready for when I went to Chester Zoo. He was a funny little man. As round as a ball, he didn't seem to have a neck, and his head always looked as if it was just about to roll off at any minute. I thought he looked like the Wobbly Man from the *Noddy* stories by Enid Blyton. I can't remember how much the jodhpurs cost, but we always paid a few shillings a week, plus an extra shilling interest when we had paid up.

On Saturday mornings we would give Aunty Mabel the money for the Tally Man, and she would pay him for us—Uncle Bill would be angry if we stopped working to go up to the yard to pay him ourselves. However, if there was an item we really needed then Uncle Bill would let us go up to the yard to buy it. Mother didn't know I bought things from the Tally Man 'on tick' and presumed I had paid for everything outright. As long as she didn't ask, I didn't enlighten her—it was more peaceful that way.

Another Saturday character was 'Thin Wally', the pop man, who always came at Saturday lunch times as we finished work for the week. We would buy pop in small bottles in wonderful flavours, and it tasted so much better than pop does nowadays. Wally was extremely tall, thin and pale. How he managed to lift crates of pop with those stick-thin arms, God knows! He always had a nasal drip ready to fall, which he constantly wiped on the back of his hand. I made sure I gave him the correct money for my purchases, as I didn't fancy being given change by hands that were still damp from the latest nose swipe—and that had just been scratching his nether regions. It didn't seem to bother anyone else, but I was definitely my Mother's child. I would thoroughly wash the bottles of pop when I got home.

The nursery employee dynamics were quite complex, so it took me a while to sort them out. Donald didn't like anyone except Bill and Mabel. He detested June, but I haven't a clue why. Winnie and Bessie didn't care for each other much, but would gang up together on poor June. Winnie never stopped nattering, mostly about sex—which according to her she didn't know much about. Bessie was bossy and always thought she knew best. Young Joe, David, Little Chris and I got on with our work and didn't take sides in the frequent rows. They all behaved if Aunty Mabel was working with us. Uncle Bill used to say 'Good owd Bessie! She'll do yer a good turn, whither y'want one doing or no.' June was a nice person and I made sure I worked next to her—and we all steered clear of Owd Donald.

If Donald was having a 'go slow' day and staring into space, Uncle Bill knew exactly how to get him to work faster. As Donald was a great fan of Morris motor cars, Uncle Bill would say, 'Tha knows Donald, if Mr Ford 'ad med aeroplanes, we'd 'ave won t'war a lot sooner.' This would annoy him, and he would start to work a little faster.

Uncle Bill would continue, 'Mr Foster[2] 'as an Armstrong Sidley yer know.' Donald's spade would go faster still. If Uncle Bill thought he still wasn't giving it his all, he would pass a really nice comment about June. Then Donald's spade would just become a blur. Bill would then pat him on the back saying, 'Good lad, that's th'way!'

Every morning as Donald worked, the contents of the packet he had in the back pocket of his jeans would start to ooze through the material. This was his lunch, which was always a fried egg butty. By lunch time it was just mush, which he would have to scoop out of his pocket with his fingers. The paper bag—that had contained what used to be a sandwich—was now almost indistinguishable from the mush. Any bits of paper he couldn't pick off went down with the rest of the mess, with much smacking of lips. Then, from his other back pocket, he would remove what had been a *Blue Riband* biscuit. He would bite the top off the cellophane packet then squeeze out the contents—which by now had the consistency of tooth paste. All of this was done, once again, with much smacking of lips. Finally, after downing the pint of tea we had made for him, he would wipe his mouth on his sleeve, burp and—much to our relief—disappear for the rest of the dinner hour.

He was a hard worker for most of the time, but was also very good at sloping off, if Uncle Bill took his eye off him. Whenever he did, the cry would go up, 'Owd Donald's buggered off again!' This was the cue for us all to down tools and find where he was hiding. The first place we would

2 *June's father*

look was the girl's toilet, as he liked to go and shut himself in there. I would rather not think about why!

One time we found Owd Donald in the summer house, in Aunty Mabel's garden. We could hear him laughing and talking to himself. I crept around the side and peeped through the window, praying he wouldn't see me. He was sitting with a *Littlewoods* catalogue on his knee, open at the bra and knickers section—touching each picture and saying, 'Crumpet, crumpet, crumpet!'

Uncle Bill arrived, dragged him out, whacked him with his trilby and said, 'Come on out y'mucky young bugger, yer not allowed in theer! Yer not fit t'be wi' decent folk!'

Donald just roared with laughter, and putting his arm around Uncle Bill's shoulder, went back to work like a lamb. Donald knew we must have told on him. He might have been as mad as a sack of ferrets, but he wasn't stupid. We were now all worried what his revenge would be—so serve us right.

At break time we had all settled down to drink our tea, when suddenly Donald took his wellies off. There was a stampede for the door, as we all tried to get out before being overcome by the fumes. He was roaring with laughter, jumping up and down and slapping his thigh in triumph. Seeing our mass exodus from the conservatory, Aunty Mabel came out of the house to see what all the commotion was about—there was no way we wanted to go back into the now pungent atmosphere of the conservatory. She went across the yard and called Donald outside, and had a little chat with him—again—about personal hygiene.

The next day, at morning break, Donald produced a tin of *Evening in Paris* talcum powder. He held it aloft for us all to see, then proceeded to remove his wellies and sprinkled it inside them. This was his idea of improving his hygiene. Toast and cups went flying as we all—once again—made a dash for the door. Uncle Bill came across this time, went into the conservatory called him a 'mucky young bugger' and whacked him with his trilby—then dragged him outside and back to work. Owd Donald couldn't have cared less, as he had now inflicted a double revenge on us all.

One day, at lunchtime, we were all talking about our holiday destinations. I said that I was going to Greystones in Ireland for a week with my sister. Pat was expecting baby number ten, and Mother said a holiday would do her good. Mother would go up to London to look after the other nine children and Pat's husband Dennis—God help him!—while we were away.

Owd Donald blurted out that he was going to Ireland for his holidays as well, with his friend Frank. So, of course—evil little devils that we were—we told Uncle Bill, knowing full well that we would have an afternoon of entertainment at Donald's expense.

We were planting lettuce seedlings that afternoon, and were keeping our heads down, just waiting for Uncle Bill to start on Donald—who almost certainly knew what was coming, and was probably now regretting letting slip his juicy titbit of 'information'.

Bill's first comment to Donald was, 'Off t'Ireland then?'

'Yes, why?'

'Well, they'll not let a mucky bugger like thee on t'boat.'

'Yes they will, Frank's bought the tickets!'

'Oh, the'll let Frank on,' said Uncle Bill. 'But when they si'thi, they'll 'and thi a pair o' watter wings[3] and say, "Sorry pal, you'll 'ave t'swim!" Or, if tha's lucky, they might throw a rope over t'side and give yer a tow.'

We were all howling with laughter by now, and fair play to Owd Donald—he was laughing as well.

Uncle Bill wasn't letting up though. 'Ave tha gorra passport?'

'Don't need one!'

'What about going through t'customs? I wouldn't want t'search through tha's bloody suitcase!'

"Don't 'ave customs."

'They will, after tha's been! Tha knows they serve cabbage wi' everything ovver theer? God lad, I wouldn't want t'be downwind of thee!'

There were more howls of laughter from us.

'Weer's tha staying?' Said Uncle Bill, not letting up.

'In a country cottage.'

'In a country cottage? When th'ask where t'lavvie is, the'll gi' thi a shovel and say, "It's ovver theer, it's cawed the Wicklow Mountains!"'[4]

Work had totally come to a halt, as we were all now weeping with laughter. This was Uncle Bill at his wicked best.

Aunty Mabel appeared at the far end of the greenhouse and shouted, 'Fayther!'

3 *'But when they see you, they'll hand you a pair of water wings…"*

4 *'When you ask where the lavatory is, they'll give you a shovel and say, "It's over there…"'*

Uncle Bill said, 'Oh Mother, gi'oer, it's only a bit o'fun. Tha knows t'little buggers work 'arder when they're in t'good mood.'

"Oh yes," said Aunty Mabel. "Ah can just see 'ow hard they're working!" So—thoroughly chastened—everyone started planting lettuce seedlings at great speed, including Uncle Bill.

Feeling a little bored one afternoon, we were very pleased to see Mrs Deakin—another Nutgrove 'character'—walking up the main path. She was an extremely nosey, local woman who had an encyclopaedic knowledge of other people's business. She liked to visit Aunty Mabel now and then, hoping to catch up on any gossip she might have missed. I don't know why she bothered though, as Mabel wasn't a gossip—and Ma Deakin wasn't one of her favourite people. If she could dodge her she would. So, if Ma Deakin didn't get an answer at the house she would come onto the nurseries and wander around, until she found someone to ask where Mabel was. Everyone she spoke to would deliberately send her on a wild goose chase.

Misdirected, Ma Deakin would go from greenhouse to greenhouse—and there were an awful lot of them— then up to the packing shed, across to the hens and back down the main path. All of the greenhouses were hot, so after standing inside for a few minutes she would go back outside, and try to fan herself with her hankie before continuing on her way.

Ma Deakin was a large lady—both in height and circumference—and always wore *Crimplene* dresses a few sizes too small. Consequently, her dress was always stretched to bursting point across her ample bosom and rear end—which left absolutely nothing to the imagination. Whether in Summer or Winter, she wore a short, thick black coat over the dress—all topped off with what Uncle Bill called her 'Chapel hat'.

After the wild goose chase up and down the paths—and in and out of hot greenhouses—she would now be the colour of a beetroot, perspiring copiously and at the point of collapse. We'd then feel sorry for her. So we'd get a high stool from the potting shed for her to sit on, and give her a glass of water. When I say we felt sorry for her, it would be more truthful to say we were worried she would expire, and that we would be locked up for manslaughter. When the poor soul finally staggered off, with her mission unaccomplished, Aunty Mabel would miraculously appear again. Uncle Bill said, 'Tha's got t'admire t'nosey owd bugger.

She's really dedicated to 'er 'obby'.

The nosey old bugger's husband, Pa Deakin, owned the local funeral parlour—which just happened to be next to a bakery. Uncle Bill's imagination ran riot, as he regaled us with tales about the Deakins. He said that the bakery did a roaring trade in extra meaty pies, and that Pa Deakin should be called Sweeny Deakin. Then he said that at Easter time the bakery had Ma Deakin suspended over the production line. As the hot cross buns got to the end, they would quickly pull a lever up and down so her backside stamped the crosses on the buns. Aunty Mabel wouldn't let him go too far, but if she wasn't working with us he would go to town, and have us in stitches laughing.

Some of the huge Nutgrove greenhouses that Ma Deakin had passed through grew Irises and Lilies, but we grew Dahlias and Chrysanthemums outside. I like Dahlias to look at, but I didn't like working amongst them, as they always seemed to be soaking wet and cold. I liked de-budding Chrysanths though, and was patiently taught how to by June. At first, Uncle Bill would only allow June to do the de-budding, but when I was up to her standard I was given the job as well. We both had long thin fingers, perfect for getting into the leaf joints to remove the buds without damaging the stems—we'd expertly leave a single bud at the top of the stem. We were proud of our specimen single blooms, and they commanded a high price at the shop in town. When I had worked at the shop, Mrs Lennon—of Lennon's Supermarkets[5]—would sweep into the shop in her fur coat, like a galleon in full sail, and spend a small fortune on them. Daddy Joe would always serve her, but one of us would have to carry her enormous and costly purchases to her car. She was a nice person, but I always made sure it wasn't me carrying her produce, as I didn't want to get near the coat made from innocent animals.

As well as de-budding Chrysanths, I loved sowing and pricking out bedding plants. The boys would fill the clamps in the potting house with Uncle Bill's special compost mix. Aunty Mabel and I would then shut ourselves in there, away from the constant natter between Bessie and Winnie—which was usually about sex, their favourite subject. Owd Donald would always try to sneak near enough to hear what they were saying.

5 *The Lennon family established a chain of supermarkets in Lancashire, Liverpool and North Cheshire through the 50s, 60s and 70s.*

I would fill the trays with compost, ready for Aunty Mabel to sow the seeds, and write the labels for her. When the seedlings had grown to the correct size, we would shut ourselves in there again and prick them out into larger trays. Aunty Mabel and I liked working together as we didn't talk a lot and preferred to work quietly. It was a relief to be on our own sometimes. Slowly the benches filled with bedding plants, and people would come for miles around to buy them. The takings for these were Aunty Mabel's pin money.

There were a few jobs I didn't like, but the only one I really detested was working in the cucumber house. It was hot and humid, and the plants were trained up both sides of the apex with the growing cucumbers hanging down. They were easy enough to cut, but the leaves were rough and would catch on your clothes and scratch your face and hands. Enormous slugs, covered in little orange mites, would be on the soil by the stems—and we had to pick them up and dispose of them. This was Uncle Eric's domain, but if he was away someone else would get the joy of working in there. If Owd Donald was available, he would go and cut. It didn't make any difference to him as he was always hot, humid and smelly—so he was quite at home.

Nutgrove Nurseries were famous for their salad crops, especially tomatoes. Vast amounts of these were sold at the shop. Customers would queue right down the street to buy Turner's home grown produce. During the summer that I had worked at the shop, I would stand all day long just selling tomatoes. I had a place just inside the shop door to weigh and sell them, and as soon as the huge trays were getting low, I would shout for Huttie to come and fill them up—I didn't have time to stop. The shop doorway was quite wide, so customers wouldn't actually need to come into the shop and could be served in the doorway. As we British are so skilled and polite when queuing, there was always a lovely straight line, and enough room for other shop customers to get in and out without any trouble. After an eight hour stint selling tomatoes, I would be aching all over.

As much as I loved Nutgrove, when my eighteenth birthday approached, my thoughts turned to applying again to Chester Zoo. So the letter was sent, and I received a reply very quickly—there was a job for me if I passed the interview, the date of which was enclosed. I asked Uncle Bill for the day off and told him why, and he wished me good luck with the interview.

Fig. I-1 Cooper St, St. Helen's, Lancashire

Fig. I-2 The Author, Aged 6, holding her doll 'Cross-Eyed Jane'

Fig. I-3 Mother, with Dick (being held) and Pat, 1931

Fig. I-4 Dick, Aged 3 (Pat in the background), in the Orchard at Sychdyn, 1933

Fig. I-5 Dick, Aged 5, 1935

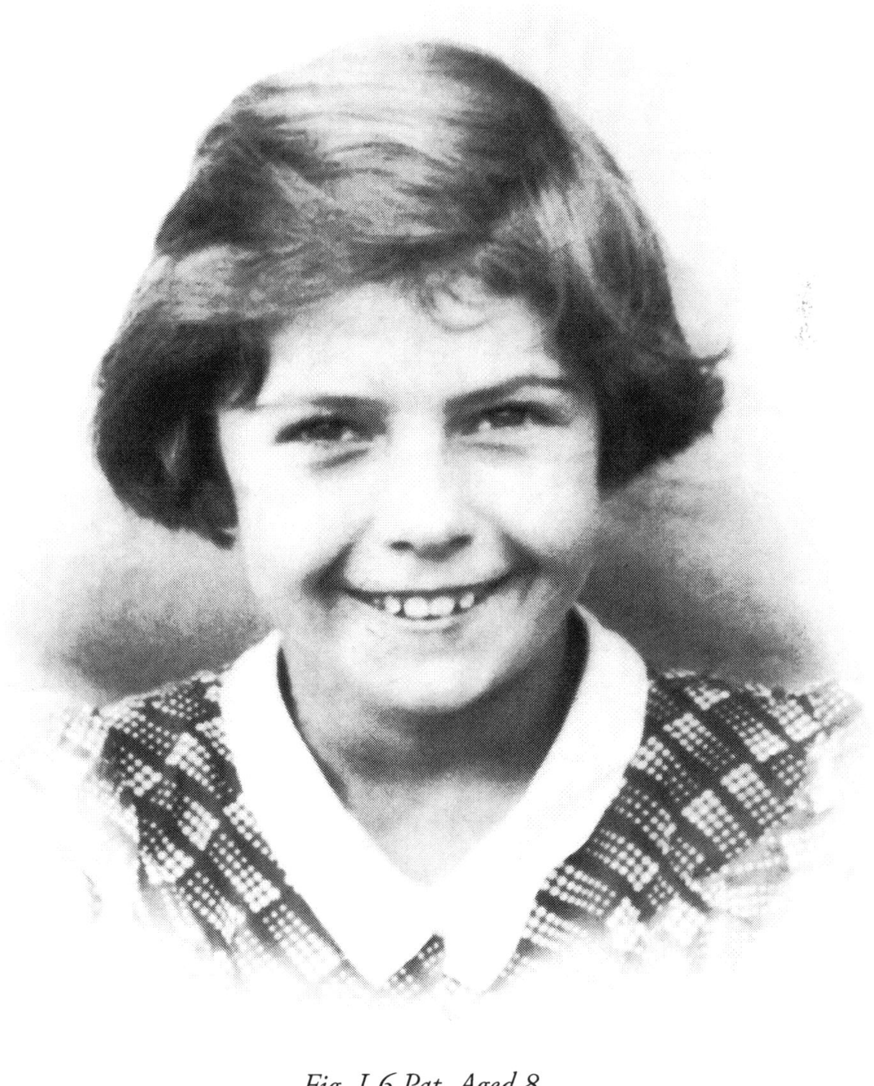

Fig. I-6 Pat, Aged 8

Fig. I-7 Dick, Age 16, Royal Naval College H.M.S. Ganges, 1946

Fig. I-8 Ship's Company, H.M.S. Theseus, 1947

Fig. I-9 Dick, home on leave in St. Helen's, 1956

Fig. I-10 The Author (second row, third from right) and best friend Doreen (second row, fourth from left), Miss Marley's Class, 1947

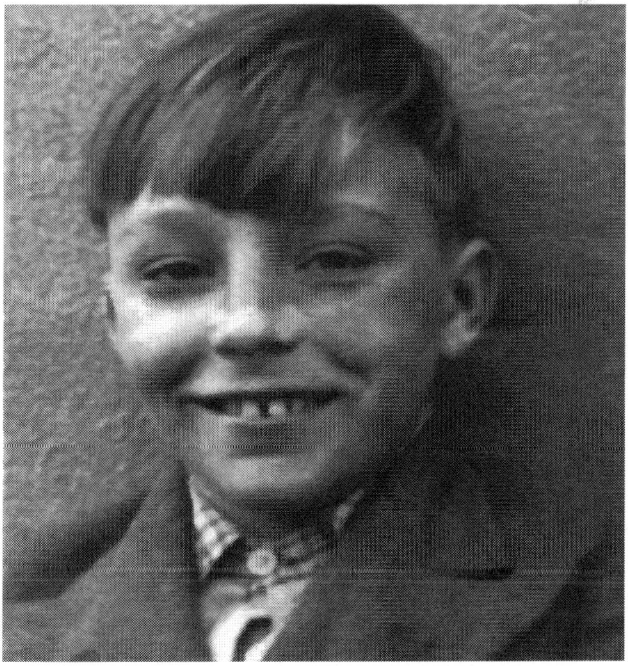

Fig. I-11 Les Stocks, Aged 8

Fig. I-12 The Author, first right, on Walking Day, St. Mark's, 1950

Fig. I-13 The Author (third fairy from the left), Red Riding Hood Panto, Mr Ormerod's Class, Windle CofE School, St Helens, December, 1951

Fig. I-14 The Author's Grandfather, Arthur Oldcorn, Age 3

Fig. I-15 House-at-the-Green, Northop (where Mother was born)

Fig. I-16 Northop, Circa 1900

Fig. I-17 Dick, Age 2, Northop, 1932

Fig. I-18 Grandpa Oldcorn & Auntie Mill, House-At-The-Green, Northop, 1926

Fig. I-19 Aughton, 1959 - From left: Auntie Mill, Mother

Fig. I-20 Books from Aughton

Fig. I-21 School Holiday, Southport, 1949 - From left: The Author, Doreen, Auntie Ada (Doreen's mum)

*Fig. I-22 Planting Hyacinths, Turner's Nursery, St Helens, 1959 -
From top: Young Joe, Nina (Dog), Owd June, the Author*

Fig. I-23 Turner's Nurseries, St Helens, 1959 - Front row, from top right: Owd June, David, the Author, Uncle Bill. Back row, from top: Young Joe, Nina (Dog).

Fig. I-24 Turner's Nurseries, St Helens, 1959 - From top: Young Joe, David, the Author. Partially in frame: Nina (Dog).

II

Zoo Quest

14: THE ZOO AT LAST

My interview was at two in the afternoon, so I set off from home at nine in the morning. I caught a bus to Warrington, then from Warrington to Chester, and then from Chester to Upton—arriving just before one-o-clock. I was to report to the time office, and they would ring through to tell Mr Bloom—the Curator—that I had arrived. A message came back telling me to go to the Fountain Restaurant and ask for Vera, who would give me some lunch, then Mr Bloom would meet me outside at two-o-clock. Feeling excited, but very nervous—and following the Zoo Guide pamphlet I had been given—I made my way to the Fountain. I couldn't eat much of the lovely lunch Vera had provided, as my stomach was doing somersaults.

Arriving outside the restaurant at two-o-clock, on the dot, I was just wondering what Mr Bloom looked like when I saw a man with a beaming smile striding towards me. I liked the look of him immediately. The saying 'first impressions count' turned out to be so true later. He shook my hand and said. 'Welcome to Chester Zoo.' He then asked whether he should he call me Miss Logan, Pamela or Pam—I said that all my friends called me 'Pam Zoo'.

'Right then,' he said. 'Pam Zoo it is!'

We walked up to his office—which at that time was behind the Zebra house—and had more of a chat than a formal interview. As I had an excellent knowledge of the animal world, I was a little disappointed I didn't get to show it off a bit more. He asked about my home, hobbies and work and I made him laugh with one or two snippets of life at Nutgrove. When the interview was over, I asked him when I would hear the result.

'I will tell you now, Pam Zoo. You will suit us very well, and you can start work with us as soon as you like, on a month's trial.' He smiled at me saying, 'Now, I will take you on a tour of the Zoo and introduce you to some of the keepers.'

I was ecstatic and practically floated around on my grand tour. I just knew that—unless I messed up very badly—my month's trial would be just a formality. I told him I could start work a week the following Monday, as I had to hand my notice in at Nutgrove. He walked me to the gate and told me to report to the time office at eight-o-clock, a week on Monday morning, and that Bill the Time Keeper would tell me which section to report to.

On the way home on the bus, reality hit me. I was dreading giving in my notice, as I knew Aunty Mabel and Uncle Bill would be upset. Over the years I had worked for them they had become like family to me, and I would miss them so much. They had helped to turn a naïve young girl into a confident young woman. When I told Mother I had got the job she said, 'Hmm, another job that necessitates the wearing of trousers, and having dirty fingernails!'

Halfway through my last week I still hadn't found anywhere to stay, then friends from the church youth club suggested the Y.W.C.A. in Chester. I rang the hostel and thankfully they had a spare bed. There was no cutting comment from Mother this time, as she approved of me lodging at the Y.W.C.A.

My last week at Nutgrove went quickly and on Saturday lunch time I said my goodbyes, with lots of hugs and tears and promises to keep in touch.

I was so grateful when the same friends who had recommended the Y.W.C.A said they would drive me to Chester on the Sunday evening. They deposited me and my luggage at the Y.W.C.A. Hostel in Watergate Street, at about six in the evening. The hostel was a large, converted Victorian House. With it still being the '60s, it had a Warden and a Cook—as breakfast and an evening meal were provided. Miss Sinclair, the Warden, welcomed me and took me to my room.

I was to share with a Japanese girl called Reiko, but she was known as 'Rebecca' by everyone. She was studying the organ and church music at Chester Cathedral, and we became great friends. After a few weeks I was given a single room. This suited me much better, as I could close my door against the constant girls' chatter and read in peace.

I always left too early in the morning to be able to have a cooked breakfast, but Mrs Jones—the cook—would make me a pile of toast as her first job, as soon as she got through the door. The butter would still be hard, straight out of the fridge, so she would slice it as thinly as she could, whack it onto the toast and wrap it up—then push it into my hand as I dashed out of the back door. It was lovely, as the butter was as thick as the toast, and I would eat it on the bus on the way to the zoo. I was always back after dinner was finished in the evening, but Mrs Jones would leave mine covered up on top of a saucepan, ready to heat up. She always left me a hefty portion—as most of the girls used to moan about the food, she was grateful for one happy customer. I don't know why they moaned, because Mrs Jones' meals were excellent—and just like Mother's.

Sometimes, I would be on late night lock up duty, particularly in the summer, when the Zoo didn't close until dusk. During that time of year, one or two keepers from each section would be on patrol—in case there were any problems with the late visitors. Consequently I wouldn't be back at the Y.W. until about half-past-ten at night. I had had my evening meal at the zoo, but there was always a plate of sandwiches left in the fridge for my supper. Mrs Jones really went above and beyond the call of duty to provide these for me, bless her. I was very grateful.

Whenever I did get back from work, I would have to knock on Miss Sinclair's door to let her know I was back, safe and sound. There were lots of rules and regulations at the Y.W.C.A in those days. Girls under twenty-one years old had to be in by ten in the evening—but you could have two late passes per week, with permission, and stay out until quarter-past-eleven. You had to sign the book when you came in, and Miss Sinclair would check the book at half-past-eleven when she locked up. Woe betide any girl who flouted the rules, as they would be out on their ear. The rules didn't bother me in the slightest—after living with Mother for eighteen years, I felt totally liberated.

Apart from a very few, the girls were a catty, discontented lot and I was surprised how nasty they could be—both to and about each other. It was another steep learning curve for me. It wasn't the good natured banter and teasing I was used to at Nutgrove, but unfettered, out-and-out nastiness. They soon learned to keep out of my way, as I had no patience with them. They were very cruel to Rebecca, but after I challenged their behaviour towards her they left her alone. I am damned sure they talked about me behind my back, but I couldn't have cared less.

I caught the bus to work for the first two weeks, then Uncle Bill and Aunty Mabel kindly picked my bike up from home and brought it for me in the Nursery van. It was lovely to see them, and they brought me up to date on the goings on at Nutgrove. Once I had my bike I didn't have to leave so early, so could partake of one of Mrs Jones' delicious cooked breakfasts. She fed me like a fighting cock, as she said I needed the nourishment working outside all day.

So I happily settled into the hostel routine.

There was always a blazing fire in the communal lounge, but I didn't go down often as the other girls were usually watching rubbish on TV. If there was a wildlife programme on, Miss Sinclair would kindly invite me to watch it in her sitting room, and Flotsam—her handsome black cat—would come and curl up on my knee. He would very often come and sleep on my bed, and I always left my bedroom door wedged slightly ajar so he could get into my room. I made sure never to make a tremendous fuss of him, as he was always being picked up by the other girls, who were always vying with each other as to who he liked best.

Once a week Miss Sinclair would give him a treat—as she thought it—of raw lamb's liver. However, this would go straight through him like a dose of salts, and in desperation he would use one of the first floor bathrooms as a toilet. Then the cry would go up, 'Pam Zoo! Pam Zoo! Where's Pam Zoo? Flottie's pooed in the bath again!'

I was the only one prepared to clean it up.

I could understand some of the fuss the first floor girls were making, as the pong was pretty ghastly. But the hordes of silly girls, screaming and running up and down the landing, flapping their hands really got on my nerves. I would push past, giving them the best withering look I could muster—a look I learned from the Master, my Mother. She would have been proud of the effect it had, as they would soon stop over acting and slope off back to their rooms. Eventually, I did persuade Miss Sinclair to stop feeding liver to Flottie.

On my first day at the Zoo, I was sent up to the small Mammal House. I met Sandra who, although a pleasant enough girl, was useless at showing me what to do. The more senior girl, Faith, was off sick. Sandra just handed me a bucket, shovel and a brush and said, 'You do that side, and I'll do the other.'

So using my common sense—and prizing information out of Sandra—I managed to get through the day. I asked her if all the animals were safe to go in with. She replied that they were. I didn't really believe her, but as they were mostly small and nervous, I took the chance. Mother had a favourite description of people like Sandra—'wet and wispy', which I thought was perfect. What Sandra should have instructed me to do, was to entice the animals into the outside enclosure whilst

I cleaned inside, and vice versa. In this section there were Fennec Foxes, Bush Babies, Malabar Squirrels, Civets, Chinchillas, Armadillos, Springhaas, Agoutis, Marmosets, Kinkajous, Binturong and a Woolly Monkey.

When Faith came back the next day, she was furious with Sandra for leaving me to my own devices. I then learned that 'Wolf'—the male Malabar Squirrel—was not to be trusted, as he would jump on your head and bite. Of the two kinkajous, 'Fatty' was not to be trusted, but 'Katie' was a darling and sweet natured. The trouble was that, until you got to know them, you couldn't tell them apart. I was very lucky not to have been bitten. 'Binty' the Binturong would pee on you if he was on a branch above you, so I also got away with that one as well.

Mr Bloom came up to see me the following day. When Faith told him what had happened, he wasn't best pleased with Sandra. Had he known Faith was going to be off sick, he would never have left me unsupervised with Sandra. Faith had assumed he would check up on me, so she hadn't worried. It was bad a mistake on Mr Bloom's part, as he should have checked anyway. He apologised profusely and was thankful I had used my common sense, because if I'd been bitten he would have been in trouble.

Sandra tried to get out of trouble by batting her eyelashes and looking sad. Reg Bloom, an otherwise intelligent man, was usually easily swayed by a good flutter of eyelashes—but it didn't work this time, and Sandra got a good telling off. To be fair, it wasn't really her fault. They knew she wasn't the brightest kid on the block. Even if I hadn't been there, she should have called Mr Bloom to let him know she was on her own. I worked with Faith and Sandra for the first week and became very good friends with Faith. Sandra didn't change though, and continued to be 'wet and wispy' for all the years I knew her.

In my second week, I was moved down to the Monkey house, which in those days was in the old part of the Zoo, near the big house. There were five female keepers—'Big' Ann, Elaine, Sue, Liz and Caitlin. Big Ann was the keeper in charge. Initially she was very welcoming and friendly, and seemed eager to show me the ropes. That lasted for all of two days before she got tired of being nice. On the third day, she lost her temper with me when I dared to take her bucket, shovel and brush. Evidently the newest utensils were exclusively hers, until they got a little tatty—at which point they were passed down the line, and she would get a brand new set from the stores. As a humble trainee, I was supposed to have taken the scruffiest set. I couldn't have given a rat's behind what tools I used, and just couldn't believe the fuss. Liz muttered to me that they had all been waiting for the 'shit to hit the fan', as two whole days of working with a smiling, amiable Ann was simply not normal. I laughed and said that I thought she was pathetic. Unfortunately, Ann was listening and had another temper tantrum. I just asked her whether she had heard the saying, 'Listeners never hear good of themselves.' I gave her my best withering look, then walked away to carry on with my work. The girls were all frightened of Ann, but I was used to Owd Donald's outbursts—she was a mere novice compared to him.

From that point onwards, I just carried out my allotted tasks and mostly ignored her. There were days when I would have loved to have thumped her, as big as she was—especially when she was bullying little Caitlin—but I knew I had to keep my nose clean until my month's trial was up.

After three weeks of working on the Monkey house—and putting up with Big Ann's nonsense day after day—it was beginning to get me down. I wasn't frightened of her, but she was now going out of her way to be unpleasant. I looked forward to the odd days when I was sent, by Mr Bloom, to work on other sections, and I got on really well with everyone. I said to Faith that if I passed my month's trial but had to continue working on the Monkey house, I was thinking of leaving. Unbeknownst to me, Faith told Mr Bloom what I had said. He sent a message asking me to go to his office.

Mr Bloom asked me about the 'Big Ann' situation and was surprised when I told him what a cow she was to work with. I said that I loved the work, but working with her was untenable. He asked why I hadn't said anything about the situation. I replied that as I was only a trainee, I didn't want to start whinging and complaining— I wanted to pass my four weeks trial before approaching him about a move. He said that I had already passed my trial with flying colours. He had excellent reports from the other sections I had worked on, and had said to Mrs Bloom—right after my initial interview—that I was going to be a 'good 'un'.

Then he said, 'Unfortunately Pam Zoo, there are no vacancies on any other section.'

My heart just sank and I thought, '*Well, that's it then.*'

Even after all the years I had dreamed about working at Chester Zoo, I was unwilling to tolerate Big Ann's nonsense. Mr Bloom could see how upset I was, and begged me to stick it out for just a little longer—he would try to think of a solution, as he didn't want to lose me.

When I got back to the Monkey House, Big Ann couldn't contain her curiosity and asked why Mr Bloom had wanted to see me. I gave her a beaming smile, tapped my nose and told her to mind her own business. Her attitude towards me improved for a few days, as I think she thought she was in trouble.

For a few days, during lunchtime, Faith and I had been going down to the Zoo Lodge—where the Blooms lived—to spend time with a baby Civet that Mrs Bloom had been hand rearing. He was almost ready to take up residence in the Mammal House, and Faith wanted to get to know him. The day after my 'chat' with Mr Bloom, Mrs Bloom told me that Reg had told her about the situation, and that she had suggested a solution—but it was up to Reg to tell me. On the following morning, I was asked to visit his office. So, keeping my fingers crossed, I knocked on the door and went in.

'Ah, Pam Zoo! Come in, come in. I have an idea to put to you. Well, actually it was Margaret's idea, as I think she mentioned.' Smiling at me, he continued, 'How would you like to be in charge of Whipsnade Section?'

Oh my God! I nearly passed out with excitement and relief.

Whipsnade section was the original part of the Zoo, built when Mr and Mrs Mottershead first came to start it up in 1930. It was called 'Whipsnade', because it mostly consisted of large outdoor enclosures.[1] Its care at the time was split between the keepers of the Monkey House and the Bear Sections and, although the animals were fed and kept clean, it needed a lot more tender loving care. Mrs Mott still took a great interest in it, and was always complaining that it wasn't looked after properly. As I had worked on it every day under Big Ann's orders—and just loved to get out of the confines of the Monkey House anyway—I was ecstatic.

'Well, what do you think of Margaret's idea?' Said Mr Bloom.

'God bless Mrs Bloom!' I said. 'Thank you so much, it's brilliant! But just one question. Does Big Ann still have an input?'

'No,' he replied. 'It's all yours and you report only to me, and if I am

1 *Named after Whipsnade Park Zoo, which had very large open enclosures.*

away to Harry Prandall.[2] I will tell Ann of my decision.'

He then told me it was unprecedented to give a new keeper their own section, and that he was sticking his neck out for me, so I mustn't let him down. I assured him I wouldn't.

For the next eight years, I worked my socks off improving this wonderful, diverse section. This kind, astute man saw the potential in a young girl, and gave her a chance to fulfil her dream.

I was now in charge of the following animals—two Malayan Sun Bears, seven Pere David Deer, three Sika Deer, three Chinese Water Deer, five Wapiti Deer, three Black Backed Jackals, two Artic Foxes, five Barbary Apes, four Lar Gibbons, two Red Pandas, two Husky Dogs, three Racoons, two Patas Monkeys, a single Sitatunga Antelope and one ancient Red Kangaroo!

It was a hell of a lot to look after by myself, but I could ask for help from other keepers when needed. Mrs Mott stopped complaining about Whipsnade section after a while, as she soon realized I loved the section as much as she did. The following year a few babies were born—and within two years babies were popping out everywhere.

Rufus, the old Kangaroo, had died by now, and so had Creaky, the Sitatunga. So when the Zoo was presented with five Rufous Bellied Wallabies[3], they took over their empty paddock. I was to have great success in breeding them, as the enclosure had dozens of small poplar trees in it. By keeping an area of short grass at the edge of the trees for them to feed, it resembled their native forest habitat in Tasmania. The enclosure might have been perfect for the wallabies, but in the autumn it was a pain in the backside for me—the amount of poplar leaves that I had to rake up and barrow away was unbelievable.

I read every book I could beg, borrow or occasionally buy about the different animals on my section. There was no Google or Wikipedia in those days, and information was a great deal harder to obtain. However, thanks to my studies— and slowly but surely—Whipsnade section improved. The Wapiti paddock was enlarged and taken right back up to the railings bordering the main road. Then Fred Williams, the Clerk of Works, told me that a new Wapiti House was going to be built. He said

---

2 *Harry was Head Keeper on the Bear section at the time*

3 *Technically Pademelons, these are one of the smallest species of the macropod family, to which Wallabies, Wallaroos and Kangaroos also belong. They can be distinguished from their wallaby cousins by their shorter, thicker and sparsely haired tails.*

that if I had any ideas about the design to let him know. So I did.

I think Fred was almost sorry he had asked. I asked for the house to have two separate areas—one for the females, and one for Woppy, the male. The hay rack on Woppy's side was to be made upright, so he didn't have to tip his head right back when he was feeding—his antlers were so heavy it was uncomfortable for him.

I wanted a feeding trough on the inside, running the length of the wall facing the paddock, with bars running down vertically. Then the females could put their heads through from outside, and I could feed them their concentrates without having to let them in.

A space was needed between the female and male area, where bales of hay could be stored. It could then be delivered straight from the Zoo farm, so I wouldn't have to barrow it up from the hay store in the maintenance yard.

Finally, an area of concrete was required outside the gates into the house, so the Wapiti's were not bringing in as much muck on their feet.

Fred went quite pale when I handed him my list but—bless his heart—I got everything I asked for. The new Wapiti house was a splendid structure and looked as handsome outside as it did inside. The builders and maintenance men teased me unmercifully for a while, and if they saw me they would shout to each other, 'Look out lads! Here she comes with another bloody list!'

Most of us were used to—and loved—the teasing and banter, and joined in. However, if you had no sense of humour—like Big Ann—it got taken seriously. Very often we would see Ann stamping out of the maintenance yard, with her blood boiling. Dave, the blacksmith, and Derek, the mechanic, were the worst for winding Big Ann up.

In the Monkey house, Ann's fiefdom, the doors to the sleeping dens were kept tight shut with big wooden wedges. This stopped the monkeys constantly rattling them. One day, Ann broke the mallet she used to knock the wedges in, so she asked Dave the Blacksmith to make her a stronger one. When completed, he sent a message to say it was finished. So off she went to collect it. She came back with a face like thunder, and went and hung it in its allotted place. It was a masterpiece—all shining steel and about the size of John Henry's hammer.[4] Up one side of the handle in big, bold welded letters was her name, 'BIG ANN'.

4 *From the 'Legend of John Henry's Hammer' by Johnny Cash. Described in the song as "a steel-nosed hammer on a four foot switch handle"*

I had had very little contact with Big Ann since taking over Whipsnade, as I now had my own food preparation area—inside the meat store, on the maintenance yard. Hearing Ann's raised voice outside the yard, at lunchtime one day, I went out to see what was happening. She was by the yard gate, opposite the Monkey House, and was shouting so loudly at someone I was able to hear her from inside the meat store. Little Caitlin was the object of her wrath.

Caitlin was in floods of tears, because Ann was now bringing very personal comments into the tirade. I went over to them and told Ann, 'You really have no right to shout at Caitlin like that, and certainly not to make personal comments about her!'

A lot of the maintenance men were now standing watching, and were muttering about Ann. She turned to me and said, 'Mind your own bloody business!'

'It is my business,' I replied, 'when I see a junior keeper being bullied!'

Big Ann then said, right into my face, 'I am a senior keeper!' Then, emphasising each word with a poke into my chest with her finger, she said, 'So don't you get bolshie with me my girl!'

'I'm not your girl,' I replied. 'I'm also a senior keeper, in case you forgot, and if you poke me one more time I'll break your damned finger!'

This raised a cheer from the work men, who all started shouting, 'Go on Pam! Thump her!'

Ann was so shocked that I wasn't intimidated by her, and that the men on the yard were objecting to her treatment of Caitlin—and siding with me—that she did what all bullies do when confronted; she backed down, then burst into tears and ran away to shut herself in the Monkey House.

I hadn't wanted to turn the confrontation into a circus for the amusement of the workmen, but I couldn't help but take Caitlin's part—and it was about time Ann got her comeuppance. I tried to talk to her later and make my peace with her, but to no avail. Poor Ann. She was so used to bullying the two maiden aunts she lived with, that it was just the way she went through life. She was excellent at teaching trainee's how to clean and keep everything shipshape, but was no good at personal relationships.

15: SMALL HENRY AND TALL SUSAN

After working on my own for a few months, Mr. Bloom called me into his office for a chat. He said that he was very pleased with my work and realized I needed permanent help, but until now hadn't had any keepers to spare. I had had a few trainees before, but most of them were useless and without a lick of common sense. With this being the most important attribute a keeper needs, they were doomed from the start. Then Mr. Bloom said that he had just interviewed a girl that he thought I would like, and that she would be starting the next week. So, the following Monday I met Margy—and Mr Bloom was right. I did like her. She turned out to be one of the best keepers I ever worked with. She was sensible, reliable, a hard worker and had a wicked sense of humour. We got along like a house on fire and we became true and lifelong friends. We were a good team, and our working day was always interspersed with gales of laughter, as we regaled each other with tales of school and previous jobs.

The only way for us to access the Wapiti pen was up past the Zoo greenhouses and nursery area—where all the plants were grown for the flowers beds and border displays, in the public areas around the Zoo. In the '60s, Chester Zoo was famous not only for its animals but also for its magnificent gardens. The Head Gardener, Mr. Philip Gallup, was a genius with plants. His designs and colour combinations, in the beds and borders, were wonderful. There must have been at least a dozen gardeners employed in those days, and I got to know most of them well. When the greenhouses were full of bedding plants or beautiful pot plants, the lads would shout to me as I passed with my wheelbarrow to come and have look.

When Margy came on the scene, 'Small Henry'—one of the gardeners—was especially keen to give us a tour of the greenhouses, as he had developed a crush on her. He became an utter pest and started to follow her. It didn't matter where we were working—his leering little face would pop up over the top of walls, out of bushes and around the corners of buildings. She ignored him at first, but then told him to 'go away' in her own inimitable style. When he started hanging around the Wapiti House every morning, and pestering her, she lost her temper with him, shouting, 'Get back on the Cathedral with all the other gargoyles!'

There was an explosion of laughter from behind the potting shed—some of the gardeners had been spying on Henry, and heard what Margy said. So Henry was teased and tormented for a while by his work mates, but it had very little effect on him. Only when she threatened to report him to Mr. Gallop did he desist. He didn't fret for long though, as 'Tall Susan' then came into his life.

Tall Susan was a trainee keeper, and was on the usual month's trial. I think she had been shunted around every section in the Zoo. She only lasted two or three days, at the most, before Head Keepers were begging for her to be moved on. She hadn't got a scrap of common sense, so the poor girl was destined for failure. Although she was shown every single job in incredible detail, she'd still get it wrong. It was just quicker to do it yourself. We had the 'joy' of having her with us for two days, and it was a mighty relief when she went to the Monkey House. Even Big Ann was defeated by her, as she took her telling's off on the chin—brave girl—and just carried on muddling her way through each day. In the end she was put on Billy Baboon duty.

Billy was a huge male Chacma Baboon, who had developed a real hatred for lady visitors in very flowery dresses. He would watch the crowds closely for such ladies, until he spotted his unsuspecting quarry. He then would start to perform a threat display, which would inevitably draw the crowds. If the nice, flowery lady happened to have made her way to the front of the crowd, Billy would gather a handful of poo—especially produced for this purpose—and with great accuracy, fling it directly at her. There would be a loud scream from the poor lady—now splattered with the extremely pungent mess—and whoever was on watch would have to take the victim to the ladies cloakroom to help clean her up. Susan was supposed to prevent these incidents, by warning such ladies not to stand too near—but she never quite managed it. In the summer though—when flowery dresses were in abundance—Billy was taken off display altogether and kept inside. Constantly having to clean up smelly ladies was not pleasant.

A neighbour of Billy's was an Olive Baboon called 'Scruffy', who was famous throughout the zoo for her greed. She would do battle with any of her kind for the smallest scrap of anything edible. She lived with a male called Harry, and their offspring of all ages. Her frequent babies would be cared for lovingly whilst suckling—but as soon as they started to eat solids, Scruffy turned into a monster. She would grab the baby by the nearest appendage then—holding it down with her foot—would force open its mouth, and scoop the food out of the poor little thing's cheek pouches with a finger. The baby would be screaming blue murder, and visitors would rush to tell keepers that a big monkey was killing a baby one. Scruffy was such a cunning madam, that we had to resort to all kinds of tricks to separate her from the others at feeding times. The key to solving this problem came, unexpectedly, in the form of a brand new food for primates. This was a powdered, vitamin enriched food, which was mixed with warm water and banana essence then formed into balls. We called it 'Gorilla Cake'. All of the baboons liked it—except for Scruffy, who refused to eat it and would just smear it all over the place. It was so funny to see the greedy madam dashing around, trying to steal food from the others—only to find that it was the hated Gorilla Cake. Although it was almost impossible to scrub her rejected Gorilla Cake off the floor once it had dried, we were glad we had introduced it, because now it was easy to separate her—she would always be more than eager to come inside for her fruit and veg. So, apart from the usual Baboon squabbles, peace reigned once more in the Baboon enclosure.

Every Friday lunch time, all the zoo staff would queue for their wage packets at the potting shed. This is where Small Henry met Tall Susan. It was love at first sight, bless their hearts. For her remaining two weeks—as you may have guessed, she didn't pass her month's trial—Susan and Henry would disappear, at lunch times, to some love nest or other. We guessed it was probably in the back of his van on the Zoo car park. They would scurry off together, with Small Henry's arm wrapped around Susan's backside, as he couldn't reach her waist. On her return, her neck would be covered with huge love bites—which made us all feel rather sick.

Margy said, 'She should be taken off public display! She's not fit to be seen!' But she continued, 'Bless her though, for being useful for the first time in her life. She's taken his mind off me!'

We presumed the romance continued after she left, because Small Henry was always so very cheerful. Some mornings, on our way to the

Wapitis, Margy and I would meet a very large plant pot that had two sturdy little legs, trotting along underneath. Emanating from the foliage of the large plant we would hear cheerful whistling. As the plant pot passed by, it would say, 'Morning!' This was Small Henry carrying a large plant to the big house—it was his job to care for, and replace, the specimen plants in the Oakfield Restaurant and the Director's flat.

16: NEW BUILDINGS AND NEW BABIES

Every department and animal section in the Zoo had an amazingly busy year in 1962. The annual Conference of the International Union of Directors of Zoological Gardens was to be held at Chester, in September the following year—and there was an awful lot of work to be done. The Zoo now desperately needed a new Monkey House and Large Cat House, so the race was on to get them built in time for the conference. Mr. Mott wanted everything perfect—and he wanted it yesterday. We all dreaded seeing him appear on our sections. Thankfully, Mrs Mott had her eye on me and kept me on my toes, so he didn't bother me too much.

Work was almost completed on a huge Tropical House, which was 'Motty's' pride and joy. Then, in the December of 1962, gale force winds caused thousands of pounds worth of damage in one night. The almost completed Tropical House lost most of its roof, and the sections of roofing were tossed all over the zoo. It was a dreadful setback, as now it would not be ready in time. It was finally officially opened in June, 1964. It was very different from the other zoo buildings, because the general public could walk along paths amongst the tropical vegetation. They could also watch—and get very close to—the many species of birds that were flying free. The keepers loved the tropical house, and had watched it grow from just the foundations into a splendid building. Faith and I liked to go in to sit on one of the benches at lunch times, to eat our sandwiches, especially in the winter. We always kept a wary eye out for Motty though, as he would not have approved and would have thrown us out on our ear pretty damned quick.

The new Monkey House was built on time, and was massive compared to the old one. There were huge inside and outside enclosures. The plate glass windows that were removed from the old monkey house, were saved and eventually incorporated into the new cat house. More keepers were needed for the new, much larger Monkey House—so there were lots of experienced keepers, from other zoos, applying for the jobs. When Big Ann moved into the new building she got short shrift from the new male and female keepers, who wouldn't put up with her nonsense. Finally, in a temper one day, she stormed out of work and never came back. Poor Ann. There was very little joy in her life, and she must have been a very lonely person. But she was just so hard to like.

Billy Baboon was moved into his new quarters, but in the inside visitor's area there was now only a large window between him and the public. Consequently when confronted with a flowery dressed lady, his behaviour was even more extreme. Although he was now only able to splatter the window with poo, he now also started to charge at the glass—jumping and hitting it with his back feet. The power behind this contact caused the glass to bow outwards. Even though it was toughened plate glass, it was deemed far too much of a risk. He was taken off display permanently, and a special enclosure was built for him inside the old elephant house—which was on my section. This was now being used as quarantine kennels, for canines that came in from abroad, and at the time just one enclosure was being occupied by a pair of Kama Foxes.

Once again Fred Williams asked me for ideas, this time for Billy's new, public free zone. So a three compartment, super-strong structure was built—consisting of a large day area, and a small middle area and sleeping area. I wanted the middle area so that, when we were cleaning out his day or sleeping area, he couldn't reach through the bars and grab us. We left the radio on for him in the daytime, and gave him enrichment[1] in the form of cardboard boxes, branches to strip and chew, nuts in their shells, old blankets and lots of straw he could spread around and throw at us. His favourite plaything was an old tyre from a moped. He would sit and turn it inside out, and back again—that should give some indication of how strong he was.

Sunday was Billy's favourite day, as he always given four ounces of sugared almonds—these were a present from Fred Blythe, the head carpenter. Every Saturday, Fred would be given them by a none-too-clean, old chap in the pub. Fred never quite fancied them, so he would give them to me for Billy. On Sunday mornings, Billy would be eagerly awaiting his sweets. How he knew it was Sunday I have no idea. Perhaps we acted a little differently, or he could smell them, because he was always

1 *Enrichment, in the Zoological sense, is introducing elements to captive animals' environments, in order to encourage their natural behaviours and to maintain or increase their wellbeing. The term 'enrichment' to describe this practice was only formally adopted in the 1970s, but the practice itself was established as far back as the 1930s.*

sitting waiting—smacking his lips in greeting as we approached. I would swing his food hopper towards me, place the paper bag into it, and then swing it back again. Billy's food hopper was specially designed to be swung on hinges with a long handle—it could then be swung towards the keeper, away from the enclosure. His food would be placed inside and swung back again, shutting tight as the latch clipped over the top. This meant we could feed him without being dragged through the bars like an egg in a slicer.

Once placed, Billy would carefully remove the paper bag of sweets, place it on the floor and rip it open. He would then select a few almonds and suck them, until all the sugar coating had gone. The now bare nuts were then pushed into a cheek pouch. He did this over, and over again until all the sucked nuts were in his pouches. He would then empty the pouches into his mouth and contentedly chew the almonds until they were all gone.

Poor Billy. I think for those few minutes every week, it was the only time he was truly happy. He was very old by now, arthritic and very lonely. Although he hadn't lived with other baboons from the time he was an adult, he had been able to see and interact verbally with others close by. I suggested that it was cruel to keep him in solitary confinement, and that it would be kinder to put him to sleep. Eventually Mr Mott agreed. On the morning of the dreadful deed, he had a slap up breakfast of sponge cakes from Vera, from the Fountain restaurant. These contained sedatives. He also had a baked potato and a boiled egg. We had wanted him to be drowsy by the time the Zoo Vet came, but it just wasn't to be and he had to be darted with sedative—and he didn't make this easy for himself or us. When finally he was asleep, and he could be put to sleep by injection, Ralph Heyward—the vet—was amazed at how many injections it took to finally make that poor old heart stop beating.

In the summer of 1963, a customs officer, based at Liverpool Docks, brought a pair of baby Black Spider Monkeys into the Zoo's Small Mammal Hospital which was based on my section. They had been confiscated from a sailor on a cargo boat, who had tried to smuggle them into the country. They were about six months old and in an appalling state—dehydrated, malnourished and their coats matted with diarrhoea, and also suffering from severe rickets. How they had survived the voyage from Guyana, just being fed on scraps of human food, was a miracle.

With their black coats, big tummies and little stick-like arms and legs, they looked just like beetles. Thankfully, we immediately managed to get about fifty precious millilitres of rehydration fluid into them by mouth, without stressing them too much.

The vet didn't hold out much hope for these poor monkey's survival. As they were clinging to each other so tightly, we didn't want to stress them any further by trying to separate them. So I wrapped their bottom ends in a towel, and put them under my shirt. I knew that body warmth and skin contact what was they needed most of all. To say that they stank is an understatement, but needs must—their welfare came first. I kept trying to make little Spider Monkey noises, to reassure them—and after about ten minutes or so, I heard a feint answering chirrup and felt them beginning to move. I looked down the top of my shirt, and saw two little faces looking up at me. The little female put her hand up and very tentatively touched my face. I just felt an overwhelming rush of love for these two poor abused little things. It was a mutual love that lasted for the whole of 'Mrs Beetle's' life. Much to the vet's surprise—but not mine—she did survive.

Both Spider Monkeys took to the bottle almost immediately, and after a wash they looked and smelled one hundred percent better. Sadly, 'Mr. Beetle' was put gently to sleep a few weeks later. His spine and legs were just too deformed from Rickets for him to be able to live a happy, normal life. But at least for those few weeks he was secure, warm and nourished—and with medication was also practically pain free. They both lived under my shirt for a few days, only transferring at night time to a heated cage—which contained a large teddy bear wearing one of my shirts.

Mrs Beetle didn't seem to miss her companion too much, as she was now fixated on me and becoming a real spoiled brat. Although she was eating solids, she was also still on the bottle. Spider Monkeys are not fully weaned until they are about two years old. Molly Badham—the owner of Twycross Zoo, who was famous for her success in rearing exotic monkeys—sent us a milk formula that would suit Beetle, and she loved it. When I was preparing her bottle, she would sit on my shoulder with her arms around my head, her tail around my neck and screaming down my ear to hurry up. She would take the bottle from me and—with a look of sheer ecstasy—close her eyes, hardly drawing breath until she had finished. She'd then look at the empty bottle and throw it on the floor.

Mrs. Beetle had another companion by now—a baby Barbary ape called 'Pip Squeak'. He wasn't the brightest kid on the block, and didn't seem to notice—or care much—how bossy Beetle was with him. He used to sit sucking his thumb, watching while the brat performed an aerial ballet over, under and around him—very often using him as a spring board. After a few months Mrs. Beetle was fit and well enough to join the colony of Spider Monkeys in the new Monkey House, and her care was taken over by the Monkey keepers. Due to the Rickets, she would always have a slight hump on her back. But her arms and legs were now straight and strong, and her prehensile tail was functioning normally. Although I was sad to hand my baby over to someone else's care, it was wonderful to see this strong, active little madam so fit and strong. All the worry and hard work fighting to keep her alive had been worth it. At first I would visit her in my lunch break, but gradually I broke contact as she began slowly integrating into the troop.

Though I left Chester Zoo at the end of 1969—just two months before I was due to have our eldest child, Christopher—I had often thought about Mrs Beetle. In 1978, on a family visit to the Zoo, I stood in the crowd watching my beloved Beetle, who was now sixteen years old. I knew it was her from the slight hump on her back. She was sitting high up on a branch, looking at the crowd, when suddenly she recognized me among the many faces. She began to chirrup to me as if she was still a baby, holding out her arms to be picked up. Even though Spider Monkeys do recognize members of their own troop that they haven't seen for a long time, after eight and a half years it was amazing. She came down to the floor, and we talked to each other for a while. Then I left her in peace. John went back to check she wasn't too distressed, but she was fine. It was just me who was left in absolute pieces. It was a wonderful feeling though, to know she had remembered me, and evidently considered that I was part of her troop. Even more wonderful, was the fact that she had produced babies of her own, and had been an excellent mother. Very often, babies taken away from their mothers early and hand reared don't make the best of parents. Mrs. Beetle was my most loved baby of the many I hand reared during my time at Chester.

In the summer of Conference Year 1963, the keepers were issued with new uniforms. Grey suits with a white shirt, red tie and peaked cap for the men. For the girl's, jodhpurs with a white shirt, red tie and brown jumper, and riding boots or shoes. We had always had grey overalls, with red collars, to wear when we were working, but an order came from Mr. Mott that from now on, all keepers must be in full uniform by 10:30 A.M. The zoo jodhpurs were poor quality, compared with the ones I had bought from the Nutgrove Tally Man, so I continued to wear those. They weren't quite the same shade but no one noticed.

By September all the animal sections had been primped and painted. We realized that all the jobs that had needed doing, for ages, on our sections—that we hadn't been able do ourselves, even the parts that couldn't be seen by visitors—were now all attended too. We had all pestered the powers that be relentlessly about them. The Gardeners had worked very hard, and the gardens were looking magnificent. The builders, carpenters, plumbers, electricians and mechanics, had been working flat out to finish the monkey house, as well as all the other jobs that had needed their attention.

We all heaved a sigh of relief once the Conference was over, as the pressure to always have everywhere—and everything—looking picture perfect was an almost impossible task, and a strain on everyone.

17: JOHN

It's time now, I think, to bring my husband John into the story.

A few days after I had started at Chester Zoo, I saw a good looking man in the canteen and I thought, 'Oh! Aren't you the handsome one!' I was told his name was John. However, as I had broken up with a serious boyfriend before coming to Chester, I wasn't ready to be interested in anyone else just yet. Keeper's paths don't very often cross if they are on different sections, and when I did see him, on the odd occasion, he was always being followed by hordes of simpering females—usually from the various cafes—giggling and batting their eyelashes at him.

One of John's jobs was to feed the Sea lions and the Polar Bears at public feeding times. Occasionally however, on John's day off—and if Harry Prandle and Young Ken were busy—I would do it. It was extremely funny to see the expression on the faces of the girls, who were eagerly awaiting John's arrival at feeding times, when they realized they had got me instead—well, if looks could kill I would be dead and buried. After a while, I decided that I would like to talk to him, but figuring out a way to get him on his own was a problem. I had no intention of following him about, or resorting to simpering or eyelash batting—but as my deviousness knows no bounds when determined, I came up with a cunning plan.

Knowing that he was very often sent to do little D.I.Y. jobs on sections, when the maintenance men were busy, I put in a report that one of the sash windows in my work area—in the Malayan Sun Bear section—wouldn't open. My plan worked a treat, and John was sent down to fix the problem. He tried to lift the window. He thumped it, then tried to lever it. He even scraped all the paint from around the joints, but all to no avail. I thanked him for trying, and we got talking. We found we liked each other, and he asked me out on a date and that was that. We have been together practically ever since. I only confessed to him many years later, that the only reason the window wouldn't open was because I had nailed it shut. Ah, the wicked wiles of women!

John had started work at the zoo in 1961, at the age of eighteen, as a trainee on the bear section—later becoming Head Keeper in his early twenties. His charges consisted of Polar Bears, European Brown bears, Sloth Bears, Asian Black Bears and Canadian Black Bears. Also on this section were Lions, Tigers, Cheetahs, Sea Lions, Bagot Goats and a Warthog called Winnie. When the new Cat House was built, he moved to the other side of the zoo to become Head Keeper of this splendid new section.

From 1960 to 1963, the zoo went through a period of animals being inexplicably poisoned. Just how, and by whom, was a complete mystery. One day, John was approached by a very well dressed gentleman. He told John that the Brown Bears had fleas, and needed washing with carbolic soap. The zoo used to get more than its fair share of visiting weirdos so, to humour him, John said he would go and give them a good scrub later. As the man turned to go, John noticed a small bottle and some cotton wool, poking out of the breast pocket of the man's jacket. Alarm bells began ringing in his head, so he followed the man until he stopped at the Emu Paddock. He then started feeding the Emus with something, so John told him to stop. The zoo had a policy to ask people to leave, if they ignore a verbal warning. John had managed to attract the attention of other keepers, while on the way to the Emus, and they had followed at a distance. As the man had totally ignored the request to stop feeding the Emus, John summoned help. Now surrounded by six male keepers, the strange man was escorted to the nearest exit, telling him he was banned. John said the man didn't utter a word as they walked along—but once through the exit turnstile, he turned around and shouted that he hoped they all got T.B. and cancer and died a painful death. All of the poisoning incidents miraculously stopped after that.

As safety is of paramount importance when working with animals, part of our training was to check that enclosures were safe to enter, and that animals were securely locked inside or outside. All doors and gates had to be bolted and locked when leaving, and if you were unsure, you had to check again. Replying 'I think so' is not the answer to give when asked if the pen is secure. When one had a trainee like Tall Susan—who was genuinely unable to understand the importance of safety checks—you have to cope and just make sure she was never ever left on her own.

Although keepers would tease and play tricks on each other, these pranks would never, ever compromise their own, other keepers or their animals' safety.

One summer, a chap came to work on the Cat House with John and his assistant, Bob Eldridge. His name was Robert Voss, and was the grandson of a Zoo Council Member. He was waiting to go to university, and at a loose end. So, evidently, some strings were pulled and he was put onto John's section for the summer. John thought Voss was strange, and found him very creepy. Almost immediately he started playing silly tricks on John and Bob, which were just annoying at first, but gradually got more and more serious. One day he poured cod liver oil into the disinfectant used for mopping the floors, which made them very slippery and dangerous. It took a lot of hard work to clean them up, and Voss got a good telling off. Then he started to annoy the big cats, by poking them through the wire with lengths of plastic pipe. So he was told off once more. Next he started locking Bob into sleeping dens—when he was cleaning them out—and Bob would have to shout for John to come and let him out. John had complained to Mr Pearson, the section officer, who then let the powers that be know what was happening. Voss was warned again about his behaviour. Finally, it came to a head when he smashed the large reinforced skylight—that was over John's office—with a heavy plank of wood. This was very serious, as the skylight was actually built into the rock formation in the outside Jaguar enclosure, and was where Khan—the male—liked to lie. Voss was evidently trying to frighten Khan by pounding on the glass. The Jaguars could have gotten through with very little effort, and John, Bob and the idiot Voss could have been killed. Thankfully he was sacked on the spot, and John and Bob breathed a sigh of relief, thankful to be at last rid of this dangerous idiot.

Not long after Voss had left, John was sitting in his office one afternoon, when he heard a loud, ripping sound coming from the boiler room—which also served as a cloakroom—next door. As the boiler room jutted out under the same rock formation as John's office, he knew what it must be. He ran outside to the front of the pen, and saw that Khan had managed—with little effort—to rip out the heavy, metal air-intake grill by the heating pump. Although it was set into the concrete, it was no match for the teeth of a Jaguar who had decided to remove it. The ripping noises John had heard, were his best uniform being shredded by the jaguar, who was now inside the boiler room. John managed to tempt Khan back through, into the outside pen, and then into his sleeping den. Thank God he had heard his uniform being ripped, because had he entered the boiler room unawares, he most certainly would not be alive today.

It can be nerve racking when a dangerous animal escapes. If gale force winds were forecast, the Lions and Tigers were always shut in their sleeping quarters. One night an unexpected, very strong wind brought a tree down across the fence in the Tiger enclosure. As Big Dave, a keeper from the Bird House, came into work early next morning, he passed the flower bed that surrounded the tiger pen. He saw the female tiger fast asleep in the pansies. He was in two minds about what to do, whether to creep past or run like hell. He crept past—brave lad. Luckily she didn't hear him, and he raised the alarm. She was lying between the wall of the polar bear dens, and the fence of the tiger enclosure, so each end of the path was blocked off with zoo vans. Slowly, she was ushered back into the enclosure, then tempted into the sleeping dens. Thankfully, she hadn't gone for a stroll around the zoo. Had Tim, the male Tiger, escaped, the outcome could have been very different.

18: DO YOU KNOW WHO I AM?

Very often we would get celebrities from T.V. and Film in the zoo—mainly of the 'Do you know who I am?' variety. For a few days we had the BBC in, filming a sequence for the most popular children's animal TV show at the time. None of the keepers liked the famous presenter of this show much, who I shall refer to as simply Mr M. On this particular day the TV people wanted to film him feeding the tigers. Before they started shooting, John gave Mr M a bucket, containing ten kilos of meat, and told him to be careful around the back of the dens. There was a small metal grill set in the den wall, at head height, and it was Tim the Tiger's 'party piece' to roar through this vent as you passed it. The power of a tiger's roar, up close, is unbelievable—it just penetrates your whole body. John was just about to warn him of this, when Mr M turned around to give John a really supercilious look—as if to say, 'Go away boy, I am an expert!'

So John withheld his advice. 'Right mate,' he thought, knowing that Tim would be crouched and waiting. 'This is going to be interesting!'

Mr M proceeded to walk toward the dens, talking in a loud voice. As his head got level with the aforementioned grill, Tim let fly with an almighty roar. Mr M instantly dropped the meat bucket as he was physically knocked sideways by the blast. Standing frozen to the spot, he was now deathly white and shaking like a leaf. The producer shouted that they would have to take the shot again.

'Why?' John thought to himself. 'It was just perfect!'

Later on that day, Margy and I were passing the tiger enclosure, and saw Mr M being filmed outside. There was a large crowd watching as he walked up and down, talking to Tim—who was lying on his platform at the far end. Mr M then climbed over the safety railings—an action totally forbidden to the public—and approached the wire fence. Initially, Margy and I had intended to just walk past—but when we saw him climb over the barrier, we thought we would wait for the entertainment to start. Mr M was so busy jabbering at Tim, that he had failed to notice the female tiger, lying totally flat and still in the grass—right against the bottom of the fence. He was still jabbering, and waving his arms about when, with a huge roar, the female shot up to her full height right against the fence—Mr M just collapsed onto his bottom. He then jumped straight up, and vaulted the safety railings like an athlete. We had been joined by other keepers by now who, like us, had been on their way to the maintenance yard, to buy break-time sandwiches from the Butty Van. Poor Mr M! His showing-off to the public hadn't had quite the effect he was hoping for, for now he had made himself look like a real twit. Of course we all enjoyed it immensely, and thought he was an idiot. He certainly got a taste of some real 'animal magic' that day.

Approaching the Gibbon enclosure one afternoon, I could see a large crowd of people. They were all watching a man strut up and down, talking in a loud voice in front of them. As I got nearer, I recognized the show-off as Peter Malloney. In the 'sixties he was a five minute wonder, on quiz and chat shows on Radio and TV. I had a job to do, so I just pushed through the crowd and, ignoring Malloney, unlocked the gate between the Gibbons' and Artic Fox's enclosures. Unbidden, he followed me through onto the path, still jabbering and showing off to the crowd. Turning around to face him, I politely asked him to leave, as the public were not allowed in keeper areas.

'Public? Public?' He bellowed. 'I'm not the bloody public! Do you know who I am?'

'I couldn't care less if you were the Shah of Persia!' I shouted back at him. 'You are to leave this area immediately!' Waving my arms at him, I backed him out of the gate. The crowd were laughing now. They thought this little fracas was much funnier than his attempt to entertain them. So, with a face dark with rage and embarrassment, he stormed off. A little while later, a message came from Mr. Mott—he wanted to see me, as he had received a complaint from Peter Malloney. I was to go up to Mr. Mott's flat in the Big House immediately.

Oh my God! I nearly wet myself, because Mottie was known to sack staff in an instant if he was in a bad mood. As I climbed the stairs to the flat—with stomach churning and knees knocking—I met Mrs. Mott, who was just coming down. She looked at me with a puzzled frown. I quickly told her what had happened. She then came back up the stairs with me, and opened the door to the flat.

Mottie was inside, pacing up and down in the hallway. Mrs. Mott said, while giving Mottie a withering look, 'Miss Logan to see you George. Please go in Pam.'

'I've had a complaint from Mr. Malloney.' Said Mottie. 'He told me that you were rude and threatening towards him! What have you got to say for yourself?'

So taking a deep breath I told him what had happened, making sure I laid it on as thick as Malloney had. I pointed out that Mr. Mott himself had told all keepers that no one, without exception, was allowed in keeper areas. I said that I hadn't been at all rude, and that Malloney was the rude one—as he had shouted and sworn at me, and evidently had delusions of grandeur.

'How could a grown man feel threatened by a girl of nineteen?' I asked, neglecting to mention that when I had backed Malloney out of the gate, I had a large yard brush in one hand, and a shovel in the other.

Mottie looked at me for what seemed to be an age, then said, 'I see, I see. Well, off you go back to work then.'

As I left the flat, I could hear him chuckling to himself and saying, over and over again, 'delusions of grandeur!', 'the Shah of Persia!'

When I got outside, I was shaking with relief. Mrs. Mott was waiting by the front of the Big House, and I just put my hand on my heart and said, 'Phew!' She just nodded her head and gave me one of her quiet smiles. I vowed if I ever met Peter bloody Malloney again, I would brain him with my brush and shovel, as the arrogant little toad had nearly got me the sack.

19: HERE, THERE AND EVERYWHERE

In 1965, the BBC TV Natural History Unit—based in Bristol—produced a new quiz programme called *Zoo Challenge.*

Zoos from around the UK were invited to bring an animal to the studio, to see if a panel of experts could identify it. When the news that Chester had been invited to take part, and that Mr Mott was going to take a keeper with him, everyone was wondering which animal and which keeper. Lots of the keepers were hoping it would be them, and lots of the keepers—including John and myself—were hoping that it wouldn't.

It was decided that the animal would be a Tayra, a member of the weasel family about as large as cat. They are found in South America, from Mexico down to Argentina. From region to region, there is a vast difference in the colour and length of coat, and also the size of the marking on the throat. Chester Zoo's male Tayra was quite small, and the colour of his coat was a very unusual light, almost pink, fawn. It was hoped therefore that he might baffle the panel.

As Mr Mott said John looked the best in uniform, upright and smart like a soldier—he could also have added, 'and very handsome'—he became the chosen keeper.

Sandra, from the Mammal House, was furious when she heard that John was Mr. Mott's choice—as the Tayras were on her section. She moaned and complained to everyone that she should have been chosen, until they were all heartily sick of her. When other keepers were gushingly sympathetic towards her, she hadn't got the sense to realise they were winding her up. She even came grumbling to me, saying that everyone thought that she should be the one to go—evidently she thought, for some reason, that I had a say in the matter. Silly girl. I lost my patience with her. 'It's nothing to do with me,' I said. 'Go and complain to Mr. Mott!'

I was worried for a while that she would do just that—she was certainly daft enough. If she had, it probably would have earned her a good rollicking or even the sack. And if she happened to mention I had told her to complain, I would have been in trouble too.

John travelled down to Bristol, with Mr. Mott, the day before the programme. The Tayra lodged at Bristol Zoo for the night, Mr. Mott stayed at a very posh hotel, and poor John at the real life equivalent of *Fawlty Towers*. When John—in full zoo uniform, including peaked cap, with bold letters clearly saying 'HEAD KEEPER', and the lapels on his jacket both saying 'CHESTER ZOO'—presented himself at the reception desk, the hotel owner just stared at him. She then looked him up and down, and said, 'Are you the man from the Zoo?'

'God,' thought John. 'She's as smart as whip this one!'

Then she said, 'Will you look at my Parrot?'

So, with great trepidation, John followed her into the living room, wondering whether this was a new slant on the 'Would you like to see my etchings?' line.

There in a small cage was the saddest looking, totally bald parrot he had ever seen. 'It keeps shivering!' She said.

'Of course it will,' John replied. 'It's cold without feathers.'

He told her that, though he didn't know much about parrots, it was cruel to keep one in such a small cage, without any environmental enrichment. Obviously, the poor thing was stressed and bored with its living conditions, and probably also had a vitamin deficiency. Ms 'Fawlty', not at all pleased with John's diagnosis, sniffed in a superior fashion, 'The Vet's given me some drops to put in his water to make him better!'

John thought to himself, '*Well, why are you bothering to ask me then? If you want to take the vet's advice, the poor parrot's problem is solved. But clearly, your vet is as daft as you.*'

When John returned to Chester, I asked him if he had enjoyed the evening meal at the 'hotel', knowing how much he liked good food.

'I've fed better food to the bears!' He replied. But at least the bed had been clean and the breakfast had been passable.

When it aired, we all watched and enjoyed the programme a great deal. On the following day, in the canteen, Sandra was tormented unmercifully by the other keepers.

'Don't you think John did an excellent job Sandra?'

'He was definitely the right choice.'

'He handled the Tayra expertly, don't you think?'

'Mr Mott must have been pleased with his choice.'

They tormented her so much, I almost felt sorry for her.

In the early '60s, keepers worked a six-day-week, so included weekends. John and I had different days off, but sometimes we could swop with another keeper and wangle a day off together. Mostly I went home on my day off, and Mother was always so happy to have me home. John would come to pick me up in the evening, so I didn't have to face the tedious bus journey back to Chester. Before leaving, I was always packed off back to Chester with a large cake tin full of Mother's delicious baking. Mother liked John very much, which was a blessed relief, as she hadn't liked my previous boyfriend—or vice versa—and the air had used to positively crackle with the negative vibes between the two of them. But it was different with John, who liked Mother a great deal too.

Just after the Zoo Conference it had been announced that, from then on, all keepers would be allowed one weekend off in four, plus their normal day off. So, of course we all would try to swop our day off to a Friday—to make it a long weekend.

We had the usual two weeks annual leave, and John and I would take one week in the early summer and one week in September. Sometimes we managed to book our week so it included our weekend off as well. For our summer holiday we would go down to Devon, and spend a few days there taking in a visit to Paignton Zoo, then travel up to Bristol Zoo—then across to London, Whipsnade and Twycross Zoos on our way home. We were always made most welcome, especially at Bristol. Geoffrey, the son of Bristol Zoo's Director, was working at Chester, so he would kindly let Bristol know when we were planning to visit. We were always met at the entrance by Les Jones, the Senior Head Keeper, and taken for a coffee before a visit to some of the sections. After a slap up lunch, we would visit the other sections, then on the Great Ape section we would catch up with Michael—a friend who used to work at Chester. It was always a wonderful day, and we were treated with such kindness.

On one of our visits we inquired about a keeper called Gerald, who also had gone to Bristol from Chester. While at Chester he had worked on the Camel, Zebra and Giraffe Section. He was very accident prone, and had lots of minor mishaps—and also two very serious ones. His first accident occurred, when one day he decided—while he was cleaning the inside pens—to have a little rest, and leant with his hand against the wire mesh dividing the pens. Unfortunately, there was a Zebra in the next pen, who proceeded to completely bite off the finger that was poking through. Later on that same year, while working with a Dromedary Camel called 'Barker'—who was definitely one of the worst tempered animals in the zoo—Gerald forgot the unwritten rule to always keep to the side of Barker. He approached him from the front, and Barker grabbed him by the head. John spoke to head keeper, Les Nield, after the accident. Les said he could hear Gerald screaming, and when he ran into the Camel House, Barker was just standing perfectly still—with Gerald's head in his mouth. Les first grabbed a brush, but then thought if he gave Barker a whack with it, the camel might bite down on Gerald even harder. Then he thought he had just better do something, pretty damned quick, so he whacked Barker on the backside. Thankfully, he let go. Gerald ran out, with his head streaming with blood. When he got cleaned up at A&E, it was miraculously found that he only needed five stitches. He left Chester soon after that, and went to Bristol. Les Nield said that he was really glad to see him go.

So, when we asked at Bristol how Gerald was faring, we knew Mr Jones—the Head Keeper—would be unlikely to give us any positive news.

'Ah Gerald,' he sighed. 'I'm afraid he is on sick leave at the moment. He was crushed between two Elephants a few weeks ago, and I don't think he will be fit enough to come back.'

So Gerald had survived a serious accident yet again, but this time it seemed his zoo days were over.

During our travels, we got to know a lot of the keepers from the other zoos, and would very often be taken to visit the latest babies. On one visit to London Zoo, we were introduced to a seven year old, hand-reared Orang Utan, called Lucy, who was still safe enough to handle. She came walking down the service passage and stopped in front of us. She was very interested in my back pack, as she could evidently smell the few *Maltesers* I had left in a box, and was looking at me expectantly. I told George—her keeper—that they were there, and asked if she was allowed to have one. He smiled, and said, 'Yes. But only one.' So I opened the box, took one out and offered it to her. She took it politely and ate it. She then took the entire box off me—which I was not going to argue about—closed the lid and, holding the box with her hands above her head, waddled back down the corridor from whence she came. Part way down, she stopped to turn around, and stared at me with a look that seemed to say, 'You are such an idiot! Only one? You have got to be joking!'

We always stayed with my sister and family on our London visit, and it was lovely to see them all. The house was always bursting at the seams, because all twelve children were still living at home then. So John and I 'camped out' in our sleeping bags on the living room floor, and very often woke to find a little person or two snuggled up to us in the morning.

After London we usually went on to Whipsnade, and after a full day were always allowed to camp in the orchard overnight. We would make an early start the next morning, with a drive up to Twycross Zoo, in Leicestershire, ahead of us. I knew Molly Badham, the director, and we always enjoyed our visits—where we would set to helping feed the latest hand reared baby Chimps and Gibbons, in the play pens dotted around Molly's living room. I first met Molly when she presented Chester with three hand reared Chinese Water Deer—they were still on the bottle when they arrived, and I took over their care. 'Pickles', 'Chutney' and 'Saucy' went to live in the paddock next to the Malayan Sun Bears. They were very popular with visitors, who loved to see these three tiny little things, with legs no thicker than a pencil, trotting behind me in a straight line.

Molly had earlier offered me a job at Twycross as a senior keeper, with more money than I was earning at Chester. I was very tempted, but was settled and happy at Chester—and as I had also started going out with John by then, I decided to stay put. It was a decision I never regretted. We were homeward bound after Twycross and were always eager to get back—even calling in at the Zoo on the evening we got home, just to check that everything was well. Of course, it always was.

In our September holiday week, we usually went to visit Reg Bloom—and Margaret, and the rest of the Bloom family—who, having left Chester, was now Director at Flamingo Park Zoo in Yorkshire. I missed them very much, as Reg had been a kind and considerate boss—if a little absent minded—who would roll up his sleeves at the drop of a hat when help was needed. And Margaret, his lovely wife, had always been a shoulder to cry on if any of us girls had problems. Also, as the zoo lodge was near to the Malayan Bear section, I had seen a lot of their three children. Peter, the eldest, who was about six when I first met him, would come and sit on an upturned bucket and chat to me through the fence. After visiting the Blooms, we would then travel up to Edinburgh Zoo. On the way, we'd visit my friend Faith, who used to work at Chester, and her husband Martin, who was the curator of Stanley Zoo in County Durham.

Zoo, Zoo and even more Zoo! This was now our wonderful life, both in work and on holiday. Traveling up hill, and down dale, in John's little *Austin A40*, packed to the gunnels with camping gear and the dog—firstly 'Cimmy', the Husky, then later 'Finn', the Irish Wolfhound. My section was expanding rapidly by then and Phillipa, another excellent keeper, had joined Margy and I. She became another friend for life, and we chatted regularly on Facebook until very recently. Very sadly, Margy died a few years ago, but her daughter Caroline still keeps in touch. We were a formidable team, as we all had the same whacky sense of humour and worked well together. Trainee keepers came and went, some of them as quickly as I could palm them off onto another section, so Margy and Philippa were precious.

The Small Mammal Hospital, that had been on my section, had moved to new premises at the other end of the Zoo. In the space left behind, the new Chimpanzee and Orang Utan Nursery was built. A spanking new Otter Pool was built, for the Asian Short Clawed Otters, opposite the Penguin Pool. A new Anteater enclosure was added, and enclosures for the newly acquired Striped and Spotted Hyenas were also built. Our day had to be planned meticulously to be able to get through the work load, and Margy and Phil were brilliant at acting on their own initiative if there was a blip in the regime. I was so lucky to have them working with me—the maintenance men and gardeners called us the three musketeers.

On my way to feed the Otters one afternoon, a lady came running towards me shouting for me to come quickly, as some boys were stealing the penguin eggs. As I started to run, I asked to her to go and hammer on the Bird House door, around the corner, to raise the alarm. I got to the Penguin Pool, just in time to see two youths climbing back over the side barrier. Giving the nearest youth a push backwards, he fell into the deepest part of the pool—and as he fell, he pulled the other one in with him. Eggs were lying smashed outside the nest boxes, and the penguins were terrified, huddling together in a corner. It was so distressing to see them and the smashed eggs—with partially developed chicks—that were lying all over the floor.

I was so upset and angry, that every time a youth grabbed onto the front barrier to try to climb out, I wacked his fingers with the metal scoop from the otter food bucket. I was trying to keep them from getting away before the bird keepers arrived. The water was up to their chins, and very cold, and they were having difficulty in getting their breath. They were crying by now, begging to be allowed out of the pool. But I had not one jot of sympathy for the little bastards.

The two Dave's, from the Bird House, came running up and were horrified to see the carnage. Big Dave grabbed one youth by the scuff of the neck, and hauled him over the barrier as if he were a feather. Little Dave, with the help of some visitors, hauled the other one out. They were so cold by now they couldn't stand, and when they did at last manage to get to their feet, they were marched to the nearest exit. A very angry crowd of visitors, led by Little Dave, unceremoniously threw them out—still shivering, dripping wet and one of them wearing only one shoe. Big Dave, all six feet six inches of him, was near to tears with the wanton cruelty caused to his beloved birds by these youths. Both Dave's had worked hard and long to get the penguins to breed, produce and incubate eggs.

Nowadays, the police would have been involved. No doubt I would be arrested for assault and battery, and the little darlings would be allowed to sue me for pain and suffering. They would have only received a smack on the wrist now, because their behaviour was due to a deprived childhood—or some such rubbish.

Dealing with the occasional nasty visitor was not pleasant, but at least now and again, as on that occasion, we had the satisfaction of giving them our own form of justice.

20: CHARACTERS

UDONG

Wearing jodhpurs brought many ribald comments from the public. We didn't care, but when you have heard the same comments over, and over again, it can get a little wearing.

I was walking past the Lion paddock one day, and saw a man shouting and waving his arms, trying to get the Lions to come over to the fence. As Udong, the male lion, started to stroll across, I thought I had better go and tell the man why it wasn't such a good idea. His friends saw me coming and gave him a nudge. He turned around, looked me up and down, and said, 'Have you lost your horse then?' I smiled and started to speak, when he said, 'Sod off, Annie Oakley!'

So I thought, '*Right mate, I will!*'

I moved back to watch the entertainment that was due to follow. Udong started to rub up and down the fence, purring loudly. By now the man was convinced he was Dr. Dolittle, and he and his friends were leaning nearer and nearer. I had been joined by Derek, the mechanic, and we were just grinning, watching and waiting. When Udong decided that these fearless lion tamers were near enough, he quickly swung around, pressed his backside against the fence and sprayed them all with pungent pee. Walking away from the two now extra-unpleasant men behind, Derek and I could still hear their shouting and swearing as we walked past the Zoo Shop. Mrs Smith, the proprietor, popped her head out as we passed and said, 'Udong's party piece I presume?'

We just nodded and laughed.

THE ADMIRAL

At Chester Zoo there is a canal system that takes visitors around the zoo in large motor boats. The man in charge of the boats when I was there was known as 'The Admiral'. He was a very smartly dressed, well-spoken man in his sixties and he kept the boats and the other drivers in good order. He was extremely odd at times, but on occasions lost the plot completely. One day we heard Police sirens coming from the Boat Bus jetty, so of course we just had to dash down to see what was happening. A large crowd had gathered around the Jetty—the Admiral was refusing to let some passengers off his boat, saying they were the Great Train Robbers. He was threatening to brain them with a boat hook if they moved. We thought it was hilarious of course. The police eventually persuaded him to let them off, and we didn't see him for a little while afterwards.

Sometimes the Admiral would refuse to let people on to his boat in the first place. If he didn't like the look of them, it was no use whatsoever for them to wave their tickets at him—they just had to wait for the next one to come along.

Another day there was again uproar at the jetty. The Admiral was refusing to let anyone at all board his boat—and there was a queue of other boats behind, waiting to tie up and offload their passengers. His reason this time was that, apparently, Princess Margaret was due to arrive—and his boat was reserved exclusively for her. He was away for a rest again after that episode, but was back as large as life after a while. We never found out much about him, except that he had been a chief engineer in the Merchant Navy and had travelled widely. During his more lucid moments, we would sit on the jetty and listen to him talk about the countries he had visited. We liked him very much, despite the fact that one day he told John that he shouldn't be courting me.

'She's related to Queen Mary you know!' Said the Admiral. 'That lot were all mad!'

Poor man. We often wondered what happened to him when he retired.

SOLDIER

When the canal system was first excavated, it left lots of little islands isolated between its channels. These were perfectly safe, natural habitats for some of the monkeys. The island opposite the boat bus jetty had Patas Monkeys living on it. Patas are mostly ground dwelling monkeys, with long legs, and are very agile and quick on the ground—but hate water. I would throw food across to them every day, and once a week the Admiral would ferry me across to clean the island, and their sleeping quarters. I always made sure my tools were immaculately clean, before and after my visit, and would take the clean straw across—and the dirty straw back—in a sack, so I didn't leave even a scrap on the Admiral's immaculately clean boat.

'Soldier' was the male Patas, who hated men, but would tolerate us girls. I would throw my equipment onto the island from the boat, then some food, so that Soldier was kept occupied while the Admiral got alongside the bank. I would then have to quickly jump from the boat—praying I landed well—onto the little flat area on the bank, and get a good handhold on the long grass. The Admiral would push off quickly, and would come back for me when I shouted him. It was quite an operation, but all part of life's rich pattern as a zoo keeper.

The zoo had a call from a local lady one day to say she had a monkey locked in her garage, and would the zoo please come and remove it immediately. So Reg Bloom, and a gang of us, set off in a zoo van with nets and a crate to capture the escapee—not knowing, until we got there, which one of the many island monkeys had escaped. On arrival at the house, we peeped through a crack in the garage door—and there was Soldier. He had thrown cans of paint everywhere, and was bouncing up and down on the roof of what had once been a very shiny new car—but was now covered in monkey foot and hand prints in various colours. Soldier was furious when netted and crated, but not as furious as the owner of the new car. Reg Bloom had to deal with her, so our only concern was getting Soldier back to his island, and finding out how he had escaped. It turned out that a Bus Boat hadn't been moored securely, and the back end had drifted over. Soldier had simply jumped onto it and made his escape. The boy responsible for this oversight was sacked. He was lucky that's all that happened to him—if the Admiral had had any say in the matter, he would have had him beheaded at the Tower of London.

MADAM

One morning, when I was working in the Red Panda enclosure, a lady came rushing up and shouted over the wall. 'It's disgusting!' She said. 'It shouldn't be allowed in front of the public!' I realized she was referring to the Wapitis in the paddock opposite, as they were rutting. I politely suggested that she could always walk away if it upset her, but she just went on and on, ranting and raving. I was quite expecting her to start frothing at the mouth, she was in such a state. She demanded to speak to whomever was in charge of 'those animals'. When I told her I was in charge, she nearly fainted to learn that a mere slip of a girl—as she put it—was in charge of rampant beasts. So to shut her up, I went to fetch Reg Bloom from home at the lodge, where he was having his morning coffee. He wasn't best pleased to be dragged away to deal with this 'foolish, frigid old bat', as he so succinctly put it.

'How can I help you?' Said Reg, as we approached the woman. Off she went, ranting and raving, waving her arms about.

'MADAM!' Shouted Reg. 'This is a ZOO, where we endeavour to let the animals live and behave as naturally as possible. As you are of such a sensitive nature, may I suggest you confine your visits to a museum in the future? GOOD MORNING TO YOU!"

Reg tipped his hat to her, and we both walked away, leaving her utterly speechless. As we walked we started to laugh, by the time we got around the corner by the lodge, we were absolutely weeping with laughter. Mrs. Bloom couldn't get any sense out of either of us for an age. Finally Reg said, 'Oh my God Pam Zoo! That was worth missing my break for!'

DAVID HIGHAM

After Mr Bloom left the Zoo, to become Director at Flamingo Park, the powers that be decided that, instead of a new curator, the zoo would be divided in two and would be supervised by section officers. The area over the bridge, in the '60s, included the Elephants, Rhinos, New Monkey House, Small Mammal House, Ankole Cattle, Emu, Ostrich and most of the hoofed mammal paddocks. This half of the zoo's new officer was Mr Norman Pearson—a big bear of a man, who everyone came to like and respect. The other half of the zoo, which included the Bird Section, Polar bears, Sea Lions, Lions and Tigers, Zebra and Giraffe Houses and Whipsnade section got Mr. David Higham as section officer—bless him. He was totally out of his depth coping with rebellious keepers and animals. Frankly, he had little knowledge of how to deal with either, and for the first few months managed to upset and annoy everybody.

He came to me at 9 A.M. one morning, and told me to go and pick up the litter outside the Wallaby pen. I pointed out that I was a senior keeper, and it wasn't my job to pick up litter. At that time in the morning I was busy preparing food dishes, and organizing work for the day. He then asked why I hadn't fed my animals when I started at 8 A.M.

'Because the baby Chimps and Orangs have to be bottle fed and cleaned out first.' I told him.

He realized I was starting to get annoyed, so went off in a huff to pester someone else. Next it was John's turn to be annoyed, as Mr Higham went behind the bear dens and asked John what the smell was.

'It's the Canadian Black Bear, in her den with cubs.' Answered John.

'Well you must clean it out!' Said David.

'I can't,' John replied. 'She's in there for the winter.'

'That's disgraceful!' Said Higham. 'You can't keep an animal locked up all winter!'

'If you knew anything about Black Bears, you would know they hibernate, give birth to their cubs and don't come out until spring,' said John. 'So who do you think cleans them out in the wild?"

So, having lost that argument, he then asked why John had a little cast iron stove blazing away, as it was far too hot in the keeper area and it was also a fire risk.

'It's not for me, and the fire risk is negligible,' explained John. 'It's keeping the wall warm, where the mother bear likes to lie. It's kept in all winter until she is let out again. Clearly Mr, Higham, you don't know how successful this section has been, over the years, in breeding and rearing cubs.'

Eventually he did realize that he wasn't endearing himself to anyone, and that if he asked the very knowledgeable Head Keepers, they would explain how their sections worked—and that cooperation was better than confrontation.

We would play tricks on him whenever we got a chance though because—God help him—he was so gullible. Every morning, he would cycle around the sections to check everything was alright. When he got to the Polar Bear enclosure, he would go up the ramp by the Sea Lions, around the wall, then down the ramp on the other side. This was a long, steep slope and he would take his feet off the pedals and come down very fast— shouting, 'Wheeee!'

So one morning, we waited until he left his bike against the railings by the Sea Lion pool, and when he went around the back of the bear enclosures, we loosened his brake blocks. We then ran and hid behind the big gates at the maintenance yard, waiting for him to come down the ramp with his feet off the pedals. He came down as fast as usual. Only this time, when he got to the bottom, the look on his face was one of sheer terror. He flashed past us, heading straight for the boat jetty and canal shouting, 'My brakes have failed! My brakes have failed!'

We were wetting ourselves with laughter, then thought we had better go and see what had happened to him. He had managed to steer himself into the Laurel bushes by the Gibbons—wise move—just before he got to the canal. We all rushed up, pulled him out of the bushes, and brushed him down—saying with great concern that he really ought to maintain his bike more carefully, as he could have hurt himself. My lord, we were so wicked at times.

Another day Mr. Higham got a bee in his bonnet about going across to the Patas Monkey Island. I did tell him that Soldier was doing fine, and warned him that he hated men—I don't know why, but he didn't believe me. So he asked the Admiral to take him across.

'I'll take Pam across, but you can bugger off!' He replied.

Having at last acquired a brief modicum of sense, Mr. Higham didn't push his luck with the Admiral. He instead announced he was going to build a raft.

This news was received with great delight by everyone, and over the next week, in the maintenance yard, the raft took shape. Mr. Higham was extremely pleased, as everyone was very helpful, and we all found bits and pieces he could use. Dave, the blacksmith, presented him with some oil drums to use as floats. The carpenters with pieces of wood, nails and tools—and the maintenance men with lengths of rope and wire, and a piece of scaffolding to use to pole himself across the canal. When he saw the large piece of wood that someone had nailed to the side of the raft, with the words '*KON TIKI*' painted on it, I think he was beginning to realize that perhaps our gifts had not been entirely altruistic.

At last the raft was finished, and the maintenance men loaded it onto a zoo lorry. It was taken down to the jetty opposite the Big House. Luckily, Mr and Mrs Mottershead were away on holiday at the time, as half the zoo had gathered for the launch—we wouldn't have dared if

Mottie had been at home. Eventually, the raft was lowered into the water and everyone gave a big cheer—much to our surprise it actually floated, nice and evenly. David was dressed in his usual immaculate white shirt, cavalry twill trousers, *Gannex* mac and highly polished shoes. Taking a deep breath, and with shoulders back, and head held high like a true Englishman—and holding on tightly to his pole—he stepped onto the raft, raising another loud cheer from us all. As he started to pole across the canal, Soldier came down to the water's edge and began to give a most impressive threat display. David was so busy watching him—and no doubt beginning to realize I had been telling him the truth—that he hadn't noticed that he was sinking. He looked down in horror as he felt water creep over and into his shoes. Clinging to his pole for dear life, he just stood stock still as the raft, with hardly a wobble, slowly and gracefully sank. We were all just howling with laughter. As the water crept higher and higher up his body, he was saying. 'Help, oh help! I'm sinking!'

We couldn't help though, as by now everyone was holding on to each other totally helpless with laughter. Finally the raft settled on the bottom. By then the water was up to his waist. He was shivering with cold, and desperately trying not to lose his balance. He looked so helpless. So a boat was pushed out to rescue him, and he was hauled on board. He got back to the jetty covered in muck and weeds, and gave us all a sheepish grin. Bless him. Then we all gave him a rousing cheer and round of applause for his bravery and entertainment value.

He never became as good a Section Officer as Mr Pearson but he did improve beyond belief, and we all came to like him very much. He left a few years later to become a partner in a Wild Life Park in Devon. On his last morning, I went to say goodbye. I gave him a hug and wished him good luck in his new venture. He told me that after learning to cope with what we had thrown at him, he felt he could do absolutely anything in the world he liked. John and I visited him and his family on one of our holidays in Devon, and he seemed very happy in his new career.

YIPPEE

Sometimes just before lunch—again while cleaning out the Red Pandas—I would see one of the kitchen girls from the Fountain

Restaurant, go scurrying past on her way to the exit by the staff car park. She was already known to be a 'lady of the night'. But evidently she was also a 'lady of the lunch time' too—as she was going to pick up a client waiting in the car park. A little while later, when I would be working in the Wapiti enclosure by the exit, I would see her being dropped off by car, van, or lorry—or whatever mode of transport the client of the day owned. She would dash back through the entrance and run full pelt up the path, scattering and terrifying visitors on her way. Every now and then she would stop, jump in the air, wave the fiver she was clutching and shout, 'Yippee!'

And that was the name she was known by to all the zoo staff.

CURLY

Curly, the female Pig Tailed Monkey, would have been a good companion for Yippee, as she always had to be taken off display when she was in season. She would pester poor Henry—her live-in lover—by sticking her bottom in his face every minute of the day, and most times he would oblige. But there's only so much a poor chap can take before the novelty wears off, and the stamina flags, so then he would get really angry and give her a good thrashing. To make matters worse, the call she would make, while alluringly walking up and down, sounded just like, 'MORE, MORE, MORE!'

REG BLOOM

Reg Bloom was a real character. A very nice man, and a kind and fair boss, he could nonetheless be taken in by a female's smiling or sad face, or the fluttering of eyelashes. He was also quite absent minded at times, as he was forever losing his bike and his dogs.

He would visit each section, every morning, on his bicycle and was not averse to rolling up his sleeves and helping out if anyone needed it. His two Rhodesian Ridgeback's, 'Sherry' and 'Sheba', always accompanied him on his rounds. He would tell them to sit and stay outside which ever building he was visiting—and like two statues they would. Quite often, he would go in through the front entrance and out of the back, forgetting about the dogs and his bike. When he did remember, he would go around asking the keepers if they had seen them. It was of no use for any of us to attempt to take the dogs back to the lodge, as they wouldn't budge. Having been told to stay, that's just what they did. In those days, we didn't have walkie-talkies like keepers do now, just the odd telephone in some of the buildings. There would always be a message in his office informing him where they were, when he got back from his rounds.

Reg and Margaret had lived in Kenya before coming to Chester, and Reg had worked with John Seago[1], who had spent most of his life working with animals in Africa. In the '50s they organized the humane catching and shipping of animals from Nigeria, Kenya and Rwanda to British and other zoos to replenish their stock after the war.

Reg knew many of the people connected to the filming and conservation world of animals. He knew both Armand and Michaela Dennis, the wildlife documentary film makers. He liked Armand, but couldn't stand Michaela and he wasn't very complimentary about her. Faith and I had some very interesting chats with him about his time in Africa. He also knew George Adamson and his wife Joy, of *Born Free* and *Elsa the Lioness* fame. He wasn't very complimentary about Joy Adamson either.

In 1962, Joy Adamson was on a promotional book tour in the UK and Reg had invited her to Chester Zoo. He brought her up to the Small Mammal House, where I was working with Faith that day. He introduced us to her saying, 'Joy, I would like you to meet Faith and Pam, my two best girls.'

Joy Adamson didn't smile, she just nodded at us and fixed us with her pale blue eyes. It was like being hypnotized. When we told Reg later that we had found her extremely intimidating, he made us laugh.

'Now you know why the bloody lions do as they are told!' He said.

GRANDAD

The zoo had many regular visitors, and we keepers got to know and like most of them. We would stop for a little chat if we had time. One visitor that no one liked was an elderly man we christened 'Grandad'. He was always smartly and expensively dressed, his ensemble including

1 *John Seago was the brother of the artist, and Royal confidante, Edward Seago.*

bowler hat and furled umbrella. He would sidle up to us and ask, out of the corner of his mouth, if any of our animals were mating. He gave us all the creeps, so we would send him on a fool's errand all over the zoo. He knew the sounds of animals mating— especially the lions—and would scurry along, trying to get there before it was all over. He'd then stand watching, with his hands in his pockets. If we could, we would intercept him and keep him talking until the event was over and then, smiling to ourselves, go merrily on our way. Outwardly he was quite posh—but to us he was just a dirty old man.

ERIC KIRKLAND

In my time at Chester Zoo, we often had visiting 'professional' photographers—most of whom shall remain nameless here. Many of them came with an entourage who always seemed to be dashing about, flapping their arms and making a lot of noise, which was hardly conducive to photographing zoo animals. Consequently most of the pictures produced were mediocre to say the least.

One chap who came in frequently was always as drunk as a skunk. At least he didn't have an entourage—just his wife, who was always just as sloshed as he was. All sections would pray it wouldn't be their misfortune to have to deal with him. Changing a roll of film was painful to watch, as both he and his wife swayed and wobbled, back and forth, battling to get the film into a camera that seemed to have a life of its own. As it was a visit sanctioned by the zoo office, we had to be present while the session was in progress. However, because he took so long many of us made the excuse that it was public feeding times for our animals, and that we were needed elsewhere. Quite frankly, I don't think he even noticed we had gone. How he made a living from photography, God alone knows.

We also had visits from press photographers who, more often than not, expected the animals to act on our command to take the pose they required. So they didn't often get the picture they had dreamed of. However, there is one pleasant, competent man who comes to mind—Johnny Walker from the Daily Mirror. With very little fuss, he always managed to take an excellent picture.

Quite often, the team from the BBC's early evening programme *Look North* would arrive to film new babies or new acquisitions. Keepers would dash home to watch the programme at 6:30 P.M. especially if they were featured in the footage.

There were also a few talented amateur photographers that visited the zoo regularly, who would kindly give keepers snaps of their animals. John and I have many of these and they have been lovely to look back on over the years. One not so talented photographer was known to us all as 'Little Des'. He always had two *Hasselblad* cameras slung around his neck. They were almost as big as him, and he made such a performance when taking pictures—which were rubbish— that he would usually draw a crowd of visitors around him, which he loved. It doesn't matter how expensive the camera is, if the photographer hasn't a clue how to use it. Poor Des had a crush on my friend Faith, from the Small Mammal House, and used to drive her crazy hanging around and following her everywhere. He kept asking her for a date and the poor deluded little soul just wouldn't take no for an answer. Faith asked Alan, a keeper from the Bird House, to pretend he was her boyfriend in the hope it would make him leave her alone—but it had no effect whatsoever. Then she resorted to being really horrible to him, and I mean so horrible that it would make us cringe—but even that didn't work. He finally stopped coming to the zoo when Faith left to get married. Such a strange little man, he gave us all the creeps.

One photographer who stood head and shoulders above them all was Mr Eric Kirkland. He was a retired dentist, who only took up photography in the '50s and was mainly interested in architecture. Then he started to take an interest in natural history, and by the early '60s was specializing in portraits of zoo animals. His photos were in black and white and were absolutely superb. He would visit the zoo most Wednesdays and his favourite subjects were the monkeys and the large cats. The camera he used was an *Agiflex II,* on a tripod. It was such an old fashioned, cumbersome thing and it took quite a while for him to set it up. He would stand for hours in front of his chosen subject very often only taking half a dozen shots when the animals were in the pose he wanted. Occasionally he would present a keeper with one of his photos and they would be gratefully received and treasured. John and I are lucky enough to own some of his 10 x 8 inch portraits of our animals. The detail is amazing as every hair and whisker is clearly defined. He was awarded two fellowships by the Royal Photographic Society—one for his architectural studies and the second for his zoo pictures. He was one of the few visitors allowed access to keeper areas and was always a quiet and unobtrusive presence on our sections when taking his photos. Such a nice man we feel so privileged to have known him.

JANE RATCLIFFE

In March 1964 I met Jane Rattcliffe, the Naturalist. I was throwing fresh browse over the fence for the Wapiti when she approached me and we got chatting. 'Woppy', the male, had just shed his antlers and Jane asked if the zoo sold them to the public, as she would love to own a pair. I said I would ask Mrs Mott, as she had the say so as to where they went. After chatting with Mrs Mott she said Jane could have the 1965 antlers. I rang Jane to let her know and she was delighted with the news. Jane and her husband Teddy became our very good friends and John and I had many lovely weekend holidays with them at their beautiful house in the Lake District before and after our children came along. Their own children and grandchildren were all living in Australia and they missed them very much. Our three children loved to visit Jane and Teddy although Jane found Matthew just a tad hard going at times his noisy, chatty, always on the go, '*Just William* x *Dennis the Menace*' character didn't always go down well.

In both Summer and Winter, if it wasn't raining too hard, breakfast was eaten in the garden. On our visits if it was cold we would sit well wrapped up, if it was raining we sat underneath picnic umbrellas armed with binoculars, eating our bacon baps and drinking piping hot coffee from a huge flask. The children thought it was a great adventure.

On one visit we watched a cock robin zooming around visiting his three wives who were sitting on eggs in different areas of the garden. This little chap would come into the conservatory early every morning for a feed of meal worms. One morning Jane had forgotten to leave the window open for him. We were all in the kitchen, and just about to go out into the garden for breakfast, when we heard a noise on the stairs. It was cock robin, fluttering his wings as he hopped down each step—the clever little chap. On finding the conservatory window closed, he had come in through the open bathroom window and found his way downstairs. He flew past us into the conservatory, where his meal worms were awaiting him.

The children and I had a week's holiday with Jane and Teddy in the summer of 1985. Christopher was fifteen, Rachael was thirteen and Matthew was eight. John had stayed at home to look after the Wolfhounds. The weather was glorious and every morning after breakfast—with hiking boots on and rucksacks on our backs, containing sandwiches and cartons of fruit juice—the children and I would walk the four miles to the ferry near Bowness. After crossing Lake Windermere on the ferry, we would hike to a different place each day. We preferred this side of the lake as it was away from the crowded tourist areas of Windermere and Bowness. After a visit to Hill Top, we each chose a place to walk to next—Beatrix Potter's Cottage at Sawrey was mine and Rachael's choice. Grizedale Forest was the boys' choice, as they said it was like 'Mirkwood' in *The Hobbit*. Wray Castle was a choice made by us all. We all enjoyed walking in the hills, and had mapped out our routes on ordinance survey maps before going on holiday. On very hot days we would find a place at the lake edge, where the children could paddle and explore. Then we would cross back over on the ferry, and walk the four miles back to Jane and Teddy's in time for tea. We probably walked between twelve and twenty miles each day. Although Matt was only eight-and-a-half, he kept up with us amazingly well—though as they were country children, they were all used to walking everywhere.

Jane was the author of three books—*Through Badger Gate*, *Fly High Run Free* and *Wildlife in My Garden* which were about the birds and animals she had reared, rehabilitated and returned to the wild. She had fought tirelessly to make it illegal to dig, injure and bait badgers and was instrumental in getting the Badger Act passed in Parliament in 1973. She was also the driving force in the fight for Badger tunnels to be built under new motorways in Badger crossing areas. Small but mighty was Jane, when she got her teeth into a problem. She was a real feisty character and would stand her ground over any wildlife issue. She once had an argument with Prince Philip at some function or other. He probably made one of his controversial comments to wind her up, and succeeded. A sense of humour wasn't one of Janes fortes—particularly where wildlife was concerned. It seems especially tragic that this wonderful, intelligent, articulate woman who had devoted so much of her life to the cause of British wildlife, should for the last years of her life have been totally lost in the awful fog of Alzheimer's. She could be stern at times, but she was very kind to us. We loved and admired her and were very privileged to have had her in our lives.

HOWLETTS

Lots of Wapiti calves had been born on Whipsnade section, a couple of years after it had come into my care. As the females were now quite elderly, it was decided to bring in some fresh blood. Three young females were acquired from Howletts Zoo, in Kent, owned by John Aspinall, and four of our weaned baby females went down to Howletts in return—we didn't want them mating with their father. I travelled down with them and was very excited at the prospect of seeing behind the scenes at Howletts, especially their famous Gorilla section.

When the Wapiti had been unloaded and settled into their large paddock, I was taken across to the wonderful Gorilla section. Just before feeding time, I went with one of their keepers to pick strawberries from a huge bed, which had been grown exclusively for them. Later I was persuaded to go into an enclosure containing six half grown female Tigers. They surrounded me snuffing and snorting in my face and although I admire these beautiful creatures, and no matter how much I was assured how safe they were, it was very foolish of me to take the risk. I was extremely relieved when I was safely outside the pen again. John really tore a strip off me when I got back to Chester and told him. John Aspinall's keepers, in those days, were encouraged to go in with all their animals—of course it is totally forbidden now. To my delight, the new Wapiti females from Howletts produced big strong calves the following year.

BAGGY AGGIE

For a few months, the Lar Gibbons that lived on one of the zoo islands were in temporary accommodation on my section. One of the females produced a baby but had rejected it, so she had to be hand reared. Kiki was the most difficult baby of all the ones I reared. The gibbons were eventually moved back to their island home after it was refurbished.

Whilst they were on my section, their accommodation was a huge domed enclosure about twenty feet high. I was on top of the outside of the enclosure one day, securing new branches and ropes—that Margy and I had just put in for them—when a booming voice rang out from the crowd below, 'Pamela Logan! Come down from there at once!'

Standing there, larger than life, was 'Baggy Aggie' my old English teacher. Wearing a multi-coloured diaphanous skirt, sandals, jangly bracelets, hoop earrings and tan make up, she looked like a very overweight member of the chorus line from Carmen. As it was more than six years since I had left school, I was amazed she still recognised me. I ignored her, hoping she would go away, but when I did eventually climb down and come back through the keeper's gate, she was waiting outside. 'Well Pamela!' She said. 'You didn't listen to my advice then! But I must say you look amazingly well.'

'*The sheer cheek of the woman!*' I thought. '*She must think I'm still 15 years old.*'

Smiling through gritted teeth I replied, 'I am well and very happy!'

'I am still convinced you could have done much better for yourself career wise!' She said.

'Quite frankly, Mrs Bagshaw, I'm really not interested in your opinion.'

'Oh dear,' she said. 'Are you cross with me Pamela?'

'No,' I answered. 'I am absolutely furious that you think you can comment on my chosen career, when you are totally ignorant of what it entails—and also it is absolutely none of your business!'

'Now,' I continued. 'If you will excuse me I have other animals to attend to!'

Margy was standing by me during the whole exchange, and as we walked away, leaving the opinionated old bat speechless, she laughingly said, 'Bloody Hell Pam! I've never seen you so angry, you were really scary! I thought you were going to whack her!'

'Believe me,' I replied. 'I was sorely tempted.'

I was still seething after the encounter so as it was nearly lunch time, Margy and I went across to the Ladies Cloakroom. Mrs Vicars and Mrs Peacock, the attendants, could always be relied upon to sooth a savage breast with one of their 'special' cups of tea—dosed with a few drops of whiskey.

These two cloakroom ladies would very often ask for my aid when children locked themselves in the loos. I would have to climb over into the cubicle to let them out. Mrs Vicars would frequently do battle with over protective Mothers wanting to bring their large sons into the Ladies Loos. As the mother would try to push the boy through the turnstile, she would say, 'You can't bring him in here he's old enough to sleep out!'

She had some wonderful and very funny sayings, and was the kindest of souls. We girl keepers could always go to both her and Mrs Peacock if we needed a sympathetic shoulder to cry on.

Every Tuesday morning at break time Margy, Philippa and I would go across to the Ladies Cloakroom because Mrs Vicars, as a special treat, would always bring lovely crispy ham rolls for us. After a cup of her 'special' tea, we would be replete until lunch time.

UPTON

Most mornings at break time we would buy sandwiches from the mobile van that visited each side of the zoo in turn. Standing in the queue one morning, behind trainee Tall Susan, we noticed she had her hair permed. Derek, the mechanic, walked up to join the queue and said, 'Good morning Susan, I see you have had your head re-sprung.'

Of course this remark just cracked us up. We had all, in our time, run the gauntlet of Derek's and 'Randy' Dave the Blacksmith's famous little quips.

Thinking back it's hard to believe how much I ate in those days. I should have been the size of a house. I would go through an excellent cooked breakfast, sandwiches at break time, down to the village most lunch times for fish and chips followed by a large cream cake from the bakery, sandwiches from the van again in the afternoon, then home in the evening for an excellent cooked dinner.

After living at the YWCA in Chester for over two years, I had moved into lodgings with Norma and Fred Blythe and their two little boys, Graham and Ian, in Upton village just down the road from the zoo. Fred was the zoo joiner and Norma was an ex-keeper, so it was just perfect. I lived with them for over five years until I got married.

Norma had a Connemara pony called Guy who was kept in a field opposite the zoo. If it wasn't raining when I left work in the evenings, I would collect him and ride him bareback down to my lodgings. This saved Norma having to go up to collect him, and as soon as the little ones were in bed she had a little extra time to groom him and maintain her tack. When riding Guy, I always prayed that there wouldn't be a queue of zoo visitors waiting at the nearby bus stop as I passed. Trying to get Guy past dozens of people, all with very interesting bags that just might contain food, was a nightmare. He would even stop at every pushchair, in the hope that some child might have a biscuit in their hand. Of course, all the people in the queue would want to pat and stroke the 'nice horsey'. I just wanted to get home for my tea, but Guy loved all the attention and wouldn't budge. So sometimes, on fine summer mornings, I would carry his heavy saddle and bridle to work. Then in the evening, with Guy tacked up, I was now fully in control of him and able to ride straight past all the visitors that were leaving the zoo.

Every evening John would pick me up about 7:30 pm and sometimes we spend the evening at the home of our friends, Meg and Frank Woolham, who lived opposite the zoo. I had first met them through a mutual friend when they were looking for a baby sitter for their boys. Frank was a keen aviculturist and the house and garden aviaries were always full of birds. Sometimes there would be frozen day old chicks or mice thawing out gently, under the eye level grill in the kitchen. These were for the Toco Toucans and the Pittas who enjoyed the occasional bird or mouse. Lying across the top of the grill would be *Ming I*, their Siamese cat—one of a succession of 'Mings' they had over the years. She would be trying to hook a mouse or chick without singeing her paw.

There was always an African Grey Parrot in the house, and the one I remember best was devoted to Frank. When he was relaxing in an arm chair with legs stretched out, she would walk up his legs and onto his chest then go to sleep with her head tucked under his chin. The boys would sometimes throw a balloon at her, and she would lift her leg and shout, 'Goal!'

The last Parrot they had was a very clear talker and had the run of the house. He loved to go behind the hall radiator, which had been taken off ready for decorating, and leant against the wall. Meg was upstairs one day when a man came to the front door, which was slightly ajar. He knocked politely and the parrot, hidden behind the radiator, shouted, 'Come in!'

The man popped his head around the door and shouted, 'Hello?'

'Hello!' Answered the parrot.

'Is anyone there?' Said the man.

'Is anyone there?' Replied the parrot.

Meg said it was very funny as was standing on the landing, peeping over the banister and listening. The poor man stood scratching his head, as he couldn't understand how the wall appeared to be talking to him. This went on for a while, until finally the parrot came out from behind the radiator and strolled casually down the hall.

The man shouted, 'Oh damn and bugger it!' And he left.

Frank wrote the text for a beautiful book, *Aviary Birds in Colour*, containing superb photographs of his birds, taken by Dennis Avon and Tony Tilford. I have it by me as I write. Looking at Frank's written dedication to John and myself brings back many happy memories from so many years ago.

Frank was the Press Officer at Vauxhall Motors and very often he and Meg were obliged to attend some function or other, hence the need for a babysitter. When I first met their boys, John was ten, Mark was seven, Andrew was two and Michael came along a year later. I loved looking after them and we became good pals. Andrew has been Team Manager of Parrots and Penguins at Chester Zoo for many years now. I see him now and then on the TV programme *The Secret Life of the Zoo*. Even though he is now a middle-aged man, in my mind's eye I still see my little Andrew, who was such a funny, happy character as a small boy. Good grief, where did the time go?

Meg was a true friend to both John and I, and we loved our evenings with her and the boys when we were courting. Frank was usually in the kitchen, developing the latest batch of zoo or bird photos he had taken. When he was developing colour slides, I would sometimes help him with the timing as it was a crucial part of the process.

In the summer of 1966 I took a wonderful trip to Nova Scotia, Canada to visit my brother. Once home again, under Frank's strict instructions, I developed the hundreds of colour slides I had taken—every one of them came out perfectly.

It was a good time to visit, as Dick was home from sea for a few months—although I didn't see very much of him, as he lived in the hamlet of Granville Ferry but was stationed two hundred miles away at the Naval Base in Halifax. He would drive home every other day, and of course be home when not on duty.

When his wife Margy was at work or young daughter, Linda, was at school I was quite content to just wander about. There were many historic sites in the area to visit and I especially liked one called The Habitation.

Fig. II-1 The Author & Faith (the first Wapiti calf), Chester Zoo, 1962

Fig. II-2 The Author, with Jeannie the Chimp, Chester Zoo, 1962

Fig. II-3 The Author, with hand-reared Sika Deer, Chester Zoo, December 1962

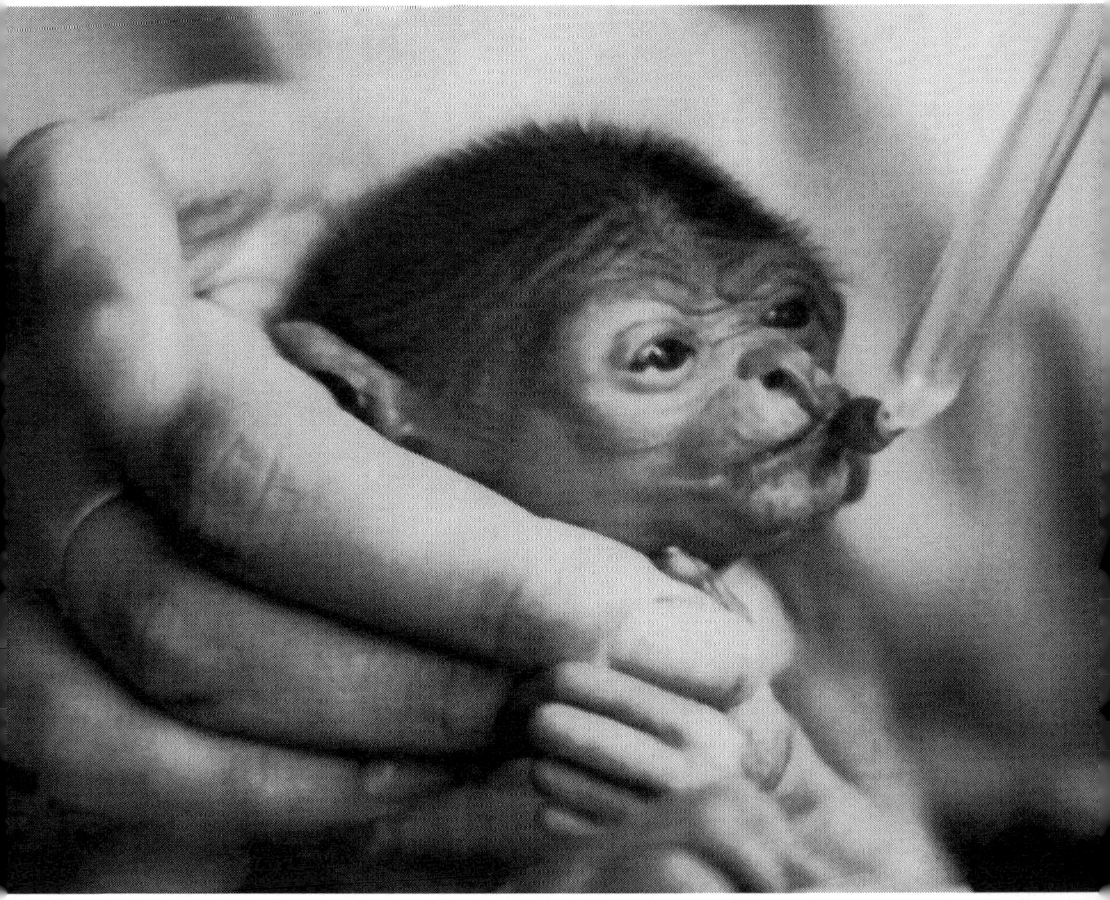

Fig. II-4 Kiki, the Lar Gibbon, being fed by the Author, Chester Zoo, 1964 - Photo: Eric Kirkland

Fig. II-5 Arabian Gazelle, 1 month old, hand reared by the Author, Chester Zoo, 1966

Fig. II-6 The Author, with Wapiti calf, Chester Zoo, 1967

Fig. II-7 The Author, with Canadian Black Bear cubs, Chester Zoo, 1964

Fig. II-8 'Big Ann' and the Author with Chimps, Chester Zoo, 1962

Fig. II-9 The Author, with Huskie pups, Chester Zoo, 1964

Fig. II-10 John, feeding Sammy the Sea Lion, Chester Zoo, 1963.
Photo: Eric Kirkland

Fig. II-11 John, with bear cubs, Chester Zoo, Winter 1964

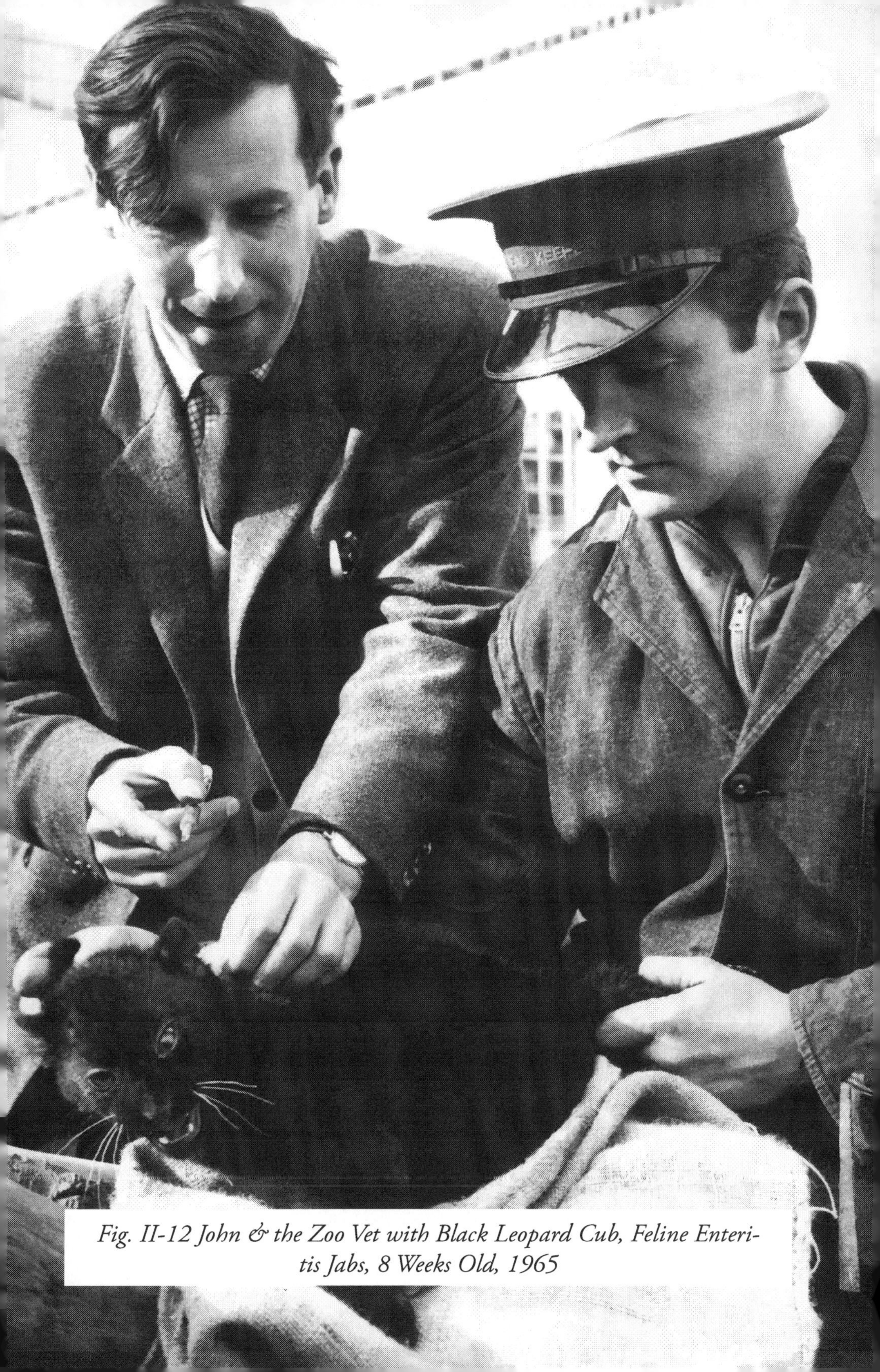

Fig. II-12 John & the Zoo Vet with Black Leopard Cub, Feline Enteritis Jabs, 8 Weeks Old, 1965

Fig. II-13 John, with hand reared Caracal Lynx and Black-Backed Jackal, Chester Zoo, 1965

Fig. II-14 John, with hand reared Caracal Lynx 'Mitzi', Chester Zoo, 1965. Photo: Eric Kirkland

Fig. II-15 Udong, the Lion, Chester Zoo, 1965. Photo: Eric Kirkland

Fig. II-16 Billy Baboon, Chester Zoo, 1965. Photo: Eric Kirkland

Fig. II-17 Soldier, the Patas Monkey, Chester Zoo, 1965. Photo: Eric Kirkland

Fig. II-18 Henry Pigtail, the Pig-tailed Macaque, Chester Zoo, 1965. Photo: Eric Kirkland

Fig. II-19 Jeannie & Polly, baby Chimps, Chester Zoo, 1962. Photo: Eric Kirkland

Fig. II-20 Andrew Woolham on Guy, (the Author out of frame), Upton, Chester, 1965.

Fig. II-21 Malayan Sun Bear. Photo: ID 14212685 © Misad | Dreamstime.com

Fig. II-22 The Author, holding Wapiti antlers, Chester Zoo, 1965.

Fig. II-23 The Admiral's Boat Bus, Chester Zoo.

III

Big Events, Giant Dogs & Larger Than Life Children

21: Married...with Children

To my surprise in June 1969, the Red Pandas produced a baby. The parents were elderly and the female rejected it. I hand reared the little chap and as John and I had just got married, he had to come on honeymoon with us. As he had to be fed every two hours, we decided to cut the honeymoon short and go back to work. You can just imagine the teasing and ribald comments I had to bear, when I appeared back at work after being away for just a couple of days.

John had left Chester Zoo before we married and was now self-employed. The Zoo had a new curator who, in Mr Mott's eyes, was the eighth wonder of the world and could do no wrong. All the keepers hated him however, as one by one he ousted all the knowledgeable keepers, either getting them the sack by lying to Mottie about things they had done wrong—or by making their lives such a misery that they left of their own volition. John decided to leave before he committed murder. I would have been for the chop as well, if I had not had the protection of Mrs Mott. The new Curator tried making my life a misery, but I complained to Mrs Mott and he soon stopped his lies and nasty tactics. God! He hated me after Mrs Mott had a go at him. This little dictator simply walked over anyone he thought knew more than him, or stood in his way of total control. It was incredibly sad, as all the keepers wanted to do was to care for their animals and go home happy at the end of the day. There was absolutely no comparison between our old curator Mr Bloom—who kept us all in order and the animal sections running smoothly, in his firm and pleasant way—and this little tyrant who only cared about his own power trip. Thankfully, as the saying goes, 'What goes around comes around', and eventually it did. Much to the relief of the keepers, the scales finally fell from Mr Mott's eyes and he sacked the nasty piece of work. Sadly, it was much too late for all the wonderful dedicated keepers who had already left.

After John left the zoo, he bought a lorry and was doing contract haulage work. The M56 was being built then, so there was lots of work to be had. The big-named contractors were disgracefully slow at paying for the work done, and John and I had some scary financial moments. The heater in John's lorry did not work, and in the winter months, he would come home frozen to the bone—especially his poor feet and legs. I would keep the oven warmed for him, so he could put his feet and lower legs inside, to thaw them out while he ate his tea. It sounds so funny now, but it was not at the time. We were choosing between heating our home and cooking a meal. It is amazing what deprivations you are willing to endure when you are self-employed.

One month the contractors were again late paying, and we had a large overdue diesel bill. Then, unexpectedly an airmail letter arrived from my brother Dick, with a money order for $200 dollars. I think that was equal to about £150 in those days, which was a huge amount in the '60s[1] and a real Godsend. Enclosed was a note saying he had won a little money in a *Reader's Digest* competition, and wanted to share it. Bless his heart.

I had not told Mother that John and I were getting married, and we waited until she went to visit my brother in Canada. I felt guilty about not telling her, but she would have wanted all the palaver of a church wedding. We did not want the fuss of a big wedding, thinking that the money it would cost could be put to better use. We were married at Chester Registry Office with just a few friends present, and Norma and Meg as our witnesses. I wrote to my brother telling him of our plans and enclosed a letter for Mother, asking him to give it to her a few days before we tied the knot.

Dick later sent a telegram, which was read out later at our little reception. All it said was:

THE WAR DEPARTMENT TOOK IT VERY WELL

John was yet to tell his mother, and was still dragging his feet about it. So, sitting in the living room at John's mum's, on the eve of the wedding, I was cross with him that he still had not told her we were getting married. I kept nudging and glaring at him, until finally he said, 'We're going to a wedding tomorrow, do you want to come?'

Dot loved weddings—and funerals—and when out and about on her bike would happily gatecrash any she passed by. 'Ooh yes!' She said,

---

1 The equivalent of ~£2300 in 2020

getting excited. 'Who's getting married?'

'We are!' Said John.

The excitement drained from Dot's face, as she flew into a tirade—as he knew she would, hence him leaving it to the last minute to tell her.

'Well, I'm not coming! I'm not!' she protested. 'I mean it, I'm not coming! Why do you have to get married this minute?'

Good God! We had been courting for six years!

'I thought you knew what side your bread was buttered!'

On and on she went until I walked out, shouting to John as I left, 'See you tomorrow!' That set her off again.

John told her the details and said that he really would like her to come. So come she did, but not in the car with John. Oh no, not Dot. She turned up on her bike, wearing her old green mac and was standing at the end of the street when we arrived. John and Meg went over and persuaded her to come in. Happily, she did not really spoil the wedding—although she did mutter and shake her head during the whole ceremony, which did put a slight damper on the day.

Poor Dot. John should have told her sooner to give her time to get used to the idea.

In the middle of the wedding reception, I realized John had disappeared. When he did appear a little later, he said he had been down to the smithy in the village to see if the welding work on his lorry was completed. Bob Jones, the Blacksmith, had commented on how smart he looked, and asked whose wedding he had been to.

'Mine,' John replied. 'I've just popped out of the reception.'

'Good God lad!' Said Bob. 'What the hell are you doing here? You'd better get back quick or your Missus will kill you!'

We quickly settled into married life, and were now living in the village of Frodsham, near Chester. I was pregnant by then, and attending antenatal classes at the little clinic at the back of the village library. The clinic usually had the same visiting gynaecologist, who I liked well enough. However, the dreaded Miss Smeaton would occasionally make an appearance.

Miss Smeaton was a very tall, forbidding looking person. As soon as she walked into the waiting room, most of the experienced mums would get up and walk out. After my first session with her, I realized why. Oh my God, was she heavy-handed! You felt battered and bruised after she had examined you. If any of the Mums were near to their time, one of her examinations would very often cause them to go into labour. I was to meet her again when in labour with our second baby, but more of that a little later on in the story.

On 11th February 1970, our son Christopher John was born in Chester City Hospital. I must admit that I thought because I had gone to antenatal classes, and worked hard at my exercises, that giving birth was going to be easy. A few puffs, pants and pushes, and it would all be over. How wrong I was! When it finally did happen, I realized the dratted nurse at the birth classes had been lying through her teeth—my labour seemed never ending. After all the animal births I had witnessed, I should have known that it was not going to be so easy.

During the birth, I was lying in the delivery room high on gas and air, but could hear some poor soul moaning and groaning. I was feeling so sorry for her that I raised my head from the pillow, to get a look at this poor woman, only to realize I was the only one in the room. I was the one making all the noise.

Eventually Christopher arrived, all 8lbs 8ozs of him. John had tired of waiting for him to appear, and had gone to his Mum's for fish and chips—the rat. He was back just after the baby was born. John remembers the midwife holding the baby up for him to see, and that Christopher was not crying but looking directly at him. As he grew, it was an inscrutable look we came to know well.

Chris was quickly whisked away soon after the birth, because I have Rhesus Negative blood type, and he was a little jaundiced. I did not see him again until the next day. The City Hospital was very old fashioned, and when I asked to see him I was told—in no uncertain terms—that it wasn't possible, there was no one available to take me to the nursery and I was to stop making a fuss. I was beginning to think something was seriously wrong with him, and was getting quite distressed, so I was given a sedative the size of a horse pill and slept for hours.

When I awoke, it became immediately apparent that the bedclothes had been changed whilst I was sleeping—on opening my eyes the first thing I saw were the words 'MORTUARY', in large red letters along the edge of the pillow case. What a sight to awaken to! Apparently, the hospital laundry workers were on strike, so the hospital was utilising every available item of laundry. They could easily have turned the damned pillow over, but that would have been the wrong way around according to their strict bed making routine.

A very nice sister came on duty the next day, and she got a porter to take me in a wheelchair to the nursery to see the baby. I learned then that it was clearly dependent on the staff on duty as to how to interpret the rules. Christopher came up onto the ward later that day, and at last, I was able to hold and cuddle him. However, cuddling babies in bed, or changing them on your knee, was frowned upon in case you dropped them. I had a real confrontation about this with the Ward Sister—who all the Mums had nicknamed 'The Southport Belle'—when she tried to scold me, as if I was a naughty two year old.

'I have changed dozens of babies' nappies!' I informed her. 'I've also changed and reared many baby apes, and have never dropped one. A human baby is a lot easier to manage than a baby Chimp or Orang Utan. So please do not to speak to me like that again!'

As soon as I mentioned baby apes, she clearly decided I was completely mad and left me alone after that.

The woman in the next bed said, 'Good on yer my duck, that told the snooty cow!'

This woman had also fallen foul of the 'Southport Belle'. Having just given birth to her thirteenth child, she was in terrible pain and discomfort from haemorrhoids. However, the 'Southport Belle' was refusing her pain relief. I can picture this poor woman now, kneeling on the bed doubled over, rocking back and forth with the pain and discomfort. When her husband came at visiting time, and saw the state of his poor wife, he marched to the nurse's office and hammered on the door. The 'Southport Belle' shot out like a bullet, ready to do battle. Ready, that is, until she saw the large and extremely angry husband. He was the size of a barn door, and ready to do murder. After a few harsh words from him, she immediately went and administered Preparation H ointment to his poor wife. She could have given this quick and easy treatment hours before. Satisfied now that his wife was being attended to properly, and that her dignity was restored, the husband stepped back out to the corridor and whistled. Immediately, a horde of children charged into the ward, descending on the Mother with hugs and kisses. The 'Southport Belle' paled when she saw so many around one bed, but she decided discretion was the better part of valour, and quickly and quietly disappeared into her office. We all thoroughly enjoyed the drama, it brightened our day tremendously, and this family's new baby girl was the most beautiful child I have ever seen. We all knew the 'Southport Belle' was just being deliberately nasty, simply because they were Romany people.

Christopher was such an easy, happy contented baby and of course, I thought it was all down to breast-feeding, and me being the best Mother in the world—never giving credit to Christopher for his own lovely placid nature.

Our daughter, Rachael Mary, arrived on New Year's Eve 1971. She was born in the newly opened maternity wing at the West Cheshire Hospital, and was baby number 28 on that new ward. They induced labour at 37 weeks, due to the incompatibility of my Rhesus Negative blood with Rachael's Rhesus Positive. She was already very jaundiced in utero, and after the last amniocentesis test, the amniotic fluid was looking like pea soup. After three days of labour pains with nothing happening, I was taken off the drip to rest overnight—which also meant I could have something solid to eat. I was sent back up to the ward, and was told I could ask for anything I wanted. I was really craving fish and chips badly, and after a little while, my meal arrived. Eagerly lifting the cover off my plate, I found a very nice piece of fish. But no chips. In my highly hormonal state, it was like the end of the world, and I just burst into floods of tears. Very kindly, the nurses sent word down to the kitchen, and a little while later the head chef appeared with a lovely, big portion of freshly cooked chips. Bless him. He apologized for the mistake, and then made me laugh when he said that his wife had just had a baby, so he knew all about raging hormones.

The next morning I went back down to the labour suite, once again to be induced into labour. After another 24 hours in labour, with nothing happening, the duty midwife sent for a consultant. To my absolute horror, in walked the ham-fisted Miss Smeaton from my neo-natal classes.

She prodded, poked, and seemed to be rolling the baby around in the womb until I was groaning with pain. Then she said, 'Come, come Mother! There is no need for all that noise!'

'There damned well is when you're so rough!' I shouted. 'How many babies have you given birth to?'

After a few more hours, labour at last started with a vengeance—it must have been Miss Smeaton's tender touch. I wanted to push now, but there was a problem as the baby's left arm was coming before the head. I am convinced this was also due to Miss Smeaton's rough treatment and her moving the baby around. Thankfully Dr Bender, the obstetrician, came on duty soon after and he tried to push the arm back up out of the way. It was agony, but after a few attempts, he succeeded. He then decided he would need to use forceps. I was absolutely exhausted by now, and the baby was in distress. I was rushed down to the theatre, as another doctor's help would now be needed to prevent the baby's arm from coming down again.

'Come on Mrs Sumner,' said Dr Bender, 'you are a strong woman! We need you to summon strength from somewhere. We have to get this baby out right now!'

Therefore, with Dr Mukagee holding back baby's arm inside, with some instrument of torture, and with the forceps in place and an almighty effort from me—that came from God knows where—Rachael was born at last, at 10:55 pm.

'It's such a shame you couldn't have held on until midnight!' One of the midwives commented. 'She'd have been the first New Year's baby. We could've had our picture in the paper!'

I felt like giving her a good slap, had I had the strength.

Desperately ill with jaundice, and having had a very traumatic birth, Rachael was rushed to the SCBU the moment she was delivered. Her poor little head was skinned raw by the forceps. They had made a real mess of me too, as I had to have eleven stitches. It is clear now, with hindsight, that I should have had a Caesarean section. Instead, I was left in labour for days, knowing that the baby was already poorly in the womb, and that her arm was preventing the birth. I would not have let a dog go through a birth like that.

John went down to the SCBU with Rachael, and was told her survival was touch and go. When the hospital Deaconess appeared—she had been sent for by the nurses, who wanted to baptize her—John was furious. He told her to go away as they were wasting precious time, and to get on with just caring for Rachael. She was so desperately ill, we nearly lost her a few times during the following days but she rallied each time. After multiple blood transfusions, she slowly started to improve and then nearly three weeks later was allowed to come home. Thankfully, her arm was not damaged, just badly bruised. Her poor little scalped head took months to heal, but her lovely blonde hair did eventually grow. Rachael's strong constitution and determined nature shone through right from the beginning, and is still shining now as a grown woman.

The Deaconess soon became a real pest, as she would frequently swoop into my room with her cape flapping like a great blue bat. She kept asking me if was there anything I needed to talk about and trying to hold my hand. I thought she was referring to Rachael's health, so I kept telling her the SCBU were very good at keeping me up to date with her progress and I had nothing to talk about to her. However, she kept on visiting. Sometimes, if I was quick enough, I could feign sleep, though even then I could sense she was standing there, staring at me. At this point, she was really starting to annoy me, so I asked one of the nurses if she had any idea why she was haunting me.

She started laughing. 'She thinks you are a pervert and need saving!' she said, pointing at the book on top of my locker.

The book's title was, *Beasts In My Bed* by Jacqui Durrell—Gerald Durrell's first wife—and had a picture of a chimpanzee on the cover. It was about the animals she had hand reared over the years, when married to Gerry Durrell.

Right! I thought. I'll have a bit of fun at this ridiculous woman's expense, next time she swoops in. A little while later, as expected, in she swooped. I was holding the book up as if re-reading it, being sure that she could see the cover and title. She kept glancing at it. 'Would you like to borrow it?' I asked her innocently. 'I've been thoroughly enjoying it, and it's very informative.'

The poor soul blanched, and practically staggered backwards with shock that I could be so blasé about my perversion. Then I burst out laughing, explaining to the deluded soul what the book was really about in fact.

'Well, I am not amused!' She said sternly, and went to leave the room.

I became furious that she had the audacity to take umbrage. 'Well I'm not amused about your assumptions about me, nor with you discussing them with the nurses!'

Glory Hallelujah! I never saw her again.

Chris adored his baby sister and was so sweet with her. She never crawled, but used to shuffle and bounce around on her bottom. Her baby babble was very strange indeed, consisting of grunts, 'raspberries' and clicks, which Chris seemed to understand. He would translate for us and as small as she was, she soon realized that she had a devoted slave in him. Her demands would send him scurrying here there and everywhere as she sat on her bottom clicking, grunting and waving her arms in the air. She learned to walk quite quickly, and once she had mastered walking only then learned to crawl. Rachael liked to do things her own way.

As they grew, Chris and Rachael were inseparable. They would go out to play together and whereas Chris would come back simply grubby, Rachael looked like a chimney sweep.

She always seemed to be in trouble and the cry of 'Oh My God! Rachael!' would often echo through the neighbourhood. It would have our next-door neighbour, Josie, hanging out of her kitchen window laughingly asking, 'What's she done now?'

One day she got into the shed and painted herself all over with green gloss paint. Thank goodness, she had her outdoor clothes and wellies on, which had protected almost everywhere, except her head, face and hands. Unfortunately, I had to cut off most of her beautiful hair. I had to remove the paint on her face with *Thawpit*, as it was all I had to hand, and it made her skin terribly sore. Afterwards, even plastered with *Savlon*, it took a while to heal.

On another day, Chris came running in to tell me that she was eating a slug. Dashing outside, I found her trotting back up the path shaking her head and trying to spit the slime out of her mouth. Salt is the best remedy for slug slime, so I whisked her into the bathroom and washed her mouth, both inside and out, with a saline solution. This of course made her vomit, and because she was screaming and struggling, she managed to deposit it everywhere, including on me. When I had removed the last vestiges of slime, I rinsed her mouth out as best I could with copious amount of water, which was not easy with a screaming child. Only then could I pick her up to comfort her. I sat on the loo seat rocking her on my knee until her tears subsided. Then I ran a bath and put her in it with her clothes on.

All through this pantomime, Chris was crying and standing in the bathroom doorway and shouting at me, 'Don't hurt her Mummy! Please don't hurt her anymore!'

As you can imagine, this made me feel dreadful and wretched, but I could not comfort him whilst covered in sick. Eventually, after Rachael and I had stripped off and had a bath in Dettol, and Chris had been soothed, we all sat in the living room—me with a cup of tea, and the children with a cup of milk. I read a story to them and Rachael, now thoroughly exhausted, fell asleep. As it was only eleven o'clock in the morning, I began wondering what other disasters the day might bring.

When Chris was five, we bought him a bicycle for his birthday. He had a few tries at riding it, but after a number of unsuccessful attempts, he clearly thought, 'Blow this for a lark!' and gave up. He went back to riding his tricycle. Rachael, aged three, decided she would have a try. She tried and fell off so many times her knees were covered in permanent cuts and bruises. She ignored these injuries however, through sheer determination. She just would not give up until she had mastered the art of riding that bike, and master it she did. Luckily, we lived very near Frodsham Marshes, where there were miles of traffic-free lanes where all the local children could ride their bikes safely. After a while, and not to be outdone, Chris decided to master riding the bike too, with a little help from his Dad. Rachael received her very own new bike that Christmas.

In the summer of 1976, I discovered I was 14 weeks pregnant, which came as a great shock. After the horrendous experience of Rachael's birth, I had said 'never again'. When our lovely GP, Dr Pepper, confirmed my suspicions, I was actually very upset and apprehensive.

'Come on Mrs Zoo,' Dr P said. 'When you hold the baby in your arms you will be so happy!'

I knew he was right, but was still apprehensive. It always felt good though, to have reassurance from Dr P.

The children adored Dr P, although Chris did fall out with him once, a couple of years earlier, when he went for his booster injection before he started school. As Chris was bending over the chair, he gave Dr P one of his inscrutable looks. 'Is it going to hurt?' He asked.

'No,' said Dr P. 'It doesn't hurt big boys.'

When given the injection, Chris let out a yell, then said to Dr P, 'You said it wouldn't hurt and it did! I am not your friend anymore!'

'I am sorry to hear that Christopher,' said Dr P kindly. 'Because I will always be your friend.'

On the way home, Chris was very quiet. At bedtime, he asked if I would help him write a letter to Dr Pepper, to tell him he was sorry and that he was still his friend. Bless him. He has always been kind and has such a big heart.

After Chris started school, he became very unhappy, because he did not like his teacher, and she did not like or understand him. Why she did not like this bright, kind, quiet child is a mystery. At four-and-a-half, he was reading well and especially loved Enid Blyton's *Mr Muddle* books. However, Mrs Bourne insisted that he must wade his way through all the *Janet and John* type books, which often had only two or three words to a page, with many replaced with pictures. Chris would read each one in less than a minute flat, and then fall into daydreaming out of simple boredom, for which he would be punished. This was simple cruelty, and he just withdrew into himself more and more. This was evidently happening frequently before I found out. Chris would not answer back, but would instead just stare at Mrs Bourne with one of his looks—which was his way of coping with the situation. The harridan eventually called me into school to discuss his 'insolent behaviour'. I was furious. He most certainly was not insolent, just very quiet and unhappy. She could see I was angry, and was on the defensive immediately.

'Is there *anything* Christopher is interested in?' She barked.

'Have you asked him?' I barked back.

I then informed her that he was very interested in dinosaurs, insects and wildlife, and loved to read about them in the many books we had at home. She then told me he did not join in with class activities, like the nature table. I looked over at the table, and instantly recognised so many things there that he had collected on our walks. I took great pleasure pointing them out to her. In fact, most of the things on the damned table were his.

'Well, I didn't realise he'd brought them!' She said. 'Why didn't he tell me?'

'Because that's not his way,' I replied. 'He's not a braggart, and just does things in his own quiet way. If you just stopped shouting at him, and encouraged him instead, he'll open up more!'

I mentioned again that he loved to read

'Well,' she said, in a supercilious tone. 'It's one thing to read parrot fashion, but quite another to understand what's being read.'

I could not believe what the woman was saying. 'Chris's comprehension is excellent!' I said, angry again. 'And you'd find that for a fact, if you took the trouble to let him read to you.'

She did try harder with him, and he tried harder with her—for my sake—but he felt that all the injustices she had heaped upon him were unforgivable. The damage was already done. She had lost his trust forever, and he now just detested the woman. He was a deep little soul for a five year old, but such a nice little boy. He had been so looking forward to going to school, and it was so sad that his first experience of it was being taught—or rather 'un-taught'—by this dreadful woman. When he went into Mrs Hall's class, the following summer, a different boy emerged. He loved her and she loved him, and with her encouragement, and at last now being taught to his ability, he absolutely blossomed.

'Christopher is a real treasure and a joy to teach,' Mrs Hall said to me, at one parent's evening. 'You should be proud of him.'

I was and still am, and as a grown man he still hates ignorance and injustice.

It was around this time we lost our first Irish Wolfhound. When dear old Finn died, we all missed him so much. We had bought him from Mr and Mrs Leatt of the Samando Kennel in 1966 before we were married.[2] He cost John the princely sum of forty guineas. We never showed him, as he was not the greatest specimen in the world, but we thought he was just wonderful. We started to attend Championship shows to watch and learn about the breed, and the whole showing side of things. The first show we attended was Crufts 1967, with Miss Hartley judging. That year Mrs Nagle took Best of Breed with one of her lovely dogs, Champion Sulhamstead Match. We would sit at the ringside in awe, watching, learning and dreaming that perhaps one day we might actually own a dog like him.

After Finn died, we decided to approach Margery and Roy Saunders of the Erindale Kennel in Kent, as we were now interested in showing. After a long chat with Marge, we booked a puppy from the planned litter by Erindale Adam, out of Champion Erindale Bernice. When it was time to pick up our puppy, we hired a camper van so we could have an

---

2 Finn's sire was Montebello Prince of Boroughbury, owned by Elsie Janes and his dam was Samando Petronella, who was mostly of Sulhamstead, Sanctuary and Ballykelly lines.

overnight stay, and be able to set off reasonably early the next morning to get the puppy home in daylight. It was dark by the time we came to settle down for the night in the van, and we could not fathom how to get the bunk beds down. We ended up with two children and two adults all squished up, in a not very wide, supposedly 'double' bed. As I was very pregnant it was not the most comfortable of arrangements, but finally, after much tossing and turning—and giggling—we managed to get at least a few hours of sleep.

When Marge showed us the litter next morning, and said we could take our pick, we were just thrilled. We chose a stunning, well-balanced cream dog puppy who was to become our first Champion, Erindale Phelan.[3] We called him 'Casey'. He was the most loving and gentle dog, and we all adored him. At ten months old, we took him to his first show, and under judge Mary Roslyn Williams he was Best Puppy, Best of Breed and then went Best in Show. He adored the show ring and always gave of his best. Our most satisfying win with him was Best in Show at Border Counties, under the famous breed specialist Bill Siggers.

At the beginning of December 1976 our third child, Matthew Peter, was born and once again—because of the Rhesus Negative problem—my labour had to be induced, but at 36 weeks this time. It was not as horrendous as giving birth to Rachael, thank goodness, but things did go awry. Unfortunately, the umbilical cord had come down, and every time I had a contraction Matthew's head was pressing on it, cutting off his blood supply. On this unwelcome discovery, I was rushed down for an emergency caesarean section. The doctor ended up kneeling on the trolley as we went along, physically pushing on the baby's head to hold it off the cord, and saying 'Ow, Ow, Ow!' as every contraction painfully squeezed his hand and wrist. I was desperately trying not to push, as we whizzed down corridors, and in and out of lifts to the operating theatre. Finally, someone slapped a mask onto my face and I sank thankfully into oblivion.

After he was delivered, Matthew was as desperately ill as Rachael had been, and at 5lbs 13ozs, much lighter than my other two. When I saw him in the SCBU, he looked like a little skinned rabbit, as he did not have a pick of fat on him, but had extremely long arms, legs and large

---

3 *Also in this litter was a pretty little grey bitch, registered as Erindale Louise. She was to become the foundation bitch of Louise Pinkney's Hydebeck Kennel.*

feet. Had he gone full term he would have been enormous. After a few days, his weight dropped to 5lbs, and he was placed under an ultra violet lamp, to help disperse the bilirubin that was causing the jaundice. He was also receiving multiple blood transfusions. Whilst under the lamp, he had to wear a mask to protect his eyes, so he looked like a little bandit. We came to learn later as he grew how very apt this was.

The units of blood for Matt would arrive by motorcycle courier from Liverpool, day and night, and someone would wake me each time to give signed permission for the transfusion to go ahead.

John and the children saw him before I did, as the Doctors and Nurses would not allow me out of bed for two days. Nevertheless, the day after this two-day recovery, and every day after that, one of the nurses would take me down in a wheelchair and leave me with the baby for an hour or so. Even with all the tubes and wires that babies like Matthew were attached to, the SCBU staff encouraged the Mums to hold and cuddle their babies. This was so very different from the old-fashioned routine at the City Hospital. I was not on a main ward, as Mums who did not have their babies with them had their own rooms. This suited me very well indeed, as I liked being by myself and I could read in peace without the constant chatter.

After ten days, I was home, but Matthew was supposed to stay at least until after Christmas, which was eleven days further away. However, the hospital rang late on Christmas Eve, to say that due to staff shortages, and as Matthew was now actually ready to be discharged, could we possibly come and take him home. Chris and Rachael were already in bed asleep, so our next-door neighbour, Josie, came to babysit while we dashed to the hospital. On Christmas morning, the children were surprised to see a baby in a Moses basket by the fire, and after giving the baby a few perfunctory looks, they got on with the job of opening their presents. We thought that, even with the excitement of Christmas, they would have paid the baby more attention. Matt grizzled for most of the morning, and eventually Rachael turned to me. Giving a big sigh, she said, 'When is the Baby Jesus going home?' We howled with laughter, realising that Chris and Rach had not recognized the baby was Matthew. However, as he grew, we came to know rather quickly that Matthew was certainly no Baby Jesus.

The tiny new human fascinated Casey, and if Matt made the slightest sound, he would look at me as if to say, 'Do something!' When I was feeding Matt, Casey would get as close as possible and lie with his head on his paws watching, already Matt's devoted friend. Matt learned to walk at ten months, holding onto any bit of Casey he could grab. He would wobble to his feet, and Casey would patiently wait until he was steady, then slowly walk with him. The bond between them was wonderful.

In September 1978, we moved to the small hamlet of Aston-by-Sutton, about seventeen miles from Chester, and Chris and Rachael would now be attending the little village school. The house needed a lot of work and the garden was a mess, but it was wonderful to have so much more room.

The children were delighted with the house and open countryside.[4] They had been used to the freedom of living near Frodsham Marshes, so were happy that they could still roam freely—only it was now in woods and open fields, and even freer than before. They climbed trees for conkers and chestnuts, made rope swings across streams, built dens and campfires and baked spuds and chestnuts in the embers. They rode the farm horses bareback, scrumped apples, damsons and pears and had great fun getting up to mischief. They would come home at mealtimes, when they heard me give two long blasts on my big referee whistle, happy, tired and very dirty. I cannot remember how I acquired the whistle, but it was an absolute beauty and they could hear it when they were many fields away, and even in the woods.

Growing up with our Wolfhounds and Shetland Sheepdogs, and being involved with their care, they learned to be kind, respectful and sensible with all animals. John and I are so happy that they all share our deep love of nature and our whacky sense of humour.

In primary school, they all loved to take the treasures they had found while 'out and about' for their classroom nature tables. Matthew, as a small boy, especially loved to pick unusual things up. So it was woe betide me if I forgot to check his coat and trouser pockets—he always had some kind of road kill, dead insects or disgusting old lice-ridden feathers secreted about his person. Finding flattened dehydrated frogs, disintegrated owl pellets, soggy wet feathers and the detritus from insects—all wrapped in loo paper—in the washing machine was not

---

4 *Having an 'upstairs' was also a source of fascination to them for quite some time.*

pleasant. Many times, on opening the washer door my scream of, 'Oh my God, I'll kill him!' would make the poor dogs go and hide in a corner. I would have to go and reassure them that I was not cross with them. Matt would always take his telling off on the chin, but usually with a comment or two. 'Oh no! That was my best beetle!' or 'My best owl pellet!' Sometimes he would even ask if I had kept the skulls and bones—of the mice and voles from the pellets—after I had picked them off the washing. I would give him one of my special withering looks, over the top of my glasses.

'OK,' he would say. 'That's a no then?'

One day, I went looking for the cause of a horrendous stench coming from the boys' bedroom. I soon discovered that Matthew had hidden an entire dead vole beneath his pillow, which had been rotting away quite merrily. When I asked 'Why?' he informed me he was saving it until it rotted away, because he wanted the 'skelingten'. From the moment he started to crawl, the boy was a menace.

When he was about 15 months, I had put Matt down for a nap in his cot after lunch, just taking off his shoes and jumper. I had just come downstairs to the kitchen, and was starting to peel potatoes, when suddenly I felt an overwhelming sense of panic. Inexplicably, I felt something was very, very wrong. I dashed upstairs and into Matt's room, to find him dangling above the floor, hanging by his neck on the outside of the cot. The collar of his t-shirt had caught and, gasping for breath, his lips had already turned blue. I snatched him up to take pressure off his neck, and managed to flip him back into the cot. Once the worst pressure was off his neck, he really started to gasp, making the most horrendous noises. Dashing into the bathroom, I got a pair of nail scissors and cut him out of his T-shirt, the neckband of which had twisted tightly around his neck. Evidently, he had climbed right over the side, catching his neckband on the release clip for the side of the cot. He had then twisted and turned, trying to free himself. Under normal circumstances, the cot would have tipped over with his weight, but John had put brackets on the legs and screwed it to the floor—as he liked to rock the cot around the bedroom during the night, keeping us all awake. He finally started to breathe normally, and his colour returned to normal. I do not know, to this day, how I sensed all was not well with him. It was very spooky. Thank goodness I had though, as we would have lost him. John was due in from work imminently, as he was on the early shift, so when he arrived home we dashed Matt down to Dr Pepper. After an examination, Dr Pepper gave him the all clear. Apart from a nasty red weal on his neck, and a very raspy voice, he was back to his rambunctious self in no time at all.

Here is a little piece, written and bought home from school by Rachael when she was six, which sums Matthew up perfectly:

My Baby Brother by Rachael

"My baby brother is nerly two years old and he has curly hiar his hiar is brown. He has Grey eyes he is nauty. He eats a lot. He is thirty nine and a half inches tall. He is a big boy for his age and one day he went in the baskit full of frut and got three bananas and two appels."

Matt was two at the beginning of December 1978, and just after Christmas I received a letter, from the Clinic in Frodsham, with an appointment for his two-year-old assessment test. I thought Oh Lord! I hope he co-operates and behaves himself!

The day of the test came, and arriving at the Clinic, I saw the waiting room was full of two year olds playing happily on their own, as two year olds are wont to do. Finding himself a toy car, Matt began playing with it quite happily until a much older boy arrived. This new arrival went around the room, snatching the toys from the little ones. There was uproar, as most of them were now crying, but the brat's Mother never said a word to stop him. The older boy, now marching up to Matt, snatched the toy car he was holding and threw it back into the toy hamper. Matt made no fuss, but instead, with a determined look on his face, got up and followed the big boy across the room. 'No boy!' said Matt, taking a firm hold of the boy's jumper and pushing him backwards into the hamper. I thought the rough justice was quite fair. All the other Mums were smiling in approval, as the brat was now flat on his back inside the hamper, with his legs dangling over the side and screaming blue murder. His mother, who was now having hysterics, ran across to rescue her obnoxious little darling. Luckily, just then Matt's name was called, so we quickly disappeared into the next room.

On entering the room, Matt immediately weighed up the health worker before the poor woman had even opened her mouth. From the look on his face, I already knew the signs were not favourable for a successful test. This was the same poor soul who had assessed Rachael at four years old, who just before she was tested had whispered to me, 'Is that lady a witch Mummy?'

You can understand then, that I was feeling a little apprehensive to say the least. The assessor was very brusque and said, 'Now, Matthew, I want you to sit on Mummy's knee please.'

Duly instructed, Matthew went and sat on a chair opposite to me. I had to get him and plonk him on my knee, keeping a smile on my face.

The hearing test came first, wherein the assessor told Matt to turn his head when he heard the sound. Standing behind him, the assessor jingled, rattled, tooted and squeaked various objects. All to no avail. Matt just stared into the distance.

'Are you worried about his hearing?' the assessor asked, of course.

'No,' I answered. 'He can hear the rustle of a toffee paper from the next room.'

'Is Matthew talking yet?'

'Yes, extremely well,' I replied. 'In fact, after eating, it's his favourite pastime.'

I do not think she believed me, and was not amused in the slightest by my little quips. The next test was balance and coordination, which required Matt to walk across the room on a wide white line, which was painted on the floor.

'Matthew, can you walk across the room, on the white path?' The health worker asked.

Matthew obliged the request by straddling the line, walking along it like a duck, and then refusing to co-operate when asked to try again.

I put on my 'very cross' face. 'Matthew, behave yourself!' I said quietly.

Next, presenting to him a wooden farm puzzle, which had seven spaces to fill in, the health worker said, 'Can you find any pieces to fit into the shapes, Matthew?'

He gave her a look that seemed to say, 'Are you daft?'

Whacking in the pieces at speed, he muttered after each one, 'Cow, horse, sheep, pig, dog, cat, tractor!'

Matt had the same puzzle at home, so I heaved a sigh of relief as I thought he was now beginning to mellow. Sadly, I was mistaken.

The next test was physical coordination. A large wooden block, with three steps, was pushed into the middle of the room. After placing a few chocolate buttons at the top, the assessor asked Matt if he could climb up the steps to reach the buttons. I watched him staring at the buttons, and knew he wanted them badly. Right! I thought. We have definitely got you this time, you little devil! I was wrong again, of course. After staring at the steps for a while, I could practically hear the cogs in his little brain whirring. Eventually, Matt walked across the room, grabbed hold of a chair, and with a great deal of effort, pushed it all the way to the back of the steps. Climbing on to the chair, he reached up and got the buttons, giving us a triumphant smile as he ate them.

The last test was eye coordination, which involved rolling different balls across the room to watch his eye movement. There was no reaction from Matt of course, until the assessor rolled a ping-pong ball along the floor.

'Can you see the little white ball Matthew?' Asked the assessor. To my surprise and delight, he nodded and watched it roll across the floor. Then he got off my knee, walked over to it, picked it up and walked over to a radiator—promptly stuffing it down the back. I dashed over and eventually managed to flick it out with my fingers, only to find the heat had melted it out of shape. By this time, the health worker looked as if she was losing the will to live.

You've only had him for ten minutes! I thought to myself, I have to live with him! Apparently, this was the only ping-pong ball they had, and there was a clinic full of lovely co-operative children still to assess. I apologised profusely, saying I would go and buy another one from the sports shop in the High Street. Unfortunately, this meant I had to walk down to the shop, back up the steep hill to the clinic to deliver the ball, then back down again to get the bus to go home. Physically and mentally shattered by now, I still had a two-mile walk in front of me when I got off the bus, as we only had a bus service to the end of Aston Lane. It was bitterly cold too, but Matt was fast asleep by now, snug and warm in his pushchair—the little blighter. I had a letter a few weeks later requesting a retest, but I ignored it. There was nothing amiss with him, either physically or mentally, and I did not intend to go through all that again.

In May 1979, when Matt was two and a half years old, we had workers repairing and replacing the house gutters and drainpipes. They were working on the house for quite a few days, and Matt took quite a shine to them. Whenever they had their tea breaks, Matt wanted to sit with them. Now, around this time he was in the habit of always removing his shoes and pants—however, his new friends had told him that he could not sit with them unless he put his pants on. Every morning, Matt would insist on wearing his 'moldyoes', which is what he called his overalls. Once kitted out in overalls and anorak, and ready to go, he would ask me to put his 'lid' up—his hood—and he would carry his little wooden chair outside. With Casey at his side, he would sit with the workers and chat away like a little old man. I would hear the men laughing at the things he said. At the time, he was still using a 'Sippy Cup' until the men told him only babies used them. He came immediately into the kitchen after this and, handing me the 'sippy', said, 'I want a man cup'. So 'sippy' at last went into the bin, thanks to Rodney and the gang. One day, whilst holding forth, he suddenly jumped to his feet. Cupping his ear with his hand, he said, 'Hark! I can hear the Oocuck!' I could hear the men howling with laughter from the kitchen.

How did he know the word 'Hark' at two and a half years old? Well, I used to sing the sonnet 'Hark, Hark the Lark at Heaven's Gate Sings' to him while listening to the skylarks in the field next to the house.[5] There were so many Skylarks in the days when the children were small, but hardly any now. It is so sad.

When the workers came to leave, I thanked them for being so kind and patient with Matthew.

'We have enjoyed every minute with that little lad and his great big dog,' said Rodney, the work gang foreman. 'They're absolute diamonds. From now on, every time I hear a Cuckoo, I'll remember little Matt.'

Round about this time, two imaginary friends called John Frodsham and John Humperback[6] suddenly materialized. Apparently, these two friends lived in the hedge on the front drive, and required regular snacks of chocolate digestives and custard creams—which were dutifully placed into two plastic bowls and pushed into the hedge.[7] I once tried to fob Matt off with just one bowl, to reduce the amount of biscuits being

5 *As you may recall, I learned this in Miss Hall's music class in my first year at Rivington School.*

6 *Do not ask, we have no idea how that child's brain worked.*

7 *It is amazing, is it not, how they liked the same biscuits as Matt?*

used in this endeavour, but I was told 'two people, so two bowls'. After pushing the bowls into the hedge, Matt would casually stroll around to the back of the house—then run back to the front, peeping around the corner to see if anyone was watching. If the coast was clear, he would dash for the hedge, grab the biscuits then go and sit in his sand pit to eat them. I would watch the whole performance from the hall window. After a while, the dogs got wise to this routine, and if they got the chance, they would snaffle the stash before Matt came back. The expression on Matt's face when he found the bowls empty was hilarious. These new 'friends' would frequent the house too, not just the hedge. Matt nearly drove Chris and Rachael mad, as wherever they went to sit in the house, John F or John H would already be sitting there. We even had to set a place for them at the dinner table. It took a lot of his energy to keep up with the pretence though, so much to our relief, after a few weeks, his brain moved on to inventing other ideas. The two invisible Johns disappeared never to return.

A few days after the workers had left, Matt went missing at lunchtime, when he would normally have been sitting with them. I thought he had gone to find them, as he had been really sad when they left. The first place I looked for him was in the field next to the house, as on numerous times he had crawled on his tummy under the hedge, to roll down the steep bank to the field on the other side. I fully expected to see him tramping across to the village with no shoes on, and up to his knees in cow poo. This would not be the first time Matt had gone 'missing' into the field, but Casey had always given the game away before by whining, and trying to get under the hedge to follow him. Unusually, this time Matt's faithful companion was lying on his bed and seemed very unconcerned. I had already looked everywhere, and there was no sign of the little devil, so after a few minutes I went up to Casey, with the intention of getting him up, to see if he would go to where Matt was hiding. To my relief there Matthew was—fast asleep between Casey's back, and the wall of his shed. I should have known from Casey's lack of fuss that they would be together.

The children always accompanied us to Championship Shows, until they were old enough to stay at home if they wished. We travelled up and down the country together most places, but John went on his own to the shows held in the far south or in Scotland. In those days, an outing in the car with a picnic lunch, and fish and chips—or a Chinese take away—on the way home, was a real treat. Quite a few Championship shows in the 70's and 80's were in conjunction with agricultural shows, and Chris and Rachael especially loved these. They would make a note of our tent, and Casey's bench number, and go off to look around and spend their pocket money—with the usual proviso that they stay together. They would come back at lunchtime to eat and drink, and then be off again.

Matthew, however, we did not allow out of our sight. In the past, I had tried pinning a label on him, in case he got lost, but he just kept pulling it off—indignantly informing me that he did not need a label, as he wasn't a parcel. Therefore, I had knitted him a special jumper for these occasions. On the back, in large letters, it said,

BALLYPHELAN
IRISH WOLFHOUNDS

On the front, in letters even larger, it said,

MY NAME
IS
MATTHEW

We were always benched next to friends. Usually, on one side would be Louise Pinkney (although she was Louise Stanley in those days) of the Hydebeck kennel. On the other side would be Sandy and Kath of the Bokra kennel. A short while ago at a show, Sandy asked me how 'MY NAME IS MATTHEW' was doing. I said he is forty now, and well, and still makes me laugh.

Traveling to the Welsh Kennel Club Show at Builth Wells one year, the children were perfectly happy until we were passing a caravan site, and a Jack Russell dog suddenly shot out across the road in front of us. John did his best, but could not avoid it and hit the poor little thing. The dog was still alive, but only just. The owners came running after him, gathered him up, and promised to take him to the Vets, but somehow we did not believe them. I think we were more upset than they were. Chris, Rachael and Matt were totally heart broken and were crying. The rest of the journey did not go too well either, as every few miles or so there seemed to be a squashed hedgehog on the road. Poor John got the blame for these as well, even though they had been dead a very long time before we drove by. For a while afterwards there would be the occasional comment from the children, 'Do you remember when we went to that show in Wales, and Dad murdered that dog and all those hedgehogs?' Poor John!

In the summer of 1980, we went to Liverpool City Show, which was a lovely day out for us all. Casey was entered in the Open Dog Show and his classes were in the morning, so we had lots of time in the afternoon to visit the fairground, produce tents, craft tents, many stalls and the parachute display. It was a glorious sunny day and Casey, showing his socks off as usual, was Best of Breed and Reserve Best in Show. After Casey had been in the ring, Chris and Rachael went off together to have a look around. They were to come back to the big oak tree by the dog show rings, and to wait if they were there before us. We took Matt up to the fairground and put him on the roundabout of his choice. Casey was not happy whenever his beloved Matthew went out of sight, but got very excited every time he came back around waving to him. However, when the roundabout stopped, to our shock and horror, Matt was on the opposite side. With lots of other anxious parents, we pushed our way through the crowd, but by the time we got to the other side, we could not see him anywhere. We were just desperate now, as he was very confident and would talk to anyone. Even though we had always told him that he should never go off with strangers, all the worst thoughts imaginable were whizzing through our heads. John said we should split up, and he would go and let them know at the lost and found tent. I went back to the tree to find that Chris and Rachael had returned, so leaving Casey with them, I went off again to search. We kept popping back to the tree in case he had come back. After about half an hour, we spotted him nonchalantly making his way down the slope to the tree. He was clutching an enormous ice cream cone, with two chocolate flakes stuck in it, and was happily licking it as he walked. Casey was ecstatic when he saw him approaching. Nearly weeping with relief, I was now sick with worry as to how he had come by the ice cream.

'Hello,' said Matt. 'I've been a bit lost.'

We all nearly hugged the life out of him. I asked him about the ice cream.

'Oh,' he said. 'I saw everybody getting ice cream from a man in a big van, so I stood 'til it was my turn.'

'But how did you pay for it?' I asked. 'You didn't have any pennies!'

'I said to the man,' he replied, '"Can I have a big one please, with two chocolates." And he just gave it to me. I said thank you, then I looked for the tree and came back.'

If I had been lost at his age I would have been so frightened, and absolutely screaming for my Mother. I certainly would not have queued for an ice cream, and then had the gumption to find my way back to a tree. Of course, I now had to go hunting for the Ice Cream man, but when I went to pay him, he just laughed.

'I thought he was with the lady behind, so didn't ask him for any money,' said the ice cream man. 'When I realized he wasn't with her, he'd disappeared. Anyway, he was the politest child I've served all day, so it's on the house.'

We were all tired by now, but Matt really wanted to see the parachute display so we stayed a little longer. He thoroughly enjoyed watching the men jumping out of planes, and drifting gently to the ground on their parachutes. He had been fizzing with inspiration and excitement, but by now was nearly asleep on his feet, so after our extremely eventful day we wended our way home. Little did I know what was now forming in his inventive little mind.

The next morning, Matt was rummaging around under the kitchen sink. I asked him what he was looking for

'Just stuff.' He replied.

I told him to go outside to play instead. A little while later, he came in and asked if he could play upstairs.

'Yes, you can.' I said, 'As long as you promise not to touch Chris's Action Men or Rachael's Cindy dolls.'

Matt had a habit of swapping Action Man and Cindy's clothes, then sitting them in a row on their beds. The sight of Action Men in frilly dresses and bikinis and Cindy dolls in combat gear was very funny. He would also sometimes take the head off Rachael's little baby doll, and push it over an Action Man's head. The sight of this large baby face on an Action Man body was grotesque, and the little devil thought this highly amusing. In truth so did I, but I always had to be suitably cross with him, as it used to drive poor Chris and Rachael mad. After promising not to touch their things, Matt went merrily on his way upstairs.

It did cross my mind briefly to query why he had his anorak on indoors, but as I was busy, I did not investigate. For a little while, all was quiet until Casey, Kerry and the Shelties—who were lying in the sun on the drive—started to make a tremendous racket. I looked through the living room window and saw that they were looking up at Rachael's bedroom window. I shot outside, knowing Matthew Sumner would be in the equation somewhere. Sure enough, there he was, with his back to me—half in and half out of the upstairs window, with one foot on the outside window ledge and the other inside. He was now without his coat, and holding on to the window frame with just one hand. The other was clutching a black plastic bin bag with string dangling from it.

Oh my God! I thought, panicking. What the hell do I do? If I shouted, it might startle him and he would fall. If I went upstairs, I still might startle him and he would still fall. I decided to run upstairs, so dashing up—and singing as I went, so he would hear me coming in the distance—I approached Rachael's room. I was cheerily shouting, 'Matt, where are you? Lunch is ready!' The ploy worked, thank God. When I opened the door, he was just climbing down off the bed.

'Hello, why were you climbing out of the window with a bin bag?' I asked.

'It's my parachute!' He replied. Seeing the look of horror on my face he said, 'It's all right Mummy, I tested it on Teddy and it worked.'

I shudder to think what would have happened if the dogs had not alerted me with their 'something's dreadfully wrong' type barking, as I know he would have jumped. Dear God Above, I thought. He is only three and a half! I'll be a gibbering wreck before he is raised.

'Play School!' I said to John suddenly, the same day. 'He has to go to Play School, to mix with other children his own age, and to give me a few hours break in the mornings. Whether he likes it or not.'

When we put the idea to Matt, it did not go down well. He said he was not going, as he was far too busy. However, at the age of four, and protesting loudly, we duly delivered him to the church hall for his first taste of Play School.

Picking Matt up after his first morning—which, incidentally, he thought was a complete and utter waste of his precious time—he did not answer me when I asked what he had been doing. When we got home, putting an arm over Casey's back, he stamped off down the hall, turning around half-way and shouting that 'Play School was poo and for babies'—and that he hadn't done anything all morning, because there was no one there. He also said that he had *not* had a drink of milk in a spotty beaker, and he did *not* eat a 'rectangular cow biscuit'.[8] Then off he went with Casey, to get on with his latest scheme. After a few weeks, he seemed to have settled and now had a friend called Graham John Waver, who evidently was very naughty. Matt would come home and sit with Casey, telling him all the things that this naughty boy got up to. The list of GJW's misdemeanours seemed endless. Casey would sit and stare at Matt with adoration while he related these events.

One day, when picking Matt up from Play School, I asked the woman in charge to point Graham John Waver out to me, as Matt had talked so much about him and how naughty he was—I did not mention that he only talked to the dog about him. She looked at me and smiled. Well, I think it was a smile—perhaps it was a grimace. It was one of those 'Perhaps we need to have a little chat...' types of smiles.

'We don't have a little boy of that name, Mrs Sumner,' said the woman, sympathetically. 'I am afraid he and his deeds are all in Matthew's head. But there were one or two little incidents which I was going to mention to you…' She then proceeded to tell me all about them.

Matt had seen me talking to the teacher, and as we walked home, he kept giving me sidelong glances. He knew, by the expression on my face, that the cat was now thoroughly out of the bag and that he was probably in deep trouble.

As soon as we got through the door, and before I even opened my mouth, he started slowly climbing up the stairs, sighing as he went and sitting down at the very top. This was the highest-level 'naughty step' achievable, and evidently he thought his behaviour warranted it. I left him to stew for a while, and then called him down stairs to discuss those 'one or two little incidents' I had just learned about.

'Why did you hit the boy with the frying pan?'[9]

'He's horrible Mummy, and hits us and spits at us!'

---

8 *Guess what the whole family now call Malted Milk biscuits?*

9 *A toy frying pan from the playhouse, not a real one thankfully.*

'Don't the teachers tell him off?'

'No, he always does it when they're not looking! He pushed Claire off the slide and made her cry, so Andrew and me waited at the bottom and when he came down we whacked him.'

'So, Andrew whacked him as well?'

'Yes, with a big plastic spade!'

By now, I was having difficulty keeping a straight face, but Matt was near to tears. 'And why,' I continued, 'do you go round the opposite way when you are dancing?'

'I hate dancing Mummy!'

'Yes you might, but you are spoiling it for everyone else aren't you?'

Matt had held the tears back for so long now, that they just suddenly spurted out in huge drops from his eyes. He was only four years old, and I felt dreadful for giving him the third degree, even if it was necessary. Gathering him up and hugging him, I made him solemnly promise not to whack any more horrible boys, but to tell the teacher instead if there were any problems. I said that I would come with him the next day, so he was not on his own when he said sorry to the playschool ladies, and to explain about the boy hitting and spitting at them and making Clare cry.

Just as Christopher started his second year at High School, and Rachael her last year at the village Junior School, our mischievous, funny, bright, happy, articulate, 'pain in the backside' little boy was due to start in the infant class. As the village school was very old fashioned, and the three resident teachers stuck in a time warp, we knew Matt would hate it. He was already reading, just as Chris and Rachael had been before starting school, and we just prayed he would not have to trawl through the one word per page *Janet and John* books. That would not go down well and, unlike Christopher, Matthew would certainly make his feelings known to the teacher.

I had Matt's uniform ready the night before, and had made a big fuss showing it to the dogs and saying how smart they thought he would look. All this enthusiasm was to no avail. Matt told me that playschool had been mostly poo, that he had no intention of going to school all day as he was much too busy, and anyway he, Casey and Kerry had made plans. I was dreading the next morning, thinking it would be awful if I had to drag him along. However, to my amazement he did not make much fuss at all. I managed to get him through the school door and into the hall, with the minimum amount of sighing, grumbling and face pulling. I felt very relieved, and walked home with Casey and Kerry with quite a spring in my step thinking, Well! That was easy!

Just after lunch that day, John was on the front drive lying under the car, mending the exhaust, when he saw a pair of familiar little feet going past.

'Oi!' John shouted. 'Why aren't you in school young man?'

'I've had enough!' Matt replied coolly.

I marched him back to school and had a serious word with the teacher, as the careless old bat had not even realized he was missing.

Some time ago, this same teacher had called me into school to discuss Rachael's inappropriate use of language in English lessons. This turned out to be her use of the word 'bitch'. As in 'we have a bitch with puppies', 'We have entered Kerry in Junior Bitch at Birmingham Show' and 'We have a bitch in season' and so on. It was a good thing Mrs Gideon evidently had not understood what 'in season' meant, or she certainly would have fainted with shock. Of course, the word 'bitch' and 'season', used in the correct context, is perfectly normal language for children raised in a household full of dogs.

Rachael had been asking for her very own dog for quite a while, setting her heart on a Standard Wire Haired Dachshund. For Christmas that year, she got all the trimmings that go with a new puppy. For her eleventh birthday, on the 31st of December, Kizzy came into our lives and Rachael's care of this wicked little dog was exemplary. The wolfhounds did not faze Kizzy one iota. She would steal all their toys, put them in a heap and growl at any of the wolfhounds who dared to try to reclaim them.

Matthew announced that he wanted his own dog too. In your dreams young man! We thought. After cogitating for a while about how we were going to tackle this latest 'Big Idea', we hit upon a big idea of our own. We told Matt that Fergus, our third wolfhound, could be his dog. As he was already Matt's other best pal, and a fellow member of his 'gang', it was an ideal solution. He was very pleased indeed with this idea, and John and I heaved a sigh of relief that we had gotten away with our ruse without any fuss. We even asked Matt to sign a copy of Fergus's pedigree, to make it look completely 'official'. The utter deviousness of parents is so necessary sometimes, especially when dealing with a determined little person like Matthew Sumner.

After a while, we decided to let Kizzy have a litter, and found a very compatible male who lived near Chester. We had seen him at shows and thought him very handsome. Although we thought his owner, Mrs Campbell, was a little strange, she was very friendly so we arranged to take Kizzy to this dog when she had her next season. The day arrived and off John, Rachael and I set. Matthew was left with Chris—who was fifteen by now—with threats that he would be hung drawn and quartered if he got up to any mischief. I said to Chris that keeping an eye on Matthew was his good deed for the day.

'That's very funny! No, it's my good deed for a whole year Mum!' He said.

On arrival at the Campbell's house, Mrs Campbell opened the door, and a dreadful stench of ammonia wafted out, nearly knocking us flat on our backs. The smell was nearly as powerful as the tiger dens at the zoo. Rachael whispered that she had changed her mind, and wanted to go home. Trying not to breathe in too deeply, we walked down the hall, with the carpet squelching and sticking to our shoes, and into the living room. It was even worse in there, with more squelchy carpet. There we were faced with dog poo, in various stages of decay, in between dirty dinner plates, cups and beer glasses that were scattered all over the floor. Rachael was now urgently whispering that she really wanted to go home. Sitting down on the sofa, John practically disappeared down into the springs. We all politely refused the cup of tea that was being offered. The expression of disgust on Rachael's face was priceless, and she was now begging to go home. We were all itching by now, and trying not to scratch.

'Please excuse the state of the place,' Mrs Campbell said. 'I haven't had time to polish today.'

How we kept out faces straight, God alone knows. We did not dare look at each other, as it would have set us all off laughing. Having made the trip now, and already suffered an assault on our senses, we decided to go ahead with the mating to make it seem worthwhile. The dog was hopeless however, and Mrs Campbell was getting in the way all the time. We did not offer any assistance though, as we just wanted to get out of there by then.

'Oh no!' Said Mrs Campbell, as the dog continued to fail to mate with Kizzy. 'He's biting her on the neck!'

'Don't be daft woman,' said Mr Campbell. 'He's only giving her a love bite, like I give you!'

As Pa Campbell had a mouth full of rotten teeth, and looked as if he had never had a bath in his life, we were all trying not to be sick. We decided then to call it a day and said our goodbyes, trying our best to put a very regretful tone into our voices.

We got in the car and drove around the corner, then just dissolved into helpless laughter. John could not see to drive properly for ages, as the tears were streaming down his face. By the time we got home, we were all vigorously scratching, so we stripped off in the outside loo, and left our clothes in there with Kizzy. After a bath and hair wash for us, it was Kizzy's turn. She had one bath for fleas, and then another because she still stank. Even after numerous baths, the Wolfhounds found us all utterly fascinating for the next few days.

In January 1982, we had a bitch visiting for a mating with Casey. As we went outside to do the deed, I told the children that if anyone telephoned they were to apologize, and ask them to ring back later. When the phone did ring Matt, aged five, got to the phone first.

'Aston 486, who's speaking please?' Said Matt politely, in his best telephone voice.

'Oh Hello, Matthew. It's Mr Clare. Can I speak to Mummy please?'[10]

'I'm sorry Mr Clare,' Matt replied. 'Mum can't come to the phone. She's outside mating with Dad on the grass.'

Mr Clare was laughing when he rang me later, and told me what Matt had said to him. I think our vicar dined out on that story for a very long time. He was such a fierce little man, but was very kindly to—and tolerant of—noisy little children in the church during the service. He thought that Matt was just the absolute 'Bee's Knees'.

I remember a baptism being held, during a morning service, when Matthew was about three years old. When he saw Mr Clare coming out of the vestry with a towel over his arm, and a bowl of water—because the font leaked—a loud voice rang out.

'Is Clare going to have a bath, Mummy?' Boomed Matthew, his voice echoing through the church. 'He will have to take his shirt off first won't he?'

---

10 Mr Clare was the vicar of St. Peter's Church in Aston.

Mr Clare had to put the bowl down quickly, and wipe his eyes on the towel, as he was laughing so much. After the service, as we left Mr Clare said, 'Oh Pam! Isn't he a just a pickle!' I thought, Well, I suppose that is one way to describe him.

In the first week of the summer holidays, in 1984, Matthew announced that he and his friends Mark and Andrew, from the farms at the end of the lane, were going to build a raft to sail on the duck pond. As the pond was only about two feet deep, I was not worried. Anything that keeps the boy busy is fine by me, I thought. The boys begged and borrowed odd pieces of wood from around the village, John's stock of nails reduced drastically and his best claw hammer and saw disappeared.

Matt spent his evenings making a flag from a piece of old sheet I had given him. Lying on his tummy on the dining room floor with the dogs, he chattered away to them as he drew and coloured his flag with some old felt-tip pens—I had already rescued Rachael's best felt-tips before he ruined them. The dogs were watching and listening to him, the tips of their tails just gently wagging. The bond between the Wolfhounds—especially Casey and Fergus—and this wicked little boy was truly special.

Finally, the day came when the raft was complete, and Matt asked if he could have a bottle of wine to launch it. After a long debate, as to why he could not have a full bottle of wine, or even an empty one—Didn't he think that broken glass in the farmyard and duck pond was a bad idea?—with much sighing and hunching of shoulders, he finally gave in to common sense. Then off he set, with a plastic bottle and his wonderful flag attached to a brush stale.

About an hour later, there was a tremendous hammering on the front door. I opened the door, and there standing on the step was a small, dirty green, slimy, smelly and soaking wet apparition. The only clean parts visible on this entity were the streaks down its cheeks made by its tears.

Looking up at me, Matt said, in a very wobbly voice, 'It sank Mum.'

The poor little chap looked so forlorn, so I was desperately trying not to laugh. Grabbing him by his shirt collar as he went to step into the house, I propelled him around the side of the house to the garden hosepipe. Trying to hose down a protesting, wriggling seven year old with cold water was not easy. His shouts and screeches were upsetting the dogs terribly—they were battering at the side gate trying to come to his rescue. Leaving his clothes and wellingtons in the outside loo, he was then allowed into the house. After a hair wash—and more protests—a bath, a cup of cocoa and slice of cake, he cheered up. Watched over by his trusty Wolfhound comrades, Fergus and Casey, who were happy now they could see I had not murdered him, he curled up and went to sleep on the sofa. God help me though, he was no doubt already dreaming up his next project.

As I have mentioned before, the stairs in our house at Aston had a dual purpose as the 'naughty steps'. The more serious the misdemeanour, the further up the miscreant went. The naughty steps, hardly ever visited by Chris and Rachael, were in constant use by Matthew. He would often just go and sit there of his own volition, choosing the step he thought fitted the crime, then wait for me to find him and dole out the requisite punishment. He reached the pinnacle of the top step for a *second* time, when, whilst playing pirates, he took the mantle clock and buried it in the sand pit as treasure. I placed him under house arrest, and confiscated his *Star Wars* figures for two weeks for that crime. It was a fate worse than death for him.

Another time, I came in from the garden to see his trusty wolfhound friends, Casey and Fergus, standing at the bottom of the stairs staring up to the top. There, sitting on the top step—for the *third* time—with his hands over his eyes, and rocking back and forth, was you-know-who.

'Well?' I said, dreading his response.

'You're not going to like it,' he said

He was correct. I did not.

Whilst jumping about, playing ball with the dogs in the hall, he had knocked off and broken one of my lovely, hand-painted china Owl plates.

'And?' I shouted.

'I am really sorry Mum!' He replied.

'How many times have I told you not to play ball with the dogs in the house? Come down this minute! You are under house arrest and on dish washing duty for a thousand years.'

He came slowly down, gradually, and as he passed me—with Casey and Fergus in tow—I heard him mutter to them, 'Beware the wrath of Sumner!'

It was all I could do to keep my face straight. Even when I was furious with him, the little devil could still make me laugh.

Chris and Rachael, in their teens, had both become members of The Sealed Knot,[11] and they would often go off to camp during muster weekends. Everything was made as authentically as possible; tents, food, costumes and equipment. Howard Talbot, an Historian and 'Gentleman Volunteer' and his wife Christine, who were family friends and had ancestral aristocratic ties to Aston-by-Sutton, kept an eye on them as often as they could spare them. The Talbot's son Charles and Matthew also joined, as drummer boys, when Charles was seven and Matt was twelve. They loved going to the Musters that took place all over the country to re-enact famous battles such as The Siege of Bristol, The Siege of Sudeley Castle, The Battle of Lansdown Hill, The Battle of Nantwich, The Siege of Chirk Castle, and many more. They would all come home, after a weekend battling and camping, authentically unwashed and smelling like a drain. Their coats, britches, and socks were made of pure wool, and they would not allow me to wash them. I had to resort to hanging them outside in the fresh air, attempting to rid them—just a little—of the smell of wet wool, mud and smoke from the campfires.

Very sadly, Howard passed away in November 2012. John, Matthew, Rachael and I travelled to Aston from North Wales for the funeral. Chris was up working in Glasgow at the time, and could not get down. Members of The Sealed Knot, from far and wide across the country, also attended his funeral. They lined the lane in full uniform and equipment. As Howard's coffin was carried from the house to the Church, we could hear in the distance the slow beat of the drums, getting louder and louder as they got nearer, and then stopping suddenly as his coffin reached the door and was carried into church. It was incredibly moving, and everyone was in tears.

11 The English Civil War re-enactment society, and the oldest re-enactment society in the UK.

22: Hafod Lwyfog

In June 1990, when Matt was thirteen years old, John and I moved to our lovely mountain home in North Wales. After about a week, Matt knew practically everyone in the village. He had a two-mile walk, to and from the bus every school day. Very often, he would meet elderly women from the village on his way, and carry their shopping bags for them. Sometimes they would stop me to ask if Matthew was my son. 'Bachgen neis,' they would say. 'Bachgen neis.'[1]

We had always tried to instil in the children the importance of being kind, and I am so happy that it comes naturally to all three of them.

The move to Wales was the fulfilment of a dream for John and me. We had decided, a while ago, that we would like to buy or build a boarding kennels, if we could find the right property. As property with land demands a high price in Cheshire, we searched over the border into Wales. We soon discovered that anything decent, within commuting distance of Chester, was still out of our price range. Looking at some of the ones we could afford, we found The Estate Agent's descriptions and photos both amusing and annoying. One property, where the photo was showing the front of the house, looked lovely. We went to view it, only to find that, unfortunately, there was a giant slate tip about ten yards from the front door. Whoever had taken the photo must have had to climb half way up the tip to get the correct angle. Another property's description contained the words 'interesting rocky outcrop to the rear'. What they should have said was, 'half a mountain jutting out, almost up to the bedroom windows'. We had liked the look of a property near Betws Garmon, only to find that the 'seven acres of land' it came with was a long narrow strip, across the road from the house, and with the access gate half a mile away.

We were getting a little disheartened by now, so we decided to look further into Wales, around the Caernarfon area. There, at last, we found what was to become our lovely home, *Hafod Lwyfog.*[2] The cottage came with almost eight acres of land, and looked out over Caernarfon Bay. The land was classed as 'less favoured', as it was only good enough for rough

---

1 'Nice boy, nice boy'

2 Roughly translated, 'Hafod Lwyfog' means 'Summer Dwelling of the Elms'

grazing, but that was fine by us.

We knew it would be a wrench to leave Aston, as we had been very happy there. However, as Chris had already fled the nest and Rachael was getting ready to, we felt that now was the time to go forward with the boarding kennel idea.

The day of the move finally arrived. We had hired a huge removal van for two days, and with help from Chris and Rachael, we packed the van with our furniture, leaving a space in the middle large enough for our six wolfhounds and me to travel in. John, Matt, Chris and Kizzy travelled in the cab. Chris had taken a few days off work to help us with the move, traveling back with John when he returned the van.

The lanes around Hafod are quite narrow, and the gateway into the property was a bit of a challenge, due to the width and length of the van. However, since the age of eight years old, John had been driving farm equipment on his Uncle Jim's farm—so he reversed the van expertly up the long, narrow, twisting drive to the house. We had been to the property a few days before to make a temporary enclosure for the dogs, as we did not want them loose in the fields just yet.

After moving to Hafod, our first job was to remove the dead sheep and lambs the previous owner had so 'kindly' left us. We found them stuffed into holes, under hedges, in the ditches or just lying out in the fields covered over with rusty tin sheets. We presumed they had died whilst lambing, and he had just left them to rot, the horrible man. We had to keep the wolfhounds well out of the fields until the job was done, but Kizzy, the dachshund, managed to escape. Later she reappeared at the kitchen door, covered in rotting sheep slime, expecting us to allow her inside the house. We put her instead in an outhouse, until she had multiple baths and smelled sweet again.

John had been working at Ince Power Station, near Chester, for many years and once we had moved, he lodged with his Mum, just coming home on his days off. Consequently, Matt and I were on our own for most of the week. When John had days off, he worked at putting in a new kitchen. All we had at that time was a sink, and three shelves supported on bricks. When the kitchen was finished, he started to build the kennels. Poor John, he used to say he was glad to go back to work for a rest.

We had since bought a goat, with two kids at foot, and four baby calves. 'Evil Alma', the nanny goat, was the worst mother in the world. We had to keep her tethered on a long chain, as she bullied not only her own offspring, but the calves as well. Both cattle and Wolfhounds learned to give her a wide berth. She was a strange old thing, and refused to eat if she was out of sight of the house. She would just stand there, staring into space, even though she was surrounded with trees, bushes, meadow grass and her favourite thistles. I would go to fetch her and move her nearer to the house, and she would run like the wind back up the path, complaining very loudly all the way. We had bought her as a milking goat, but soon found milking her was easier said than done, as she was very uncooperative. She just would not stand still, and refused to let her milk down. Determined to get something from her, one morning John put a harness on her and suspended her lightly from a beam in the barn, so her feet could not quite touch the ground. I had only managed to get about half a pint of milk from her, when we realized she was so comfortable suspended like this—gently swaying in the harness—that she had gone to sleep and was snoring. The cantankerous old madam had beaten us once again, so we had to acknowledge defeat and gave up the idea of having lots of lovely goat milk for the dogs.

The first contact I had with our nearest neighbours, was when they came to complain that Matt had been scrumping their apples. It was hardly the crime of the century, and scrumping is what country boys do for fun. However, Winifred and Tom, who were not natural country people, did not quite understand the concept, and took the deed very seriously. I made Matt go down to their house and apologize, which he did. He also offered to do some odd jobs for them, in payment for the two whole apples he had scrumped. They were very pleased with his apology. When they got to know him, they realized that although he was a rip at times, he was a very nice boy and not a juvenile delinquent.

I introduced myself to our two other neighbours, Del and Janice, who lived on the smallholding behind ours, and Ivor from the farm in front of us. Ivor was especially kind and said I was to go to him if I was worried about anything when I was on my own. He would notice when we bought in new calves and would just come over and disbud and castrate them for us each time. When the cattle trod on his toes, or tried to kick him, he would swear at them in Welsh. The swearing must have been particularly strong, as he would blush with embarrassment and beg me not to tell John.

'It's sorry I am for the bad words!' He used to say. 'Don't you say those words or tell the Master!'

He would never take any payment for his trouble, and used to get cross with me when I offered. So instead, I would leave a bottle of his favourite whisky, along with a fruitcake, inside the metal post box on his gate.

I decided to take Welsh lessons, as I knew Ivor would be pleased if I could say at least a few phrases in Welsh to him. After a few lessons, I thought I would give it a go, so I spoke a phrase to him that I had made up for my homework.

When he finally stopped laughing, he looked at me. 'Bloody Hell girl, speak English!' He said, wiping the tears of laughter from his eyes. 'BBC Welsh that is! Too posh, all wrong.'

What I thought I had said was:

'I hope that my husband buys me lots of books for Christmas.'

Apparently, what I had actually said was:

'I am going to receive lots of milk from my husband for Christmas'

Ivor gave me a hug, still chuckling and apologising for laughing, but I did not mind in the least as I thought it was funny too.

As we were living in a Welsh-speaking area, I asked Ivor if he minded us English folk buying Hafod Lwyfog. He said it did not matter to him at all. He was just glad to see someone looking after the old place, as the last bugger had been Welsh and he was a bad man. A few years after we had moved to Hafod, Ivor retired and sold the farm. He went to live on his other farm near Pwllheli. I missed him so much, as he was a real character and such a good friend to me. Sadly, he is now no longer on this earth, but I think of him often and hope he is managing not to swear too much in front of the heavenly host.

One day, not long after we had moved, I was working in the garden when I heard growling coming from the far end of the house. I ran around the corner to find Del, from next-door-up-the-hill, standing perfectly still with his hands down by his sides, eyes tight shut and trying not to shake. Circling around him slowly and growling deep and low, was Saxon, one of our wolfhounds.[3] All the other hounds were in the grass

3 *Ballyphelan Celtic Legend*

enclosure by the main path.

'Oh my God, oh my God,' Del was saying, repeatedly. 'Oh my God, Oh my God.'

Every time Del so much as twitched, Saxon's growl deepened further. He would not have bitten him, but probably would have knocked Del down flat if he had tried to move.

Poor Del had come over the fence, and down our back field, to ask if he could borrow John's big axe. As Saxon did not know him, he did not intend to let him go any further without permission. When I spoke to Del, Saxon relaxed and stopped growling, but still escorted us to the kitchen door, keeping an eye on Del all the way. He was such a gentle, friendly hound but the clever boy was protecting me from an intruder. Unsurprisingly, Del always came up the path from that moment on.

Working hard on his days off, it took John almost two years of relentless graft to build the kennels. In between his kennel building, there were fences to put up and maintain, fields and hedges to mow and cut and dog shows all over the UK to attend. I did a lot of the mowing when John was away, and looked after the cattle, calves, goats and wolfhounds—and kept Matthew fed too which was a full time task in itself, as the boy had hollow legs.

A few weeks after moving in, I was cooking the evening meal for Matt and myself when I heard him kicking the front door. I was cross to start with.

'Stop that!' I shouted. 'Now go away, your dinner's ready yet!'

The kicking continued however, and now Matt was shouting, 'Mum! Mum!'

I dashed to the door to find him standing there, holding up his arms for me to see. His forearms were quite evidently broken, as both were now shaped like a letter 'V'. Apparently, he had fallen from the rope swing on the big beech tree onto the drive below. He was in a lot of pain, so I carefully bound both arms across his chest and rang for an ambulance. On being told the ambulance would be at least an hour, I phoned for a taxi to take us to Ysbwty Gwynedd in Bangor, which was fifteen miles away. A&E was packed of course, and we waited two hours before someone finally saw him. He was X-rayed and then admitted, as he had to have surgery to set both arms. The Doctor laughed when asking Matt's name, as this was the third Matthew with broken arms they had seen that night. Although Matt had gone one better, and had broken both. He was home after a few days and off school for a week or so, until he mastered the art of using his arms without bashing everything in sight. The plaster casts were like lethal weapons, and Matt has always been fond of waving his arms about when talking. When the plaster casts were removed, and his arms were fully functional again, it was my turn to have an accident.

As the soil at Hafod is only a few inches deep before you hit rock, John had made a large cold frame for me, so I could grow a few salad crops in grow bags. After lifting the top of the cold frame one morning, to water the plants, I slipped and my left arm went straight through the glass. I felt what I can only describe as a 'thud' to my wrist, and knew immediately that I had done some serious damage. Confirmation of this came a few seconds later, when blood started to spurt everywhere. My first reaction was panic, as John was away and Matt was at school. Then the sensible part of me took over. Squeezing my wrist, whilst holding it up in the air, I began chanting very loudly, and repeatedly, 'Don't panic! Stop the bleeding, get to the phone.'

I made my way back to the house. I had to let go of my wrist to get a clean tea towel out of the drawer in the kitchen to make a tourniquet. Of course, as soon as I let go, blood began spraying everywhere again. I rang Janice, from the farm behind us, and she came and took me to hospital. The outside wound had sealed by now but blood was still leaking into the tissue of my arm. On arrival, I was admitted then taken straight up to a surgical ward to be prepped for theatre. As I had just finished bucket feeding the baby calves before I cut my arm, I was not in the most hygienic of conditions. I did not smell very sweet either. At least I had managed to remove my cow poo covered wellies, and put my slippers on, before getting into Janice's car.

After delivering me to the hospital, Janice kindly went back to the house and wrote a note for Matt to explain what had happened, and then cleaned up all the blood in the kitchen, and by the phone in the living room—so that Matt did not come home from school to the sight of blood all over the place.

Rachael came to visit me that evening, bless her, as she had taken time off work to come and look after the dogs, livestock and Matt, as John couldn't get home until the weekend. I was allowed home three days after my operation. I was so glad to get out of hospital, as I was on a mixed ward and hated it. There were many old men in there, who all seemed to have an aversion to wearing pyjama pants. They would walk about with their dressing gowns wide open, displaying their dangling credentials. It was not a pretty sight. For some reason, they always seemed to have to stop and chat to each other opposite my bed. Rachael stayed with me until John came home. He went back to work after a week, so I had to manage on my own, but as I am left handed, it was doubly awkward, only having the use of my right hand.

Whilst in hospital, I was told that I had not only severed my Ulnar artery, but the Ulnar nerve too. I had now lost the feeling in part of my hand and my fingers. A little while later, I had a second operation to try to repair the nerve a little better, followed by electric shock treatment at Walton Hospital in Liverpool. Thankfully, the shock treatment did give me a little more feeling in my middle finger and hand, and I could use my forefinger and thumb. I knew it would never be right again, but I was so relieved to still be able to knit, sew and craft.

After two years, the kennels were finished and we were finally open for business. We slowly started to acquire customers and a good reputation. We also started to work with a local dog charity called PAWS. They did not have their own premises, and relied on local kennels freeing up a few kennel spots they could use. We did not want the stray dogs in the same building as the boarding dogs, so John built separate accommodation for them. However, PAWS would also take in dogs from private households that had suffered bereavement, illness or divorce. If these dog's inoculations were up to date, we could house them in the main kennel building.

The dogs we took in from prior owners were much easier to home, as we knew their history. However, some of the strays would come to us in a dreadful state and it would take weeks of kindness and good food to get them right again. It was very hard work turning them into dogs suitable for adoption. Occasionally, a dog would come in so physically and mentally damaged that it would have to be put to sleep. It was heart breaking to see dogs covered in cigarette burns, or who had had paint thrown on them. Dogs would frequently come to us so covered in mange or fleas, and very often both, that they had scratched themselves raw. Some of the dogs were terrified of any sudden movement, as they had been used to being beaten or kicked. Even bitches in whelp would come in to us, and some of them were so emaciated it was a wonder they survived the whelping. Nevertheless, survive they did, and the majority of them were wonderful mothers. It was lovely to see the difference in their eyes after a bath, a nourishing meal and lying in a warm comfortable bed, realising that we could be trusted.

Here are just a few stories of the dozens of rescue dogs we rehabilitated over the years.

Hannah

Hannah was a Boxer bitch, who came into rescue from a puppy farmer who lived locally. She had been bred from every season, and consequently was thin and undersized. The owner had had a stroke, and his wife had asked the vet to come and put all the dogs to sleep. Most of them were euthanized, but homes were found for a few puppies. Our vet thought that Hannah, one of the breeding bitches, deserved a chance. She was signed over to PAWS, and then she came to us. After a few baths to sort out her skin infection, and a few weeks of good food, she was ready for adoption. She had the sweetest nature, and was very soon homed.

The evil puppy farmer had now recovered from his stroke, and had started breeding Bulldogs. God help them! I thought.

I asked our vet, Gill, if there was any way of stopping this man from breeding dogs to destruction. Unfortunately, she said that as long as the dogs had food and water, and a dry bed, the law tied her hands.

'I'd like to tie his hands together, and throw him in our septic tank!' I replied.

Bert and Ernie

Two little mongrels, Bert and Ernie, were rescued—along with a few other dogs—from a local woman who was a hoarder. Their coats were so thick and matted that they could not turn their heads, and Bert could not even stand up properly. He just shuffled along on his bottom. It took me hours to clip Bert's coat, but he was a little star. Even though it must have been very uncomfortable for him, especially around his matted feet, he hardly moved as I pulled and clipped.

When I released the matting on his stifles, he could at last stand properly and although a little stiff at first, he was soon walking normally. After I had totally removed his coat, and bathed him, he was so happy that he ran round and round in circles, jumping and barking. Ernie was not quite as bad as Bert, but bad enough. At least he had been able to stand upright and wag his tail.

A woman who was interested in adopting Bert came to see him, and when she saw how attached he was to Ernie, took them both. Bless her heart. There are some really good people in the world.

Faith

One evening, in April 1995, a local farmer brought a Greyhound bitch to us. He had found her in a ditch at the roadside, and was only just about alive. The poor thing had terrible mange, and a large open infected wound on her right shoulder. The sides of her earflaps had been cut away, and were an infected mess. This had evidently been done so she could not be identified by her tattoos. As both ears were mutilated, this was evidence that she was an ex-Irish racing dog. Her skin had split in numerous places, as she was so emaciated and dehydrated, and she really needed to go on a drip. However, I knew she had given up, as the spark had gone from her eyes, and I did not think she would make it through the night. Therefore, after syringing some rehydration fluid into her, I just wrapped her in a duvet and—continuing with the fluid, little and often—I held her in my arms all night. She just lay looking at me, and I thought that at least for her last few hours on earth, she would be warm and feel loved. In the middle of the night, she went into a deep sleep and I thought it was the end. Imagine my surprise in the morning to see her lifting her head to look at me. I was so happy that I just burst into tears.

The vet came out to see her and gave her antibiotics, and we decided that rather than distress her—poking about trying to raise a vein to attach a drip—I would continue with the rehydration fluid. She was now managing to lap a little, if I held her head steady. It was still touch and go, as we did not know how much damage her prolonged starvation had done to her internal organs. After twenty-four hours, she was trying to get up and could stand if I supported her. There was a dramatic improvement by the third day, and I allowed her a little solid food, which I added to her liquid diet. I do not think she had been offered chicken ever before in her life, as she nearly ate the dish as well. After a week, she was walking and on almost a normal diet, and looking one hundred percent better than when she arrived.

The only downside of this tender loving care was that now I had Sarcoptic mange mites, burrowed in on my midriff, neck and arms. It was very difficult not to scratch myself raw, as the itching was nearly driving me insane. It was indescribable. Then of course, John started itching and scratching as well. Having obtained some foul smelling, potent chemical skin wash from the Doctor, we stood naked in the bath pouring it over each other. It was pretty noxious stuff. The fumes were so unpleasant we had to leave the bathroom window wide open, whilst we applied the unction to our now freezing bodies. The potion eventually worked, thank Goodness, though even weeks later just the thought of mange would set us off scratching again.

Faith was with us for five months, until she was fully fit. She was the most loving, trusting and obedient dog and we would have loved to have kept her. However, our own old, ex-rescue Greyhound, Nellie, was such a grump we knew she would not tolerate her, so we reluctantly put Faith up for adoption. I am usually happy to see rescue dogs go off to their new homes, but it broke my heart when Faith was finally adopted.

We will never know the identity of the evil person who neglected her and threw her in the ditch to die. Whoever they are, I hope they rot in Hell.

Nellie

Nellie was a greyhound who had been found, lost and wandering, on a beach on Anglesey. When we first started to take in dogs for PAWS, the majority that came to us were ex-Irish racing greyhounds, found after being dumped on the beaches. Our theory was that they had been unsuccessful, or been injured, at race meetings in the UK—so it was easier for their evil owners to dump them on this side of the water, rather than take them back on the ferry to be dumped in Ireland.

Nellie was very depressed when she came, so we brought her into the house to be with us, and the Wolfhounds, just to give her the extra love and attention she needed. She ended up then staying for the rest of her life.

She shared a bed with our Wirehaired Fox Terrier, Pip, who John had found abandoned as a puppy. We had to be careful with the Nellie-Pip friendship. Although he was her best friend in the house and front garden, if he started to move faster than a trot, Nellie's eyes would glaze over—and her muscles would tense—as the chase-to-kill instinct took over. I have no doubt that she would have caught and killed him if they had both been running loose in the fields.

In all the years she lived with us, she was always very sparing with her affection, so to have her wag her tail when being stroked was lovely. If she came and laid her head on your knee it was so wonderful it would make me want to cry. Although a lot of her behaviour was due to how she had been reared and treated, before she came to us, most of it was just Nellie's own temperament—as all the other poor, abandoned greyhounds we took in were always very affectionate.

One morning we realized Nellie was missing, and although we searched high and low, we could not find her. Later in the day, to take a break from searching, I went into our bedroom. I immediately noticed a strange, large bump under the bedclothes, so I pulled them back. And there Nellie was. She did not even raise her head as I pulled the bedclothes away—she just opened one eye, giving me a look that seemed to say, 'Bugger off!'

Nellie was terrified of thunder and one day, during a storm, she broke through a pane of glass in the kitchen door and bolted across the fields. Once again, we searched the lanes and asked people in the nearby villages to look out for her. She had not been handed in at the dog pound, and after five days, we had given up hope of ever seeing her again. On day six, we saw a couple strolling up our drive with a black greyhound on a lead and realized that it was Nellie. Evidently she had appeared in the garden of a nearby holiday cottage they were renting, and realizing how traumatized she was they had kindly taken her in, hoping they could find out who she belonged to. During the time Nellie had been with them, she had walked part way up Snowden, travelled on the train to Llandudno, walked on the beach, walked up the Great Orme and had also been for a long walk along Black Rock Sands, at Porthmadog. They had just happened to notice our kennel sign, as they were walking around the lanes that morning, and came to ask if we knew whom she belonged too. As the old grump had given no sign that she recognized us, when we made a fuss of her, they were amazed when we told them she belonged to us.

We asked them in for a cup of tea, and as we all walked into the kitchen, Nellie pushed past us. Climbing into her bed with Pip, and giving a sigh, she curled up and went to sleep. She slept so deeply for the next twenty-four hours that we kept poking her to make sure she was still alive. She was by now at least twelve years old and must have been absolutely worn out after all her adventures. She lived for another year, then sadly, she developed bone cancer in her left back pastern, on the site of an old injury she must have sustained while racing. She was such a character, and we all missed the funny, grumpy old thing when we knew the time had come finally for her to be put gently to sleep.

As John and I have a quirky sense of humour, we find many of the situations with our clients—and the clients themselves—sometimes extremely amusing. Weird and wonderful people seem to flock to us like moths to a flame.

The majority of our clients are very nice, but we do get the odd grumpy, whacky or eccentric ones. A couple of stories follow of two of the latter, who sadly are now gone, but are certainly not forgotten.

Miss Euphemia Pratt was a small, genteel old lady, who never had less than five adopted rescue dogs of all shapes and sizes. Her dogs would board with us when she went on holiday. On the days she was bringing her dogs to us, we could hear her car chugging up the drive, with gears crunching and coming to a juddering halt next to the kennel van. Always parking too close to the kennel van, she was invariably unable to open her door. So instead of reversing, she would shuffle and scramble over the seats, gear lever and handbrake—with legs flailing and pink drawers flashing—and exit via the passenger door. Why she did this every time, God alone knows.

This performance took quite a while, and the car would be rocking from side to side by now, as the dogs in the back had worked themselves into a frenzy of excitement. We always tried to stop her before she opened the back door to let them out—but usually it would be pandemonium, as they would all start fighting, setting off our wolfhounds on the house yards. She would try to help, but only made things worse. She would stand by the car, wagging her finger at them. 'Sit! Sit!' She would shout.

'Oh dear, dear me. What naughty dogs!'

When we finally managed to grab the dogs, as they whizzed past us doing the 'Wall of Death' around the car, we could get them into the kennels. Then Miss Pratt would spend an age patting them on the head, telling them she would see them again soon.

Checking the inoculation cards was like a nightmare. Very often the ink had run, stuck together as they were with dog slobber, old dog food and covered in teacup stains. With admission forms finally filled in and signed, she would then hand me the weird, wonderful and over-the-top feeding instructions for each dog. I always promised to follow the instructions to the letter, while keeping my fingers crossed behind my back, so it was not a lie—unless they had genuine special needs, I fed them a normal diet for the duration of their stay.

When it was time for her to leave, John would stand at the corner of the kennels waving his arms, attempting to prevent her from reversing into the wall. Again. Finally, we would wish her a happy holiday and wave her off, feeling badly in need of a holiday ourselves by now.

She was such an old dear though, who loved her dogs very much. Occasionally an old or infirm dog, who was unadoptable, would come into rescue—and Miss Pratt would take it and care for it, for as long as it lived. All of her dogs were fed on—and slept on—her once beautiful antique furniture, in her once lovely old house.

Even all these years later, there is still a large crack in the wall of the outside run of kennel 12. Bless you Miss Pratt—you were a very special lady.

Mrs Pritchard was another of our elderly clients. She had a darling old border collie called Jenni, who was always immaculately clean, and groomed to perfection. Jenni was a little stiff in her joints and could not get out of the car without help. As Mrs P would not let me lift her out, we would have to endure a performance with 'the ramp'. This she kept in the boot, and was a huge handmade contraption, containing enough wood to build a bungalow. As Mrs P did not want her car's paintwork scratched, she would insist on removing it and putting it in place herself. With much grunting, puffing and struggling the ramp would finally be in place, and Jenni would stroll down it like a model on the catwalk. After settling Jenni into her kennel, I would then have to read the itemized feeding and exercise regime Mrs P always handed to me. Scheduled to start at seven in the morning, this itinerary did not finish until ten o'clock at night. I would just nod my head agreeably, making all the appropriate noises, whilst once again crossing my fingers behind my back. When, I thought, does she think I'll have time to look after all the other dogs?

She was a nice person really though, just very 'correct' and 'old school'. Whenever she came to collect Jenni, she always brought a 15kg bag of *James Wellbeloved* food for the rescue dogs. At Christmas, she would bring another bag of *James Wellbeloved*, deposit £50 in the charity collection box and there would be a box of chocolates for John and me. She was such a kind and generous woman, but she was a little fierce at times.

A man once rang Hafod, asking if he could view the kennels.

'Yes, certainly.' I said. 'Come any time between 1:30pm and 5:00pm.'

I then heard him discussing this with his wife in the background.

'Can we come at 12:30?' He asked.

'No. I'm sorry,' I said. 'That is our lunch time, and it is precious when we are busy.'

'Oh,' he said. 'My wife wants to come with me, and she can only come at 12:30.'

Not wanting to lose a prospective client, and through gritted teeth, I agreed.

They duly arrived and, with much crunching of gears—reminiscent of Miss Pratt's visits—their car stopped with the bumper about an inch from ours. As the man got out, I asked him to ask his wife to park in the allotted space. However, I could see her sitting bolt upright in the driver's seat, with a face like thunder, making no move to get out.

'Are you getting out?' He asked, opening her door. 'It's safe, there are no dogs loose.'

'No!' She said, slamming the door shut, nearly chopping off his fingers.

So just the husband and I went into the kennels. He had been looking around for about two minutes, when his wife—who was still in the car outside—started honking the horn and revving the engine, provoking all the dogs into a fit of frenzied barking. I was feeling really angry with her now, and went over to the car.

'Please stop making such a noise!' I said. 'You're upsetting the dogs.'

I asked the man why she was being so awkward.

'She's in a temper,' he said. 'She doesn't like driving around this area. The lanes and your driveway were too narrow. And she doesn't like dogs.'

'Er... So does she like your Labrador?' I asked, bemused.

'Oh no,' he said. 'He's not allowed to come into the house.'

Why on earth, I thought, had she made such a fuss about coming with him, and at 12:30, if she doesn't like dogs and had no intention of viewing the kennels?

Evidently, she was a control freak, and I had actually given up my dinner hour for this obnoxious old bat.

Just then, John appeared. Everyone who knows him knows he is very friendly and loves to chat. Seeing the woman sitting in the car on her own, he opened the passenger door and stuck his head inside, starting to chat away to her. He was completely oblivious to the woman's foul mood. Even when she started to reverse to get rid of him, he just carried on chatting, giving her advice on reversing safely. John was walking backwards by now, and only when she changed gear and started to pull forward did he decide to give up. Her husband, realizing that she was actually driving off without him, snatched the passenger door out of John's hand, shouting at her to stop. Just before she put her foot down on the accelerator, the brave man managed to throw himself into the passenger seat, without breaking his neck, and off they went now at great speed down the drive. John just stood there scratching his head looking bewildered, wondering what the hell was going on.

Where was I, you might ask? Well, I was leaning against the kennel wall with my legs crossed, trying not to wet myself, absolutely helpless with laughter. Oh, my word, we really do get them. Honestly, it had been like a Brian Rix Whitehall farce.

In the summer months, visitors to the area quite often ask us if we can board their dogs for just one day; as they would like to take the train up Snowdon, and don't want to leave their dog in the car. If we have room, and they have their dog's current inoculation card with them, we will accommodate them.

One day, the phone rang and I answered.

'Hello? Hello? Is that the kennels near Esau?' Said a man's voice.

'Do you mean Rhos Isaf?'

'I have no idea, but you'll do.'

'How can I help you?'

'I want to put the dog in kennels for one day. We're going up Snowdon.'

'Are the dog's inoculations up to date? And do you have the inoculation card with you?'

'The what?'

'The card from your vet with the record of his injections.'

'Oh that, yes we have.'

'What date do you want to bring your dog?'

'Don't know. We haven't made our minds up.'

'Well, I need to know the precise date, so I can tell you if we have room.'

'We don't want a room, we are camping. We just want a kennel for the dog.'

Oh dear God, I thought, give me strength.

Eventually I managed to book their dog in, and they duly arrived on the designated morning. A large battered transit van rolled up, driven by a small, scruffy looking little man. A very handsome Border Collie was sitting on the front passenger seat, complete with car harness. I asked the man if I could see the inoculation card.

'Oh,' he said. 'I'll ask the wife where she put it.'

Wife? What wife? I thought. I see no wife.

Sliding open the van's side door, the man revealed an interior packed to the roof with a settee, mattresses, suitcases, *Calor Gas* bottles and camping gear.

'Avril?' The man shouted inside. 'Where's that card for the dog?'

From the van's interior, a disembodied female voice answered, 'Hang on a minute, it's in my bag. I'll come down.'

'Well hurry up!' Said the man.

Two human feet suddenly appeared from on top of the pile of van contents, followed by a pair of legs, then finally the body of an extremely thin woman. Sliding slowly on her tummy down the pile, she was clutching the handles of a large handbag, which got stuck between a mattress and the top of the door frame, and she had to give it a few good tugs to free it. Once 'Avril' was on terra firma, she then proceeded to rummage in the cavernous interior of her bag, until finally she produced the card. John had walked away and left me there, as he could not keep a straight face—it was hard work keeping my own face straight, believe me. When at last the dog was in his kennel, they drove away with Avril now proudly sitting in the passenger seat. Well, at least for a little while, until they collected the dog, who would undoubtedly want his seat back. John reappeared then, and we just fell about laughing.

Oh my word, I thought. That's yet another little tale for my book. I must go and jot it down.

We were expecting new clients one afternoon, who had booked a kennel for two Pugs. Eventually, a shocking pink—and I do mean shocking pink—VW Beetle, with pictures of Barbie dolls plastered all over it, arrived. Out of this vehicular vision stepped two of the biggest, butchest women I have ever seen.

My face must have registered my amazement, which I quickly tried to hide. The driver shook my hand a little too firmly, and the passenger gave me what she must have thought was a friendly 'pat' on the back.

'I can see we took you by surprise,' she said. 'We just love making an impression!'

I thought, Well you have succeeded. My fingers feel like they've been through a mangle, and I probably have an excellent impression of your hand on my back!

Both GPs, they actually became very good clients of ours over the years, and we liked them a great deal. Their whacky sense of humour was just like ours, and we really missed them when they moved to live in Birmingham.

Some tales can seem so bizarre as to be unreal. I assure you however, that every word of this next tale is true. Proving the old adage, that truth really is stranger than fiction.

A car rolled up one morning, and a very small woman got out. On her left foot was a single roller skate, and on her head a very jaunty straw hat, that looked like a miniature boater. Sticking out from the top of this hat was a wire, on the end of which was a plastic daisy.

I thought, Oh Dear God! Not another one!

John took one look and disappeared—the rat—leaving me to deal with the apparition.

Trying desperately to keep my face straight, I asked how I could help her.

'I've brought my dog,' she said. 'He's booked in for the weekend.'

'I'm sorry,' I said. 'But you haven't booked in with us, we're full.'

'Oh yes I have!' She said

'I'm sorry,' I said again. 'But you haven't.'

This woman was quite a feisty little soul. Getting extremely angry now, she was determinedly trying to get to the kennel door. Perhaps she thought she could claim sanctuary once she got inside. Unfortunately, we have slate shale and gravel on our driveway, and try as she might her roller skate just would not roll. The more irate she got at her lack of progress, the more the daisy on her hat waved about.

It was almost too much to bear. I knew if I started laughing, it would become one of my long, loud 'weeping with laughter' sessions.[4] Taking a deep breath, and composing myself, I suggested that she must have the wrong kennel.

'No!' She shouted. 'It's not the wrong kennel! I wrote the name down!' She then handed me a piece of paper. Written on it were the words:

ELNA KENNELS

'Madam', I said. 'This is not Elna Kennels. This is Hafod Lwyfog, which is written in very large letters on the sign at the entrance.'

At last, she conceded defeat and made her way back to the car, this time plonking along on her uncooperative, non-rolling skate, and one good foot. Getting back into the car, she remembered to duck her head so as not to dislodge the lovely daisy on its wire, which was still merrily waving in the air. Finally, she drove off. How she could drive wearing a roller skate I have no clue. As she disappeared down the drive, John appeared again.

'Who the hell was that?' Said John, bemused.

I just went into one of my laughing meltdowns, and had to lean on the kennel wall with legs crossed once again, trying not to wet myself.

---

4 My family are very familiar with these, and are used to them.

Living where we do, on a hill on the edges of Snowdonia National Park, we often get some very challenging weather. What follows is a tale of when the elements almost proved a little too challenging.

On Christmas Eve, a few years ago, a gale force wind had been blowing for most of the day. We had shut the boarding kennel dogs in early, and were looking forward to an evening by the fire.

After tea, John had gone out to get more logs for the fire. After a while, I realized that he had been gone for an awfully long time. Knowing that something must be wrong I grabbed my coat, John's padded jacket and a torch, and went out to look for him. As I got near to the kennels, I heard a shout. Looking up I saw John sitting on the edge of the kennel roof, trying to stop the wind from blowing it off. Thank goodness that he had gone out when he did. Had the roofing sheets at the edge been taken by the gale, then the whole lot would have come off like a pack of cards.

The poor man, now frozen to the bone, had shouted himself hoarse. He knew I would not have been able to hear him, but thought that perhaps the wolfhounds might alert me by barking. However, there was fat chance of that—they were all fast asleep on their beds.

I dashed up the ladder that John had wedged against the front of the kennels and, crawling on my hands and knees, reached the side edge. After helping him on with his coat, and tying the hood very firmly under his chin, I joined John on the edge of the roof. The wind had just started to get up under the sheet next to the one he was sitting on, so I plonked myself on it, praying that between us we could save the roof if we sat it out. It was very frightening, as the wind was lifting us both up and down as well.

To keep our spirits up, we talked—or rather shouted—to each other, trying to sing Carols, scanning the sky for a glimpse of Santa and his sleigh. We were trying not to think what would happen if the roof went and took us with it. The physical effort of holding the roof down was exhausting, and it was so cold we had lost the feeling in our faces and limbs.

After a few hours, the wind abated enough for John to risk leaving me on my own, while he went and fetched some large rocks. Thankfully, he had a large pile of suitable material, from a wall we had taken down.

He disappeared into the darkness with the wheelbarrow, and seemed to be gone for a very long time. He reappeared eventually, with his barrow full of rocks, and dumped them by the ladder. Repeating this three times, until he had enough rocks to put along the edge of the roof, he then carried them one at a time—and with just one hand—up the ladder. Grabbing hold of each rock as they reached the top, I rolled and wobbled them all into place, until at last the damned roofing sheets stopped lifting.

Staggering back down the ladder, with numb and aching backs, legs, arms and faces, we re-entered the wonderful warmth of the house. We then spent the next few minutes moaning and groaning, and almost weeping with pain, as the warmth and feeling came back into our extremities. It was now past midnight, so we wished each other Happy Christmas, and after a hot drink dragged ourselves off to bed.

Going out early on Christmas morning, we greeted a bright crisp sunny day and an intact kennel roof. Feeling extremely pleased with ourselves, we set to our work, soon finishing feeding and cleaning the boarding dogs and our own dogs. Deciding to leave moving the rocks off the roof until Boxing Day, we went inside to enjoy Christmas afternoon.

When we did come to move the rocks, we were amazed to find they were so heavy that John could hardly lift them. I could not even budge them an inch. Yet just two days before, John had carried them up a twelve-foot ladder one-handed, and I had pushed them into place with frozen hands. Now though, it took our combined effort to push them off the edge of the roof and onto the drive.

It just goes to show what panic, sheer bloody-mindedness and a surge of adrenalin can do for two old codgers' strength and capability.

Whoops!

A while ago, John was away for a few days visiting his Mother in Chester, and being on my own I was busily dashing around, as the boarding kennels were full.

The last job in the morning is emptying the dog poo buckets into the sump of the kennel septic tank. This morning, I was carrying two heavy full buckets of canine excrement, when I slipped on the slope by the sump. I landed flat on my back, the buckets flew into the air and their contents covered me from head to toe—even getting into my mouth and up my nose. Totally winded, I lay there like a beached whale, snorting, spitting and swearing—and doing a fantastic impression of Victor Meldrew.

It was only a few months since I had had surgeries for breast cancer, and had recently also had a fracture of a thoracic vertebra. You have done another good job on yourself Pam, I thought. You clumsy old bat.

After a few minutes, I managed to sit up and was relieved to find only my head was hurting, where I had whacked it on a rock. I got up and ran to the nearest hosepipe, which was by the house gates, and washed myself down. Normally, I would have been able to use the shower in the kennel grooming room, but we had a delivery of dog food stacked in the doorway, and it was impossible to get in. So unfortunately, it had to be the hosepipe—being covered in poo, I could not go into the house either. When I had washed the worst of the effluent off my head and face, I stripped off my sodden stinky clothes, down to my bra and pants—not a pretty sight—and started to hose myself down again. Blue with cold now, and just trying to get the last vestiges of poo out of my hair, I heard a vehicle coming up the driveway. A wave of panic washed over me. The nearest place to hide was in the outside loo, so desperately trying to get my wellies back on my wet feet, I made a dash for it—shutting the door just as the postman arrived. As we have a post box at the front gate, I knew he must have been delivering a parcel, because he always leaves them in the outside loo if there is no one around. He's going to have one hell of a shock if he opens the door! I thought. Luckily, it was Adrian, our regular postman.

'Pam, I have a parcel for you!' He shouted,

'Leave it by the kennels please!' I shouted back, answering from the loo.

'I can't,' he said. 'It's got to be signed for.'

Muttering to myself, and doing my Victor Meldrew impression once again, I opened the door slightly. Poking a wet, smelly brown arm through the gap, I signed the pad.

'I'll explain the next time I see you,' I said, sheepishly from behind the door.

Laughing, he said, 'I don't think I really want to know!'

After he had gone, I emerged from the loo, and threw the clothes I had been wearing into the bin. I did not want the disgusting items even to go in the kennel washing machine. Thankfully, my immune system must have been up to scratch, as I did not have an upset tummy after ingesting dog poo. Most importantly of all, there were no problems in the back and bosom departments.

Unfortunately, even after numerous showers, people were still wrinkling their noses as I passed by. In the end, I doused myself in TCP and that worked a treat.[5]

The moral of this tale is always to proceed slowly, on your big flat feet, when carrying buckets of dog poo down a slope.

---

5 Miss Livesey, my old head mistress at Rivington School, always smelled strongly of TCP and I am now wondering why!

23: Going International

Early in 2006, while exhibiting at Crufts, Ute Spatt approached us, who had travelled to the UK especially for Crufts.[1] She had noticed our big red wheaten boy, Ballyphelan Red Admiral—'Simba'—and wanted to know if we would be willing to let her and Margit Honsa[2] use him on Ailysh, one of the bitches they had bred—owned by Franz and Doris Schenkermayr. Ute and Margit admired Simba so much that they were willing to travel from Austria by car.

I did not know an awful lot about the Northern Forest Kennel, except for the fact that their dogs were well known for their health and longevity. This is an enormous plus in Irish Wolfhounds, so we were very interested. Unfortunately, during Simba's last heart test the cardiologist had detected an extra ectopic beat. This was not serious, but could mean he might possibly develop Atrial Fibrillation or Dilated Cardiomyopathy later in life. In common with most others breeders of Wolfhounds, we regularly test for health problems, trying our hardest to only breed from healthy dogs. Consequently, of course, Simba was not fit for stud. Although Ute was disappointed, she quite understood our reason. Noticing her disappointment, we asked if she would like to use Ballyphelan Boatswain—'Bo'sun'—instead, as his heart test was clear. We said we would send a copy of his pedigree for her and Margit to peruse and discuss. Ute agreed to this happily.

Eventually, in June of the same year, Franz and Doris brought over their adored bitch, Ailysh, to Bo'sun. In early September, she produced four puppies, and they kept a bitch, calling her 'Jemima'.[3] During their visit, the weather was glorious, and it was the start of our deep and lasting friendship. They have been back to see us many times over the years.

Franz and Doris kept begging us to visit them in Vienna, but it is hard to get time off together when you own a busy boarding kennels, especially when you do not employ any staff. John said that I should go, and he would stay at home and hold the fort. Bless him. In the past, I had talked to Franz and Doris about wanting to see the Viennese

---

1 *Of the Spatthausen kennel in Austria*

2 *Of the Northern Forest kennel*

3 *Ute selected the only male in the litter*

Christmas Markets, so they suggested I come in December. It was a deal.

In 2007, off I went to Vienna for a week on my own. It was truly magical, with everything covered in snow. Franz took me to a different market in Vienna every evening and even all the way to beautiful Salzburg to see the markets there. I just wish I could have afforded to buy some of the beautiful hand crafted items that were on sale. I loved the mulled wine they sold at the markets—the Viennese call it 'punch'—it warmed you right down to your toes. I still have the punch mug they bought for me at the Maria-Theresien-Platz market, to remind me that I had said that was where the best 'punch' was sold.

In 2009, John and I actually managed a holiday together, as Rachael came to look after the kennels and the wolfhounds for us. So on the 30th July, off we both went to Vienna. As before, during my original visit, Franz had arranged and timed an itinerary in his meticulous way. The number of places we visited during our stay was amazing. We had a lovely walking tour of Vienna on the 31st, made so much more interesting by Franz and Doris explaining everything, and knowing the best places to go. Our walk around Vienna included a tour of the most fantastic ice cream shops in the world.

We set out very early on the 1st August for the 200-mile journey to Salzburg. Part way there, we stopped at Mondsee to eat breakfast overlooking the lake. Then on to Salzburg, where we walked through the magnificent gardens of the Schloss Mirabell, took a stroll down the narrow, picturesque medieval Getreidegasse, which had shops to die for. Mozart had been born on this street, so we visited his birthplace, and then took a tour through the huge Feste Hohensalzburg, the 11th century castle overlooking the town,[4] which is reached by a cable railway. Everywhere we went, the wolfhounds Ailysh and Jemima came too. They even got into one of the little cable cars, and travelled up to the castle without turning a hair. They were not allowed inside the castle however, so Doris sat outside in the shade with them, while Franz took us on a tour of the interior. We all enjoy walking and history, so it was a wonderful day.

Setting out early again on the 2nd August, we travelled to the Wachau valley, famed for its vineyards and apricot plantations. Visiting Burgruine

---

4 Construction on this fortress began in 1077, and it was expanded numerous times right up to the 17th Century. Refurbishment began in the late 19th Century

Aggstein, a ruined castle high on the right bank of the Danube, we ate a picnic brunch in the courtyard. The view from the castle, looking down on the Danube wending its way through the valley, was breathtaking. Descending back down from the castle, we paid a visit to the magnificent Benedictine Abbey at Melk. Driving home through the valley, all the little houses we passed had apricot trees in their gardens, with the owners selling the fruits at the roadside. We stopped to buy two huge baskets of the heavenly, delicious, ripe, sweet, warm, plump and juicy fruit. They bore very little resemblance to the hard, tasteless objects that pass for apricots in UK Supermarkets.

When we arrived home, Franz and Doris's children, Matthias and Leonie, were back from their holiday with their Grandparents. We rounded off our lovely day all together, with a meal at Haus an der Weinstraße, near the ancient town of Modling. We had eaten so many apricots during the day, it is a wonder we managed to find room for anything else. However, we all managed to do justice to the lovely meal without much persuasion.

On the 3rd August, we paid a visit to Vienna Zoo and had a wonderful day. We were introduced to Ramon, who is a senior keeper on the Elephant Section. He is a friend of Doris and Franz—and has a wolfhound himself—and treated us to a 'behind the scenes' tour of the Elephant, Big Cats and Orang Utan sections, by their respective keepers. Most of them spoke a little English, but as Doris and Franz both speak excellent English, they translated when we wanted to ask questions. This visit to the zoo was incredibly special. Franz had gone to a great deal of trouble to arrange it for us, by seeking permission from the zoo authorities for our behind the scenes visits. It was such an extra special day.

After lunch on the 4th August, we took a boat trip down the Danube, which was just lovely. Following our river trip, we stopped for a meal at a very posh restaurant on the Kahlenberg, overlooking Vienna. The meal, though lovely, was a little expensive, and we all thought it was nowhere near as good as the food at the other restaurants we had visited.

On the 5th August, the day before we travelled home, we visited the Schloss Schönbrunn, the palace where the Emperor Franz Joseph and Empress Elizabeth[5] had lived. John and I took a guided tour inside part

5 *'Sisi'*

of the Palace, which is so huge it would have taken a week to see it all. We then walked around the beautiful gardens with Franz and Doris. A quick visit to the ice cream shop, on the way home, was our last adventure in what had been an amazing week with our wonderful hosts.

Bohemian Rhapsody

Opening my morning post one day, I was extremely pleased to receive an invitation from Edita Berasova to judge the Tullamore Cup competition, to be held on the 15th September 2012 in the Czech Republic. This is a show held every year for Irish Wolfhounds from all over Europe. The venue was a lovely campsite near the town of Trutnov, in sight of the Karkonosze—a mountain range straddling the Czech-Polish border in the North East—and is a truly beautiful area.

Doris and Franz kindly suggested that I spend a few days with them first. They would then drive me to the show, and stay for the weekend. So on September 11th, with case packed and John nagged—to the point of suicide—about the boarding kennel regime, my journey began.

On arrival at Manchester Airport, I said goodbye to John, not forgetting the last few nags, then left him with a look on his face that seemed to say, 'For God's Sake woman! Go!'

Passing through security, the scanner alarm went off as I walked through it. I was pulled to one side to be frisked very thoroughly, and then examined by a hand held metal detector, which went off as it reached my stomach. Confused at first, I suddenly realised why. Just as I was leaving home, my trouser zip had broken, and because all my decent pairs were already packed, I had quickly looked for a safety pin to hold the zip together. Unfortunately, all I could find was a truly enormous kilt pin. Acutely embarrassed, I lifted my shirt to show the security officer the offending item. As the security woman gazed at the enormous pin, I tried to make a joke of it. 'I hope that won't be classed as a lethal weapon!' I quipped. Her stony expression told me she had not found this at all amusing. I think they pick the most humourless people for this job. On the other hand, perhaps it is just that they get more than their fair share of idiots like me.

When I finally got through to pick up my hand baggage, I found it was sitting all alone on the 'naughty passenger' table. I knew had not left a water bottle inside, as I had on a previous occasion, so I stood and waited nonplussed for the security man to come over. He was still talking to the woman who had frisked me, who no doubt was telling him about the giant pin across my pants. When asked to empty my bag, I was surprised to find the offending item was a small stick deodorant shoved in a side pocket. This had to go through the x-ray machine to prove it was safe, and my bag had to go back through as well. Finally, I was waved on my way. Feeling like an utter fool, I vowed that I would double check everything for my return journey.

The flight to Vienna via Zurich was very pleasant. I had a two hour wait between flights in Zurich, so I thought that I would stretch my legs and gammy knee by having a stroll around the very posh shops. Looking at the ridiculously expensive clothes, I thought that some of them looked like ten year olds had made them in a sewing lesson at school. The two hours wait passed quickly, as Matt had kindly loaned me his Kindle and had downloaded four books for me.

Arriving in Vienna, and met by Doris and Franz, I was gasping for a cup of tea, and was soon whisked away back to their home. Franz, being his usual superefficient self, had again organized everything down to the last minute. It was so lovely to be with Franz, Doris and the children again, although the children—Matthias and Leonie—were going to stay with their Grandmother whilst we were away. I also had a wonderful welcome from the wolfhounds, Aylish, Jemima and Solo. Even Ginger, the cat, came to say hello.

As I was going to spend a few days with them before my judging appointment, they asked me if there was anything special I wanted to do in Vienna. I said that I would love to see the Gustav Klimt exhibition at Schloss Belvedere. Therefore, on the next day, off Doris and I went. What an artist Klimt was—it was simply amazing. One tends to think of Klimt's paintings such as *The Kiss*, and others of that style, but his portraits and paintings of the countryside are also incredibly beautiful. All the way around the exhibition, I was thinking of my friend Pat Crawshaw, who was a great fan of Klimt. She would have loved it.

I decided to hire English headphones for the exhibition, so Doris could enjoy it herself, without me nattering and asking for translations. I queued for ages at the counter, and when I eventually got there, they would not let me hire them without proof of identity—which I did not have with me. I had left my passport in my room, in case I lost it whilst 'out and about'. They suggested I put my backpack into the cloakroom, and they would take the ticket to hold as identity. Having no choice, I left the queue for the headphones, and joined the queue for the cloakroom. After depositing my backpack, and with ticket in hand, I queued for the headphones once more.[6]

After we had looked at the exhibition, I wanted to buy something for Pat Crawshaw from the shop. Unfortunately, my purse was still in my bag, in the cloakroom now located down three flights of stairs. Descending the stairs, and joining the cloakroom queue once again, for what seemed like an age, I finally retrieved my purse. Staggering back up the stairs, with my gammy knee now giving me hell, Doris and I had a spontaneous fit of giggling. It was the kind of giggling where you just cannot stop, and when you are out of breath produces the most peculiar noises, which only made us laugh more. It is a wonder no one came to escort us off the premises.

On the way home, Doris bought a big basket of wild mushrooms picked locally in the forest. For dinner, we had homemade veg and mushroom soup. It was delicious and, I am ashamed to say, I had far too many helpings. It was a lovely end to a lovely day and I climbed the stairs to bed, feeling happy and replete.

The next day, as a surprise, Doris and Franz had booked tickets for a then brand new enterprise called '2,000 VIENNA YEARS'.[7] This is a 5D cinema, where you are strapped into your seats as you travel through time in three dimensions. The sensation of rushing forward is amazing as the seats move, and you find yourself holding on for dear life as you whiz through the historical periods of Vienna of the past 2,000 years. Seemingly flashing through time, we passed through The Roman Occupation, The Turkish Siege, The Plague in the Middle Ages—where the sensation of rats running through our legs and over our feet made everyone scream—the Hapsberg Dynasty, the Mozart and Strauss eras. We went into a bunker during the allied bombing of WWII, and this part was very, very frightening. We flew through the establishment of the Austrian State Treaty, then up to the present day, where we found ourselves travelling around in a horse drawn carriage—except the carriage was flying above all the buildings. It was an amazing show, and we all

---

6 *Please Schloss Belvedere, hire more staff!*

7 *This was the first season of the 'Time Travel Vienna' attraction on Habsburgergasse.*

thoroughly enjoyed it.

In the evening, I was taken out to dinner at the Panorama Restaurant, up in the mountains overlooking Vienna. It is absolutely gorgeous, and had already become one of our favourite places to go when I visit. They only serve Austrian food, so I had to pretend reluctance when ordering my usual local rump steak on a bed of vegetables and herbs. It was so tender, so delicious and so large that when asked later if I would like a sweet, I declined at first. 'Perhaps though,' I thought. 'I could squeeze just a little ice cream into the corners…' Unfortunately, I had forgotten how big the servings were, and when my extravaganza of apricot ice cream arrived, there was enough to feed a family of ten. It was wicked to have to leave so much on my plate, but there was too much even for an ice cream addict like me. As I retired after another wonderful day, I knew that I had eaten just a little too much for my own good. At two o'clock in the morning, I became extremely thankful that I had packed my *Rennies*.

Early on Friday the 14th, we set out on our journey to Trutnov. Franz had kindly decided to take the scenic route across country, through lots of small towns and villages, so that I could see as much of the Czech countryside as possible. Arriving at the venue after a five and a half hour journey, we dumped our luggage in our allotted cabins and went for a walk around the lake with the dogs. We had only stopped once for a coffee on the way, and to let the dogs have a pee, so Jemima and Solo were more than glad to stretch their legs properly. Aylish had been left with friends, as she getting old now and was not up to long journeys anymore.

Many people had already arrived, and I was amazed to see dozens of Irish Wolfhounds all running loose, and happily interacting, whilst their owners unpacked their cars. As the site borders a forest, I was impressed that the dogs stayed within sight and sound of their owners. Most of the exhibitors had their families with them, so there were many children playing with the dogs, running in and out of the forest. I love children, so it was lovely to see them so free and happy, sliding down the banks and climbing trees. In the evening, we had a barbeque and everyone wore something with the colours of green, white and orange, to represent the Irish Tricolour.

Judging started at 9 am the next day, and I had an entry of 86 dogs. For the uninitiated, judging entails a head to toe, hands on examination of each dog, then watching how they move when they are told to run around the show ring—to ascertain that everything is as near to the breed standard as possible. Exhibitors had come from the Czech Republic, Poland, Germany, Slovakia, Austria and Russia. The quality was excellent, and I was thrilled to have a chance to judge so many lovely dogs. The final line up of all the class winners was very pleasing, and walking up and down the line—trying to decide who my ultimate winner would be—I just kept coming back to the Best Puppy winner, *Farchar Really Irish*. Such a stunning puppy, he was my choice for Best In Show. When I was able to study the catalogue, after judging was finished, I found out that he was one of a lovely litter by *Ch. Wolfhouse Toscanini* x *Ch. Dechtire Really Irish*. Some of his siblings had also been entered, and they too were lovely specimens of the breed. I did not finish judging until 5pm, as there were so many extra classes. These fun classes gave everyone a chance to win one of the amazing prizes that were up for grabs. I must give notable mentions to several people here: Petra, my highly efficient ring steward, who spoke amazing English and kept me running on time. Edita, who organized the show, took the photographs and kept everything outside the ring running smoothly and of course all the other helpers who worked so hard in the wings. I take my hat off to you all.

After judging, I was introduced to many breeders and owners I had only heard of before. It was so nice to meet them 'in the flesh', put faces to names and see their lovely dogs. Everyone seemed to have enjoyed themselves. I know I did.

I was due to give a talk at 7:30 pm that evening, but the restaurant was a little slow serving dinner, and everyone was feeling a little tired by now. Instead, it was decided that we should all sit round the tables, where I would pass around photos of past and present Ballyphelans. This worked really well, and many in-depth questions were asked, as well as fun ones. With Petra and Edita once again translating, I managed to get across what I wanted to say in an informal way, instead of lecturing. Some of the German people could speak Czech, some of the Czech people could speak Slovak and Polish, and some Polish people could get by in Russian, so it took a while for the questions to be asked and answered, as they passed through several layers of translation. Almost everyone spoke enough English to get by in basic sentences, but it was hilarious at times when the odd word was translated incorrectly.

After a highly enjoyable but tiring day, I finally said good night to everyone and retired to my cabin. It was a very nice cabin, as cabins go, but a lamp on the path right outside my bedroom window stayed on all night. As I am used to total darkness at home, it had taken me ages to get to sleep the night before, with the room illuminated like Blackpool Pier. I really needed a good night's sleep, so I took the duvet off the spare bed, dragged the chest drawers over to the window, climbed on top, opened the balcony windows at the top, and wedged the duvet in them. This worked a treat, but I forgot to remove it the next morning. I expect the cleaners were cursing me when they came to refresh the room.

The next day was the coursing competition, held in a huge field. All dogs entered were given numbers, drawn out of a bag, and two dogs at a time chased a lure[8] over quite a distance. The lure changes direction as the dogs chase it, and they are scored on their speed and cunning as they chase. Being a knock out competition, the winners of each chase are drawn against each other, until there is just one left. Quite a lot of the show dogs lure-course as well, and love it, getting so excited waiting for their turn. This is why most of the dogs I had judged were extremely fit, with excellent muscle tone. Wolfhounds are the most loving and gentle souls, but they are sight hounds, and it is their nature to run and chase. This is why, at home, our own fields are well fenced, as sheep surround us on three sides. Anything else that dares to show itself in our fields, be it rabbit, pheasant, mole, mouse or vole, is chased and very often caught and eaten there and then. We stayed and watched the coursing until lunchtime, then headed for home, as Doris and Franz had to pick up Aylish on the way from their friends Karin and Freddie.

Living in a large traditional house in the wine district in Lower Austria, Karin and Freddie's house is to die for, as it is full of beautifully carved traditional furniture. The flagged and marble floors are covered throughout with beautiful rugs, and everything is shiny and spotless—even with a houseful of Irish Wolfhounds. I just wanted to stay and live in that house forever. Aylish, though pleased to see us again, would have quite happily stayed with Karin and Freddie.

Just before lunch the next day, I was taken off to my favourite ice cream shop, and we sat at a pavement table in the sunshine, under a magnificent Horse Chestnut tree. There were lots of lovely, big shiny

8 *Most usually, a white cloth attached to a wire, pulled by an electric motor.*

conkers lying all over the pavement, and I could not resist picking up two huge ones and putting them in my pocket. After pigging out on numerous varieties of ice cream, we dashed back home, collected my luggage, then set off for the airport to catch my flight to Zurich. This time, I double-checked my hand luggage for contraband—and the pinned pants were now in my case—so after one last cup of coffee, saying a tearful goodbye to Doris and Franz, promising to visit again soon, I made my way to security.

I walked into the scanner, without a care in the world this time, but the alarm went off at full throttle. A woman, with a face like a funeral, then ran a hand held detector over me, which went off as she scanned my left boob. Oh my God! I thought. I must be radioactive from all the radiotherapy treatment two years ago. All I had in my breast pocket was a small packet of Kleenex tissues, which I removed and handed over. However, as I did so I could feel something hard inside. Then I realized what was in there. At the Klimt exhibition, I had bought two keyring fobs of his paintings, to clip onto my kennel key ring, and had stuffed them into the Kleenex packet. Putting them in the pocket of the clean shirt in my case, so I would not lose them, I had forgotten all about them. As this as was the only clean shirt I had left to wear, I had put it on for the flight home. The detector went off again as she scanned the tissues, so they were put in a box to be x-rayed. She continued down my shirt, and the detector went off again. This time, metal press-studs on my shirt were to blame. I had to open my shirt, to show there was nothing concealed, and then she went around my back and down my legs. As she went across my trainers, the detector went off again, due to the metal eyelets on the lace holes. So now, I had to take my trainers off, while she checked my feet. Finding no explosives between my toes, she came back up the front of my legs, her eyes stopping at the two large bumps in my trouser pocket. At her request I emptied the said pocket, and smilingly produced the beautiful, shiny horse-chestnuts I had picked up earlier. She looked like she wanted to slap me, and frankly, I would have wanted to slap me by now too, if I had been in her shoes.

'What is?' She asked.

'Conkers!' I said.

It is such a silly word that I just burst out laughing—though it does not take much to set me off. So, desperately trying to stop laughing—

and before I irritated the poor woman even more—I just shrugged my shoulders and she flounced off to x-ray the conkers. Of course, the scan showed they were harmless, so with a scowl she at last waved me through. I thought that perhaps she should have been a little more gracious, as after all, had I not been a good practice exercise? She should have been very grateful to me for making her boring day more interesting. Ye Gods! I thought. I am worse than one of our Kennel's nutty customers!

Putting my watch back on, I realised my gate would be closing in ten minutes, as all this palaver had taken such a long time. I ran—well I say 'ran', it was more of a fast toddle really—for what seemed like miles, and thankfully got there in time. Once on board I settled down with my Kindle. The change at Zurich went smoothly as always, and so leaving the sunshine behind I eventually arrived back in cold, wet miserable Manchester. I went through the 'Nothing To Declare' gate, trying not to look worried or guilty, and holding my breath just in case they pounced on me.

It had been a wonderful trip, with marvellous hospitality, especially from Doris and Franz. They had once again made an enormous effort to make my visit a memorable one. Thank you my dear friends, you are so special.

Note to self: *Triple* check baggage and pockets next time.

24: A Very Crafty Person

I have always loved making and designing things. One of my earliest memories is of sitting on the garden path as a tiny tot, armed with a very large claw hammer and a tin of nails, making patterns as I hammered the nails into the ground—then using the claw on the hammer to pull them up again. Apart from the odd bashed finger, I never really hurt myself and it helped my hand to eye coordination tremendously. There were no helicopter parents in those days.

At the start of the 1980s, I had knitted jumpers for the whole family with a pattern of Irish Wolfhounds on them. Taking note of these when seeing us out and about, friends in the breed were asking if I could knit one for them. Therefore, I decided to buy a knitting machine to cope with the requests. The orders came in thick and fast, and although I loved designing the patterns and logos, I never really took to the machine. The children told me, years later, that in the evenings when they were in bed, the constant 'ziz-ziz-ziz' noise as I knitted used to drive them mad.

Late in 1982, I had an order for twenty jumpers from a woman in the USA, who said that a friend of hers was going to be at Crufts in February 1983. She thought that perhaps if I was attending the show, I could give the jumpers to her friend personally and save on postage. I agreed to this, and began work on this large order. Once completed, I packed them all lovingly into boxes and stored them away, ready for delivery at Crufts 1983, which was now less than a two months away.

At the beginning of 1983, I had what I thought was a tummy bug that seemed to be going on forever, and I was feeling a little rough to say the least. Oh God, I thought, please do not let me be pregnant. I have to go to Crufts to deliver the jumpers! Ill or not though, I still made the journey to London, deciding that when I got back, if I was still poorly, I would go and see Dr Pepper.

At the station, I managed to manhandle the two large boxes of jumpers, and my case, onto the train. I had opted to travel first class, so was very comfortable and I slept most of the way. As I was staying at my sister Pat's house, two of my nephews, David and Jim—who both worked for the railways—met me at Euston Station. Once back at Pat's, I was tucked into bed and pampered by them all. I was dreading the journey to

Earls Court on the tube the next day, but Pat came with me and insisted we went by taxi instead. Finally, at the venue, the jumpers were safely delivered—and gratefully received—but I did not feel well enough to stay to watch the Wolfhounds being judged. I just wanted to crawl back into bed.

Once back home again, the nausea subsided but I was still feeling extremely odd. My brain and body seemed to be in overdrive, and I started to do the most peculiar things. One day, the coal bucket mysteriously went missing, and John found it in the cupboard under the stairs. Another day, instead of using the fireguard, I had placed a plastic clothesbasket in front of the fire—which melted all over the hearth. On yet another day, Rachael found a missing teapot in the bath and John once found me cleaning the windows at 3 o'clock in the morning.

We all thought my antics were hilarious, but I really thought I was going mad. Although I was feeling desperately tired all the time, I just could not keep still and was rapidly losing weight, even though I was eating enough to feed an army. John said that we would have to take out a second mortgage to be able to afford to keep me. My heart rate was so high at this point that it must have been nearly off the charts. At last, having struggled along for the best part of a year, I went to see Dr Pepper.

'What can I do for you, Mrs Zoo?' He said.

'You can shoot me!' I replied.

'Hold your arms out straight in front of you,' he said, looking at me appraisingly. 'Can you see the tips of your fingers trembling?'

I nodded.

'I believe you have Hyperthyroidism. But don't worry, we can fix that!'

After a blood test, and now with medication and beta-blockers, after a few weeks I was feeling a little better. However, by the end of the year I had not improved as much as Dr Pepper would have liked, and referred me to a specialist. When I went to see the endocrine specialist, he said—in a very sniffy voice—that Dr Pepper had been in touch with him and was not happy with my progress. An appointment for an operation would have to be made. Expecting to have to wait for up to 6 months, I believe Dr P had pulled some strings—because in January 1984 I went straight into hospital for a thyroidectomy.

For three days before my operation, I had to drink 45mls of neat iodine, twice a day.[1] Oh my God, the taste was indescribable and just lingers in your mouth forever. Through trial and error, I found the best thing to take the taste away was lashings of cold sweet tea. In hospital, I would ask for extra cups every time the tea-lady came round. The other women on the ward would also ask for extra cups, and then give them to me. I had to hoard them out of sight in my locker, as the ward cleaners would throw them away even when I asked them not to. One nurse, on opening my locker, nearly feinted when she saw the rows of paper cups full of cold tea. She thought I had lost the plot until I explained.

All the women on the ward were very nice, except one who was a really nasty piece of work—she swore and complained about everything. She was on a special diet, and every day when her lunch arrived, would remove the cover and shout, 'Where's my gravy? There's no f----- gravy!'

'For crying out loud!' We would all shout. 'Please give her some gravy to shut her up!'

This obstreperous woman objected to every procedure. One morning, when she had to have her bloods taken, she barricaded herself in by pulling her bed across the corner and holding her bedside chair across the bed, ready to defend herself against all assailants. She made the poor nurses' lives a misery. However, I was due to go into theatre that morning, so I never learned the outcome of that battle.

In the recovery room, when I awoke from my operation, I was shivering violently, and amazed to find myself wrapped in a foil survival blanket. Apparently, the heating was off in the theatres, and even in some of the wards—in the middle of January. I and two other women, who had had major operations themselves that morning, were shuttled by ambulance to the Infirmary in Chester. At every bump in the road on that journey, I thought my head was going to fall off, as it now seemed only attached to my body by the dozens of enormous clips across my throat.

Putting us all in a small side ward, on the gynaecology wing, the lovely nurses had warmed our beds with fan heaters, and put in hot water bottles for our feet. Oh, the blessed warmth of that bed was wonderful! The nurses then brought us a lovely hot, sweet cup of tea. We were chatting amiably to the ward sister, and just starting to enjoy feeling

1 Ingesting liquid Iodine reduces the blood supply to the thyroid gland, making it safer to operate on.

comfortable and warm, when we heard a commotion in the corridor. The ward doors opened suddenly, and two porters wheeled in the 'Where's my gravy' woman, swearing at the top of her voice.

All three of us said, as one voice, 'Oh no, please don't bring her in here!'

After explaining to the ward sister, much to our relief, she immediately arranged to have 'Where's my gravy' housed elsewhere. The nurses on that ward were just so caring with all their patients, that I cannot praise them enough. I moved onto the main ward in the evening, as there was a bed spare. The next morning, a little Irish nurse came on duty. As all the other women on this ward had had hysterectomies, she quickly noticed the incongruous gash across my throat.

'Oh, Holy Mother of God!' She said jokingly. 'The knife must have slipped!'

Everyone burst into fits of laughter, with me holding my slashed and clamped throat, and the other women holding their stitched abdomens. This nurse was such a funny, competent little soul, and everyone loved her immediately.

At visiting time, John and the children came to see me.

'When are you coming home Mum?' Matt asked. 'Dad makes lumpy Ready Brek, and he made me go to school in pink underpants!'[2]

Initially, John had taken a week's holiday while I was in hospital, but my stay had now lengthened. During the week, Dr Pepper had rung John to see how I was.

'She seems OK,' said John. 'But I'm worried, as I have to go back to work soon.'

'OK, John,' said Dr Pepper. 'I want you to come see me tomorrow.'

Unsure about why he needed to be there, John went to see Dr P the next day.

'How's your bad back?' Said Dr Pepper, looking at John with a poker face.

Nonplussed at first, the penny quickly dropped. 'Oh,' replied John, playing along. 'It's not too good.'

'In that case,' said Dr P. 'I'll give you a sick note for a fortnight. That should be time enough for it to right itself.'

Suddenly, John was able to be at home to look after the children, and

---

2 Due to a red football sock in with the whites

be there to help me when I came out of hospital. Seeing Dr P a few weeks later, I thanked him.

'Ah well, you see Mrs Zoo,' he said. 'Now and again I will tweak the rules for hard working folk, who are not at the surgery every five damned minutes.'

I smiled, and thanked him again.

'But,' he said, tapping his nose. 'It's our secret, don't forget.'

I always have a craft project on the go, and love cross-stitch, embroidery, sewing and knitting. I had always wanted to learn to spin, so soon after moving to Wales—thirty years ago now—I was taught to spin by two very talented and patient ladies, Peggy and Margaret, from the local craft group. Along the way, I also learned about the many breeds of sheep, and the vast difference between their fleeces. My favourite fleece to spin came from Blue Face Leicesters, and I knitted myself a very nice jumper with the resulting wool.

I was absolutely thrilled when our craft club included me in their team to represent Caernarfon, in the Spinners and Weavers Guild Gwynedd finals at the North Wales Show. Each team had eight members, and from a raw fleece each team had to card, spin and ply the wool, then knit a child's jumper from a pattern supplied by the judge—all in just five hours. The pattern also specified what ply the wool had to be, and to what tension we had to knit.[3]

At first we all carded the raw wool, which entails pulling lumps off the fleece, then combing it between two wired paddles—until it was all knot free, and lying in the same direction—then rolling the wool with our hand against our knee into a loose cylinder shape. When we had just enough fleece carded to begin spinning, it was given to Peggy and Margaret—the two best and fastest spinners—who got cracking on spinning. When enough fleece had been carded for the rest of the team, we all started spinning. When enough spun wool was ready to begin the knitting, I started to knit, because I was the fastest knitter. As soon as enough wool had been produced for everyone, four of us knitted and four kept on spinning. We were extremely pleased to come second out of nine teams, as we had worked so well together. It was such a lovely, happy, fun day. I remember it with great fondness.

---

3 In knitting, tension is defined by the number of stitches and rows per inch

About twenty years ago, while browsing through the craft magazines in W.H. Smiths, I came across one called *Dolls House World*. On the cover was a picture of a tiny little kitchen table, with the most realistic little items of food displayed on it. Fascinated, I bought the magazine and discovered a whole new craft world. After looking at all the different projects—ranging from making furniture to furnishings and dolls—the miniature food was the one that really excited me. I just had to have a try at making it.

The miniature food items are made from polymer clay, and I mostly use the *Fimo* brand. It comes in wonderful colours, and can be blended to make the exact shade you want. It sounds easy, but I had many disasters and a lot of wasted clay before I got it right. The first items I made when I started—which I thought were wonderful at the time—now make me cringe. I had bright green apples, eye-bogglingly bright yellow bananas, pillar-box red meat and so on; they were all terrible colour blends, out of scale and very childlike. Like with everything, practice makes perfect.

As the final process to finish a piece, the clay needs baking at 130°F to harden it off. This process was a learning curve in itself, as the baking times all depend on the thickness of the items. One day, I forgot about the items I had hardening in the oven, and they burned to a crisp—filling the kitchen with smoke and fumes. The fumes from polymer clay are extremely toxic, so it was not a mistake I made a second time.

When I first took up my new hobby, I would make little items of this and that, which is so time wasting. The way I work now is to concentrate on one or two items of the same type, and make a whole batch. Therefore, I will have a cabbage and cauliflower session, or a meat, fish, bread or cake session. When I have many different items made, I will have a dressing session for tables and kitchen preparation boards or shop displays. These items sell well at craft fairs, and very often people who do not even have a dolls house will buy an item to put into a display cabinet.

There are some very serious collectors of dolls houses out there. Many have houses ranging from the Tudor period up to the modern day. The food for these collectors, therefore, has to be accurate, realistic and to scale, and I had great fun researching the different eras. The Tudor period was very interesting, and I found some weird, wonderful and outright disgusting concoctions at the wealthy end of Tudor cuisine. However, the poor people lived mostly on 'pottage', where anything they had went into a single pot over the fire, to be eaten with coarse brown bread.

I also love making items for miniature shops, and a few years ago was commissioned to make a shop for the local butcher, which he now displays on his counter. This has brought him extra trade, as the local children drag their mothers into the shop to see it. The mothers then of course feel obliged to buy something, once they are inside.

I used to have a stall at many Craft Shows and Dolls House Fairs. I would do very well, very often meeting and selling to the same regular customers. My daughter, Rachael, would sometimes come and do a stint on the stall with me. At certain venues, we needed eyes in the backs of our heads, watching for two women known to have 'light fingers' who would regularly prowl some of these events. We knew who they were however, so word would pass from stall to stall to watch out for them. These women would walk around first to look at the stalls, deciding what to steal. Hardly ever would they be caught, as they worked together—one would buy a small item to distract you, while the other one helped herself. If I did spot them approaching, I would pointedly go and stand at the front of my stall. This put them off, so they would glide off to try their luck somewhere else. They always went for the unusual and more expensive items, and when there are many people around your stall, it is impossible to watch everything that is going on. Sometimes stallholders, who had more than one person working on their stalls, were able to spare someone to police the event. They took it in turns to follow these women around, practically breathing down their necks so they knew we were aware of them. When looking at these two well-dressed, middle-aged women you would never have suspected that they were thieves.

Although I mainly make food items, sometimes I will make a room box. This is wooden box open at the front, and sometimes at the top. The interior can be a shop, a room in a house, a garden or even a tiny garden shed full of paraphernalia—the subjects are limitless. I decided to make one resembling a Victorian farmhouse pantry, and enter it in the craft section at the North Wales Show, with the title 'Pantri Nain'.[4] On the evening before the show, I was putting the finishing touches to it. All I had left to do was to stick on the little wooden doorframe, around the false door on the back wall. I reached into my workbox for the tube of

4 *'Granny's Pantry'*

wood glue I thought knew was there, to realize that it only existed in my imagination. Panic set in. What the hell could I do? It had to be finished, as I had an early start for the show next morning.

As it was getting late, I thought cogitating in the bath would help me come up with a solution. Lying in the bath, muttering to myself, I suddenly had a 'Eureka' moment. The answer, of course, was *Super Glue.* I shot out of the bath—well, it's more of a slow creaking exit these days—to finish the piece. Not bothering to get dry or dressed, I just flung on a bathrobe. With the robe edges flapping, I dashed to the kitchen, praying there would be a tube of *Super Glue* in John's 'useful drawer'. Hallelujah! There was a new unopened tube. Cradling the precious tube, I went back up to my workroom in the cog loft.

Anyone familiar with Super Glue will know that the tubes are rather small, so when making a hole in the tube, I made it a little too large—consequently using far too much glue. However, I stuck the doorframe in place quickly and, without thinking, went along its edges with my fingertips to remove the excess glue. I then went to wipe my hands on my apron as usual. Only there was no apron, of course. Just nice, bare pink skin. I sat for a few seconds in quiet disbelief, staring at the fingers of both my hands—which were now firmly superglued to my thighs.

John was away visiting his Mum, so I could not call for help and I had no clue how to unstick myself. There must be information on the tube, I thought. Unfortunately, it was the wrong way up, and my hands were out of action, so picking up a craft knife with my mouth, I flipped the tube over—only to watch it fall and land on the floor. Bending down as far as I was able, I still could not read the instructions, so now it was a case of having to get down onto the floor myself. It is very tricky trying to kneel down, when your hands are stuck to your legs, so I sat on the armchair and slowly slid down the front, until my bottom touched the floor. I shuffled across to the glue tube, which thankfully was now instruction side up, but also oozing copiously into the carpet. Still unable to read the writing, I rolled onto my side so an eyeball would be right up to the tube—praying that my nose and face would not come into contact with the pool of glue. I had a vision of the headline in the local paper:

Missing Mad Woman's Dead Body
Found In Loft Glued To Carpet

At last, after managing to read the instructions, I discovered that in order to unstick myself, I needed either acetone or vegetable oil. I did not have acetone, but there was a bottle of Flora oil in the kitchen, so now all I had to do was get down the stairs. Needing to stand up, I figured the best way was to shuffle on my bottom across to the door, which thankfully was still open. By sitting sideways, placing my feet a few steps down and pressing my back against the wall, I managed partially to stand up. As the treads on the loft stairs are quite narrow, we normally go up and down sideways. Therefore, by bending down, and sticking my elbows out as far as I was able, for balance, I made it down sideways to the back hall without breaking my neck.

The journey to the kitchen was easy, as I could open doors on the way by pressing my chin on the handles. Once there, I stopped for a moment to work out my next move. Plan One was to just try pulling my hands free, and although I am sure I could have done it with brute force, it would have removed my fingers tips and been extremely painful. I quickly cancelled Plan One. Racking my brain as to how I was going to pour oil onto my hands, I realized that whatever the solution was, it was going to make one hell of a mess.

Plan Two it was then.

I thought the best thing would be to get into the bath, as it would be much easier to clean up afterwards. However, first I had to get the oil somehow. So grabbing a spoon from the sink using my mouth, and holding it in my teeth, I was able to flick open the cupboard door containing the Flora. Bending down and picking up the bottle with my mouth, gripping it firmly in my teeth—and gagging at the taste of oil—I knew I would have to remain bent double to carry it any distance. Giving an excellent impression of Quasimodo, waddling back to the downstairs bathroom, I placed the oil bottle on the loo seat. I then moved the bathroom chair towards me with my feet, and sitting on it, swung my feet into the bath. Then by swinging my body back and forth, I gained enough momentum to stand up. I had thought that perhaps I could wedge the bottle between the taps, and unscrew the top with my teeth to let the oil pour over my hands—but there was too much space to wedge it tightly. I realised that the only way I could manage it, was to lie down in the bath, and by picking the bottle up with my feet, allow the oil to pour down my legs until it reached my hands. Therefore, pushing the plug in with my toes, and leaning over the end of the bath, I picked the bottle up from the loo seat with my mouth. Pressing it against the side of the bath with my knees, I unscrewed the top with my teeth then placed it between my feet and ankles. However, lying down was far more difficult than I had anticipated, as I could only get part way down. I just had to let myself go with a wallop, cracking my head on the other end of the bath in the process. Thankfully, the oil was still upright.

As the bath is cast iron it was freezing cold, so turning the taps on with my toes, I let my poor, cold aching body lie for a while in the glorious hot water. Eventually, lifting the bottle with my feet, I was able to pour enough oil down my right leg to reach my right hand. After a few minutes, it was free. The rest was easy once I had one usable hand, and after an application of oil directly on the correct spot this time, my left hand was free as well. After washing the oil off myself and cleaning the bath with gallons of washing up liquid, I finally got rid of the oil slick. Hells Bells! I thought. What a palaver! By now wishing that I had never entered the damned craft show.

It was now well past midnight, and I was cold again, worn out and now smelling sweetly of lavender soap—with just a hint of Flora Oil. Off I toddled to bed, with two hot water bottles, a cup of hot chocolate and a lump on my head the size of an egg—vowing in future to treat the dreaded *Super Glue* with more respect, if I ever had occasion to use it again.

I did not tell John when he came home, as it would have just confirmed his suspicion that I am totally loopy.

25: The Tail Ends

The kennels are still in business, but we do not take in rescue dogs anymore. We will carry on for as long as we can, as I do not relish living on just our pensions.

I judged in Sweden in 2018, and the Boston Championship Show near Peterborough in January 2019. I made the decision that those will be my last judging appointments, at home or abroad.

John had been asked to judge the Irish Wolfhound Club Open Show in 2020. At the time he said that he would, as long as he is still alive and standing upright. However, due to the Coronavirus restrictions there have been no dog shows held in the UK since March. Other countries have managed a few, but certainly not the usual number.

With almost no shows being held in 2020, the Irish Wolfhound Database decided it would be fun to hold an International Photo show for veteran hounds via the internet.

I was honoured to be asked to judge some of the classes along with 4 other international judges. The judges were:

- Lloyd Simmons, Canada — 7-8 year olds
- Pam Sumner, UK — 8-9 year olds
- Deborah Sanders, USA — 9-10 year olds
- Velda Clark, Ireland — 10 + years
- John Lewington, Australia — Breeder classes and Best in Show

I thoroughly enjoyed sitting at home judging my allotted classes. It was not at all the same as a proper 'hands on' assessment, but most of the photos of the side view of each hound were very clear—so I was very happy with my placements.

My choice for the best exhibit from the 8-9 year classes was:

Anna Vydra B&G (*Santir Vincent* x *Vianho Dama*)
Breeder: J Biljan
Owner: Edita Berasova

My critique read as follows:

"This beautiful quality bitch is all sweeping curves. Lovely head on a well arched neck. Excellent front assembly. Strong well angulated hind quarters, with good length of second thigh and low hocks. Excellent tight, well knuckled feet."

I was delighted when she was awarded Best In Show in an entry of 250 hounds. I was doubly delighted when I looked up her pedigree on the database, after the show, to find she had a little bit of Ballyphelan in her breeding.

I write this ending sitting at the kitchen table, with wolfhounds lying fast asleep and snoring all around me, and proudly looking at the walls covered in Kennel Club Certificates, Breeder Awards, Best in Show awards, Best of Breed awards, Champion Certificates and Challenge Certificates. I am also looking at the pictures of our children and grandchildren, squashed in between all the dog paraphernalia, who have brought so much love and laughter into our lives. I am reminded of something Matthew said to me once, 'How come the dogs always get fed before us?'

I have been so lucky to have had such a happy life, with the ups far outweighing the downs. Of course having a sense of humour, and being just slightly weird and wacky has helped tremendously.

Fig. III-1 The Author, with hand-reared Red Panda, Chester Zoo, July 1969.

Fig. III-2 The Author with Billy Goat, and John with Finn, our first Irish Wolfhound

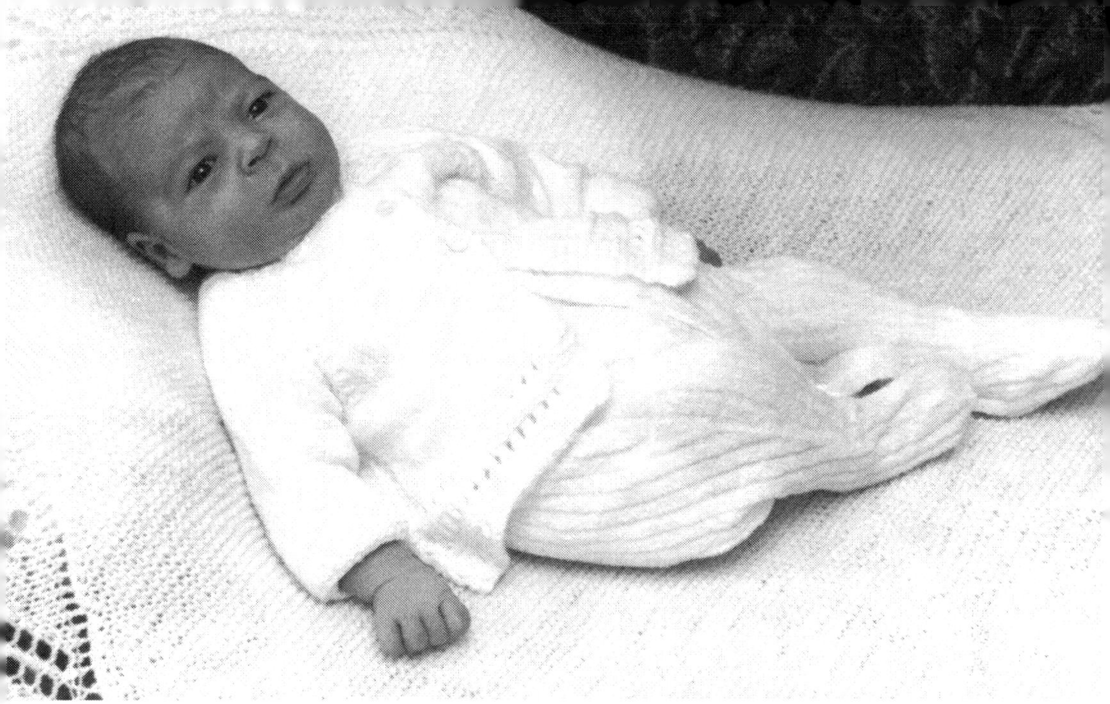

Fig. III-3 Christopher John, 2 Weeks Old, 25th February 1970

Fig. III-4 Finn, with baby Chris and Shetland Sheepdogs: Muffy, Blue and Simon, John's Mum's house, Upton-by-Chester, 1970

Fig. III-5 Christopher John, with our dogs, Marsh Lane Caravan Park, Frodsham, 1970. Dogs from left: Shetland Sheepdogs - Blue, Muffy. Irish Wolfhound - Finn

Fig. III-6 Chris, aged 16 months.

Fig. III-7 Rachael & Chris, not smiling at the photographer, 1972

Fig. III-8 Rachael, aged 8 months, and Chris, aged 2½, Summer 1972

Fig. III-9 Rachael, aged 3, with 'Flat Rabbit', 1975

Fig. III-10 Chris & Rachael, on Chris' first day at school, January 1975

Fig. III-11 Chris, Rachael and Finn, 1976

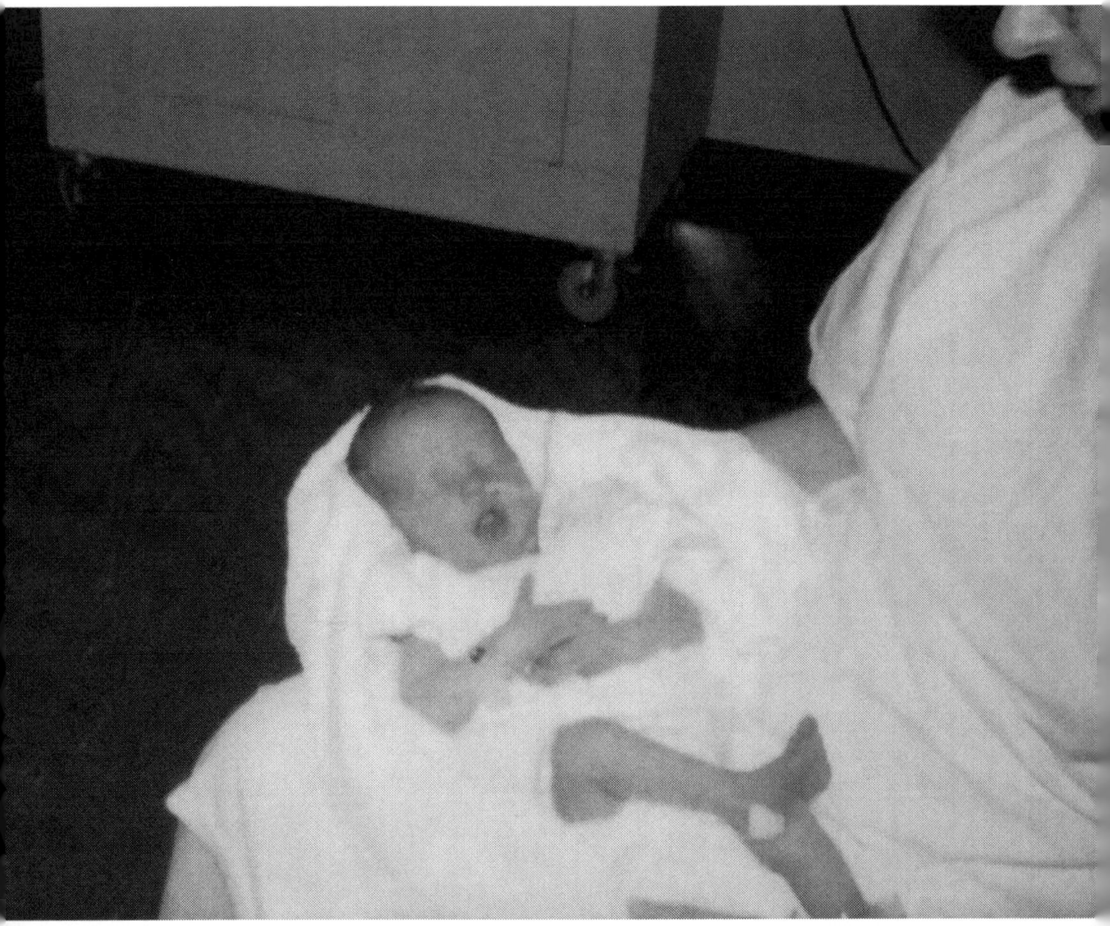

Fig. III-12 The Author, holding Matthew, SCBU, December 1976

Fig. III-13 From back-left: Marge (Dick's wife), John, The Author. From front-left: Matt, Rachael, Chris. Chester Zoo, 1978

Fig. III-15 Chris, Matt and Rach, bathed and ready for bed, Aston-by-Sutton, 1978

Fig. III-14 Matt, with no shoes or pants on again, Aston-by-Sutton, 1979

Fig. III-16 Rach, Matt and Chris, Matthew's 3rd Birthday Tea, Aston-by-Sutton, December 1979

Fig. III-17 Rach, Chris and Matt, with Casey, Aston-by-Sutton, 1980

Fig. III-18 Chris, Matt and Rachael, snowed in at Aston Lane, Aston-by-Sutton, 1981

Fig. III-19 Rachael, Matt and Chris, Matthew's first day at school, Aston-by-Sutton, September 1982

Fig. III-20 Matthew, mischief personified, October 1982

Fig. III-21 Matthew, sitting with Kerry's litter, Aston-by-Sutton, 1982

Fig. III-22 Rachael with Matthew, coming home after his first day at school, Aston-by-Sutton, 1982

Fig. III-23 Matt (Celtic warrior) and Fergus (Irish Wolfhound), winning first prize for Fancy Dress, Irish Wolfhound Club Rally, 1984(ish)

Fig. III-24 Rach, Matt and Chris, Windemere, Lake District, 1985

Fig. III-25 Matt, singing solo at Aston Village School, Aston-by-Sutton, 1985

Fig. III-26 The Village School, Aston-by-Sutton,

Fig. III-27 St Peter's Church, Aston-by-Sutton. © Church of England - Diocese of Chester

Fig. III-28 Hafod Lwyfog entrance

Fig. III-29 Arial view of Hafod Lwyfog

Fig. III-30 View from Hafod, looking South West

Fig. III-31 View from Hafod, looking North West, showing the Irish Sea and Newborough Beach, Anglesey

Fig. III-32 Matt, aged 13, in the living room at Hafod, not long after moving. Hafod Lwyfog, Gwynedd, Wales, 1990

Fig. III-33 Rach, with Berwick, Hafod Lwyfog, Gwynedd, 1990

Fig. III-34 Sunset across the Irish Sea, seen from Hafod

Fig. III-35 Haymaking in Hafod meadow

Fig. III-36 Matt, visiting with his Uncle Dick, Nova Scotia, Canada, 1991

Fig. III-37 Pat, relaxing at Hafod with Kizzy looking on, 1991

Fig. III-38 John, master builder, building the kennels, Hafod Lwyfog, 1991

Fig. III-39 The kennels, completed and occupied, Hafod Lwyfog, 1993

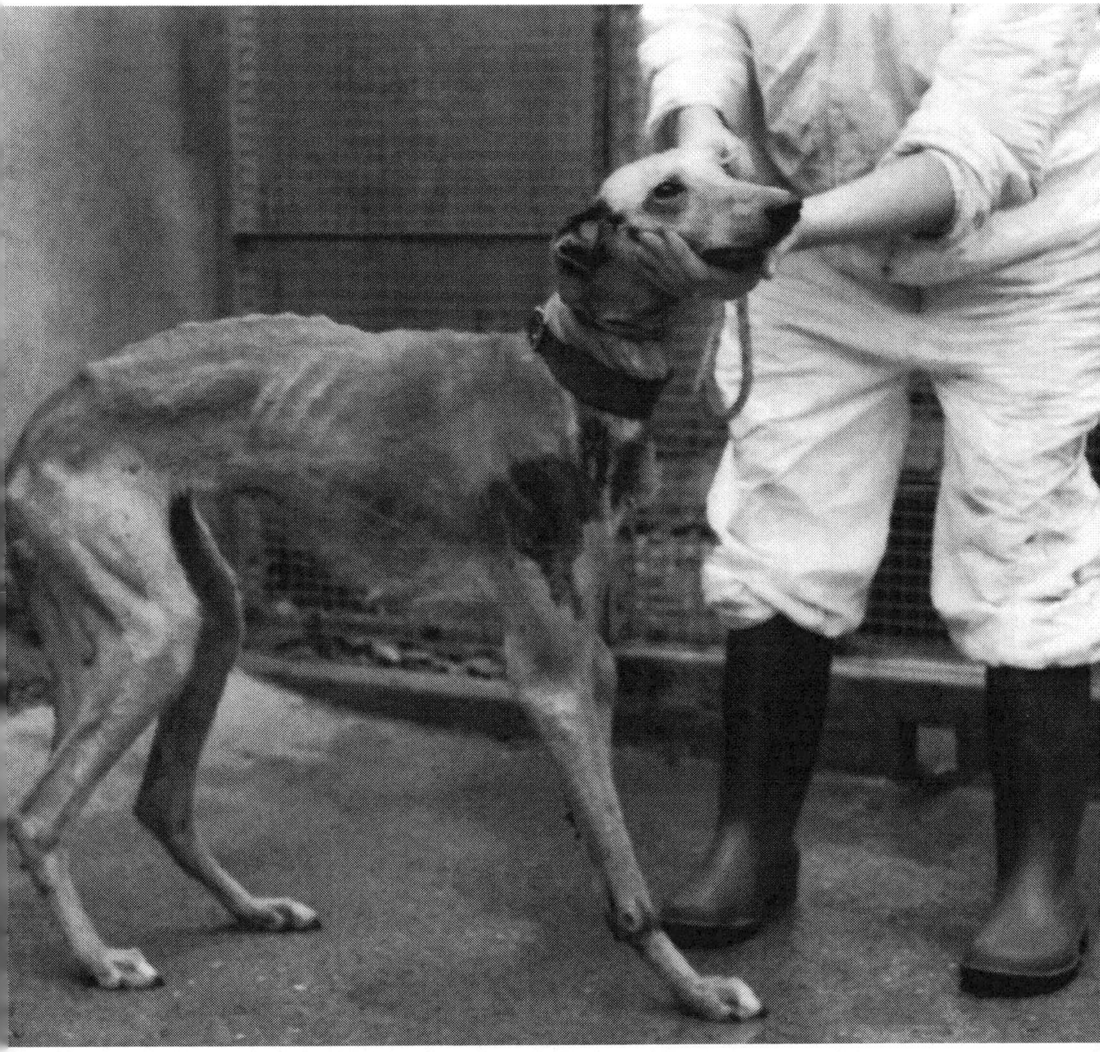

Fig. III-40 Faith, the rescue Greyhound, being helped to stand by the Author, one week after coming to Hafod. The dark patches on her skin are Terramycin Wound Spray (antispetic)

Fig. III-41 Faith, the rescue Greyhound, restored to full health, four months after coming to Hafod.

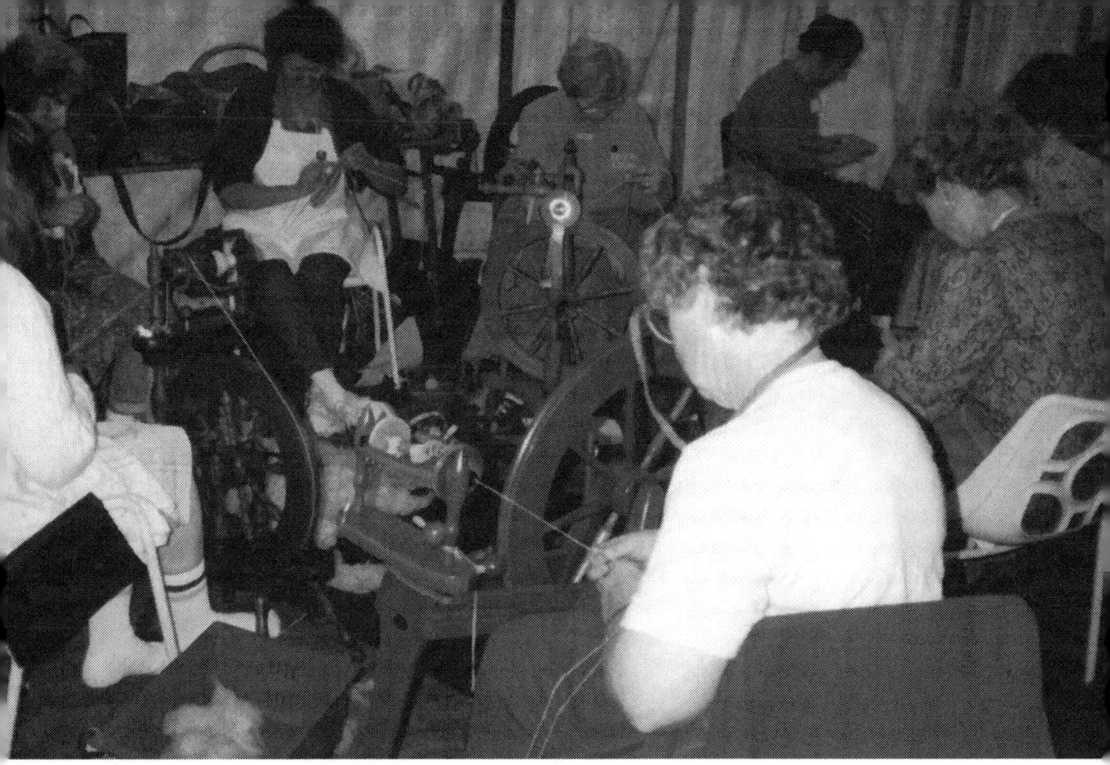

Fig. III-42 The Author, third from the left, North Wales Show, Spinning & Knitting Competition, Caernarfon, 1991

Fig. III-43 Baby Knitwear, knitted by the Author whilst waiting for grandchildren

Fig. III-44 Doris, Franzi, Children and Wolfies

Fig. III-45 Birth Sampler, crafted by the Author for her first grandson William, 1999

Fig. III-46 Birth Sampler, crafted by the Author for a commission, 2015

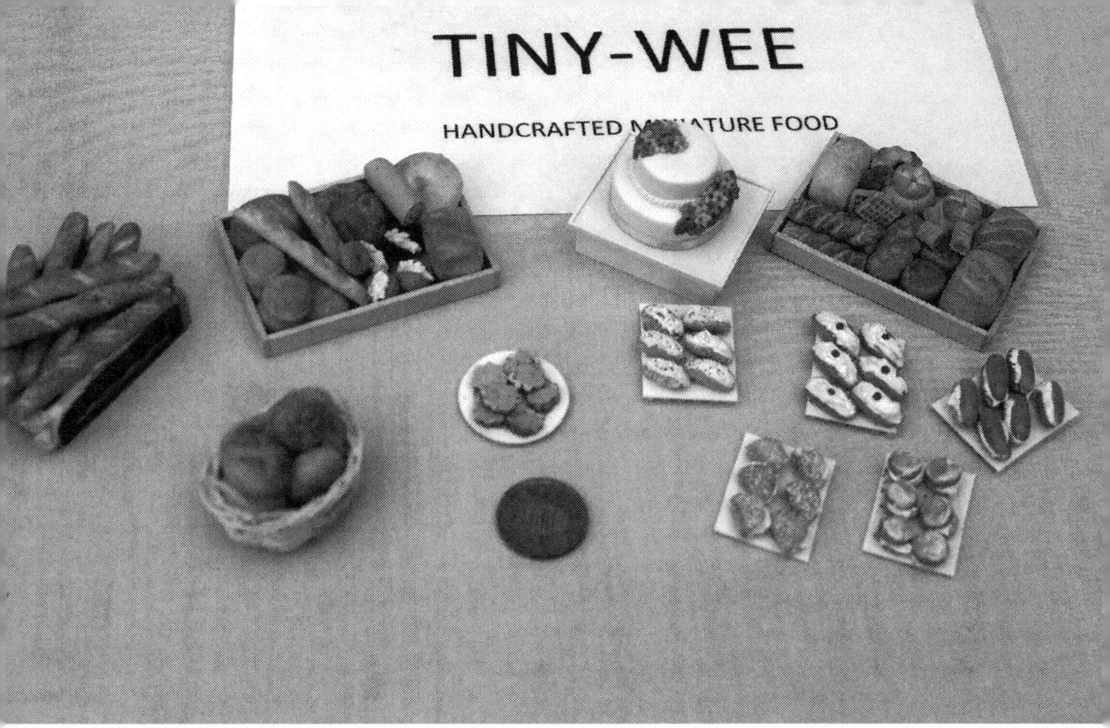

Fig. III-47 Cakes, Bread & Pastries, Handcrafted Miniature Food

Fig. III-48 Cheese & Meat shop counter displays, Handcrafted Miniature Food

Fig. III-49 Cheese Counter, Handcrafted Miniature Food

Fig. III-50 Beehive, Rhubarb and vegetable barrow, Handcrafted Miniature Food

Fig. III-51 Grocer's market barrows, Handcrafted Miniature Food

Fig. III-52 Assorted kitchen boards, Handcrafted Miniature Food

Fig. III-53 Victorian kitchen, Handcrafted Miniature Food

Fig. III-54 Fishmonger, Handcrafted Miniature Food

Fig. III-55 Basket of mushrooms, Handcrafted Miniature Food

Fig. III-56 Rachael, holding new-born William, the Author's first grandchild, Hospital, 1999

Fig. III-57 The Author's grandsons, William, aged 10 and Josua, aged 7, 2009

Fig. III-58 Chris and Matt, Ty Coch, Porthdinllaen, 2013

Fig. III-59 Rachael at hound show, 2013

Fig. III-60 Josh, aged 15 and William aged 17, at Hafod, 2016

Fig. III-61 Matt's 40th Birthday Bash, Bangor, Wales, 2016. From left: Chris, Will, John, the Author, Josh, Mandy (Chris's wife), Rach, Matt

Fig. III-62 Chris, with his wife Mandy, at home in Kirkby, Christmas, 2018

Fig. III-63 Kayleigh, the Author's step-granddaughter, in her ACF Sergeant fatigues, holding her award from the Lord Lieutenant of Merseyside, 2017

Fig. III-64 Tom, the Author's step-grandson, with his fiancée Laura, New York, 2017

Appendices

I: Snippets and Scraps

Here are just a few odds-and-ends that I could not quite shoehorn into the book without disturbing the flow too much. Nevertheless, they deserve a place, so here they are…

§

Whilst still living in Frodsham, one day Chris, Rachael and I were waiting to catch the Chester bus. Rachael would have been about four years old at the time. My heart sank when an old lady we knew from the village, Miss Sephton, joined the queue. The dear old soul had quite a lot of facial hair, and I knew that Rachael would not be able to contain herself without commenting.

'You are not to say anything nasty about her beard!' I whispered to Rachael. 'She can't help it, and it makes her sad when people say cruel things.'

When our bus arrived, we hopped on and went to sit on the bench seat at the front. To my dismay, Miss Sephton came and sat opposite us. Rachael kept flashing the most cherubic smiles at her, and I kept flashing warning looks at Rachael, knowing she was gearing up for a comment. It was a such a relief when we reached our stop without incident, and we stood up to get off the bus. However, as we passed Miss Sephton, Rachael placed a friendly hand on the old lady's knee.

'I think your beard is very lovely,' she said, looking up at her angelically. 'It's just like our dog's, only longer!'

§

'Oh!' Said Chris, aged five, on being told that his Aunty Margy was expecting a baby. 'I didn't know she had been in season!'

§

Chris, aged eight, had been expressing an interest in the breeding process of the dogs and although he knew about mating, he had never actually seen one close up. When asked if he would like to be present at the next one, he replied that he would, so we allowed him to watch.

'Is that it?' He said, after the mating was over. 'Well, yuck! I am telling you now that I am never, never, ever getting married!'

§

Getting onto the Chester bus with Matt, aged three, I realized that, unfortunately, the only empty seat was next to an old man with a wart on his nose. Matt could not take his eyes off it, so during the journey I desperately tried to distract him. I really thought I had succeeded. However, as the old man got up to get off Matt said to him, 'You won't pick that spot will you?'

§

At the 1979 Irish Wolfhound Club Championship Show, we were standing at the ringside watching the judging. John had Matthew, aged two and a half, on his shoulders. Standing in front of us was a man with a perfect Monk's tonsure. Matt was staring at the very pink, very shiny baldhead poking up above the hair, looking very puzzled. Then he leaned forward, patted the dome with an outstretched hand and asked, 'Is this a little bit of man?'

§

Chris and Rachael had always had a special bond and rarely quarrelled. They loved their little brother most of the time, but found him extremely hard going at times. One day, when Matt was about five—after yet another serious telling off from me—I could see their point. This time Matt had painted, and ruined, some of Christopher's very special and pristine Corgi cars with green enamel modelling paint. He had very thoughtfully spread newspaper on the bedroom carpet before commencing the task though. I was absolutely furious with him, and after his telling off, he informed me that he was going to run away because, as he put it, 'There's no laughing in this house!'[1]

He stomped off upstairs to pack his little suitcase—one of his many Car Boot Sale treasures, bought for ten pence. I found him a little while later sitting on the hall chair, with his hat and coat on and his case packed. Casey was lying at his feet and the Shelties, Muffy and Blue, had also joined the merry band.

'Hello,' I said. 'I thought you were leaving home?'

'I haven't had my tea yet!' He said indignantly, looking at me as if I were an idiot.

At teatime, he came to the table carrying his case, and still wearing his hat and coat. After tea, I told him he would have to run away on his own, as the dogs would be staying.

'Oh well,' he said, giving a big sigh. 'It's too dark to find my way now, so I'll have to stay.'

§

One morning, Matthew was misbehaving at the breakfast table. I told him to go and stand in the hall, and only to come back when he could behave himself. After a few minutes, he strolled nonchalantly back into the room, as if nothing had happened, and got back up to the table.

'Oh good,' he said, taking the top off his boiled egg. 'I timed that perfectly. My egg is exactly the right temperature to eat now.'

§

Although Matthew, as a small boy, was an absolute little terror, he was always polite and good mannered with adults—and an unfailingly kind little boy to anyone in need. He would stand his ground with much bigger boys, and always go to the rescue of any child being bullied—or any animal, bird, worm or creepy crawly that he thought was being treated cruelly. He was such a confident, outgoing little chap he made friends easily and was very popular at school.

Once Chris and Rachael reached their teenage years, they preferred to stay at home when we went to dog shows. Therefore, from the age of

---

1 This is yet another of Matt's sayings that the family have used ever since, to indicate when someone's sense of fun and humour fails them.

about eight, it was just Matt, John and I. Shows were held indoors in the winter, and very often, there would be an elderly lady or two who had come into the venue for company and warmth. Matthew would inevitably attach himself to one of these ladies, who he thought looked lonely, and would sit chatting to her. We would see him across the hall, arms waving in the air, as he animatedly related some very exciting and interesting stories to his elderly friend, who would be laughing at his tales. At lunchtime, he would come and ask me for money to buy her a cup of tea, and would then share his packed lunch with her. I got so used to this that I started to pack extra sandwiches. Twice a year at the Bolton Show, and at the Heywood and Radcliffe Show, he would renew his acquaintance with the same elderly lady. There was genuine pleasure on both their parts when they saw each other again.

After his very first encounter with this lady, I had asked what it was they talked about. He told me he talked about all the things we had done, and she told him all the exciting things she had done during the Second World War. She also told him, 'I wish my grandson was nice like you, and not a horrible little shit!'

Of course, like all small boys, he loved the excuse to repeat the word 'shit' as many times as he could get away with when retelling the tale. I shudder to think what juicy family secrets the perceptive little brat revealed during these conversations.

§

At the Bolton Show, on New Year's Day in 1979, I was at the ringside watching the Any Variety Hound class, standing behind two old dears who had probably come into the venue for warmth and company. John was in the ring with Casey, and standing at the end of the line behind the other exhibits, who all happened to be Dachshunds. The old dears were watching the judge lift up each exhibit, one by one, for examination. It was just getting near to Casey's turn for examination, when one turned to the other.

'Come on Phyllis, let's go an' get a cup o' tea.' She said.

'Nay Kitty. 'Ang on a mo.' Said Phyllis. 'I want t'see 'ow they get that big bugger ont table.'

'See yon?' Said Kitty. 'That's an Irish Wolf that is!'

'Ee, never!' Said Phyllis. 'I wonder 'ow they got it 'ere, all that way from Ireland?'

§

At the same show, again at ringside—this time watching an Any Variety Terrier class—I was standing next to a group of old dyed-in-the-wool terrier men. Sitting directly in front of us was a middle-aged woman, who was very loudly making derogatory comments about the dogs and the standard of judging. After a while, one of the old men leaned over, and tapped the man sitting next to the woman on the shoulder.

'Hey mister,' asked the terrier man, pointing at the woman. 'Is she thine?'

The man nodded.

'Well,' said the old chap. 'Tek the bugger 'ome!'

II: The Ballyphelan Story

As I write this, John and I have owned and loved Irish Wolfhounds for 54 years. Back in 1966, and wanting our first Wolfhound, we wrote to Sheelagh Seale, the owner of the Ballykelly Kennels in Ireland. She had no puppies for sale at the time, so she put us in touch with Mr & Mrs Leet, of the Samando Kennels in Sibford Gower, Oxfordshire. They had a litter by *Montebello Prince Of Boroughbury* x *Samando Petronella*. We went to view the litter when they were five weeks old. John decided to buy a grey brindle male, and at eight weeks old he came home to us. He cost 40 Guineas, which was a tremendous amount of money for a badly paid young zookeeper to spend.

Samando Pluto, or 'Finn', as we called him, was predominately of Sulhamstead, Sanctuary and Boroughbury lines. He was not a great specimen of the breed, by any means, but we thought he was perfect and adored him.

On holiday in 1967, we made an appointment and travelled down to see Elsie James, the owner of his sire, and ask her opinion of Finn. We were expecting her to say that we should show him, and that he would probably go Best in Show at Crufts. After looking at him and scratching her head for a while, Elsie let us down very gently—bless her. She pointed out all his confirmation faults, the worst of which were his undescended testicles, but did kindly say how fit and healthy he was, and in lovely condition.

We reared Finn in the same way as the big cats and canines in our care at the zoo, as we were given very little information by his breeders with regards to his feeding regime. His diet consisted of raw horsemeat, fish or chicken with brown bread, cod liver oil, bone meal and any veg scraps left over from our meals. He never had a day's illness in his life, until the very end when he developed a tumour in his jaw. He was almost ten years old when we lost him.

A few months after acquiring Finn, we realized what an amazing breed we had chosen, and became very interested in the showing side of owning a wolfhound. We started to attend Championship Shows all over the country, as our work commitments allowed, to learn as much as we could about the breed. By now we were both Head Keepers, so it was not always possible to have time off together. Attending shows all over the country, each on our own, was not as much fun as going together—we did not know anyone in those days, and were in awe of all the famous kennel owners. After a while, we were fortunate enough to come to know many of the famous pre and post war breeders:

- Mrs Nagle (Sulhamstead).
- Miss Harrison and Miss Atfield (Sanctuary).
- Miss Hudson (Brabyns).
- Elsie James (Boroughbury).
- Mrs Dunlop (Delorne)
- Mrs Pringle (Baldeagle)
- Ruth Jenkins (Eaglescrag)
- Ron & Helen Baird (Outhwaite)
- Bill Siggers (also once kennel manager for J.V. Rank, at the famous Ouborough Kennels of Irish Wolfhounds and Great Danes).

John especially got to know many of the ladies. Who could resist a pleasant young man with a handsome face?

After marrying in 1969, we continued to take a great interest in the breed and dreamed that one day we would own a top quality show hound.

During the '70s, we decided to buy a puppy from the Erindale Kennel of Marge and Roy Saunders. They had a litter planned by *Erindale Adam* x *Ch. Erindale Bernice*. When we went to collect the puppy, to our surprise Marge told us to choose the one we wanted. We chose a very eye-catching, well-balanced cream dog. Also in the litter was a very pretty, little grey bitch who was being registered as *Erindale Louise*. She became the foundation bitch of the Hydebeck Kennel. Her owner, Louise Pinkney—who was still Louise Stanley in those days—always benched next to us at shows. We became good friends, and still are to this day.

Our puppy, *Erindale Phelan*—'Casey'—was to become our first champion. He was a hound who looked good as a youngster, and kept his form all his life. He also adored the show ring, and always gave of his very best. He was not as good a specimen as some of our later dogs, but he was extremely eye catching, a great showman and just sparkled in the ring.

As a youngster, he won the RCC at Crufts under Tom Horner. This was our first important win. I had stayed home with the children, and when John rang to tell me the news, I was so happy I danced all around the house. The children thought I had gone totally mad.

In 1979, Casey won Best in Show at the Border Counties Championship Show, under the famous breed expert Bill Siggers.

'Well done young man,' he said, as he handed John his Rosette. 'He's a grand dog.'

We came to know Bill over the years. He was a real character, and had a wicked sense of humour.

By 1979, we also now had a son of Casey's, *Brooksborne McShaunessy* ('Fergus') and a big cream bitch, *Erindale Phase* ('Kerry'). We had a litter from Kerry, but disappointingly, the puppies' confirmation did not quite come up to our now exacting standards. However, they were an amazingly long-lived litter and all went to wonderful homes. They all lived to almost ten, and one bitch to eleven-and-a-half. Mr and Mrs Cross, the new owners of this bitch, became our very dear friends. They were two of the nicest people one could wish to meet, and our children adored them.

Kerry's top line wasn't quite right, as the rise over the loin started a little too far forward, a confirmation fault she passed on to her pups. This was not important for pet dogs, but not correct for show dogs. So remembering the advice of Judge Tom Horner, which was always to breed from the very best bitch possible, our next move was to find one.

A very good friend of ours, Maggie Brooks, offered us pick of litter bitch from her litter by *Ch. Eaglescrag Lysander* x *Erindale Harmony Queen*. And so, at 12 weeks old, *Brooksborne Carina* came to live with us. She was so lovely we could not believe how lucky we were. She was a sweet natured, but strong willed bitch and should have gained her title easily, but she could be extremely stubborn. Often refusing to move in the show ring, it was very embarrassing at times. Always eager to go to shows, she would trot quite happily to the ring. Then 'the look' would come on her face. Oh God, I would think, she is not going to move today!

I remember Carina refusing to move when being shown under Joe

Braddon, who was another famous old judge. However, he must have seen her trotting quite happily to the ring, as he told John to take her out and go around the outside of the ring, then run her back in and stand her. Sure enough, the naughty madam moved and stood perfectly. It would not be allowed nowadays, but back then many of the old long established judges were a law unto themselves. Carina had so many RCC's we could have papered a wall with them, but sadly she never did gain her title. We had lots of advice from friends and other exhibitors, who thought they could get her to move. John would hand the lead to them with a knowing smile and wish them luck, but they soon gave up when they realized that no amount of talking nicely, being firm or tempting her with morsels of delicious food worked. When Carina said 'No', she meant it.

Fortunately, she made her mark as a Dam and was a wonderful mother, and was Alpha Bitch for many years. The pack did not argue with Carina—her word was law. From her first litter, by *Ch. Erindale Callan Of Finloren*, a handsome wheaten dog puppy we named 'Rogue' was exported to Australia and became *Ch. Brooksborne Rogue*. Carina had some wonderful offspring in her second litter by *Ch. Hydebeck Reginald Snuffson*, who was a grandson of Casey's litter sister, *Erindale Louise*. A bitch puppy from this litter, *Ballyphelan Celtic Song*, went to Norway, and a very handsome dog puppy, *Ballyphelan Celtic Knight*, went to our friend Maggie Brooks. We kept two from the litter, *Ballyphelan Celtic Legend,*—'Saxon'—and *Ballyphelan Celtic Charm*—'Ginty'.

Saxon was a very handsome black dog who, unfortunately, broke a toe as a youngster and consequently we could never show him, as he was never quite sound on that foot. Ginty had won two CCs and three RCCs when one day, when running through a clump of willow trees in our fields, she whacked her tail on one of them. It was so badly damaged it had to be fully amputated so, disappointingly, that was the end of her show career and she never gained her title. It took her a while to adjust after the amputation as, like all wolfhounds, she used her tail to balance when changing direction while running fast. Most of the time our dogs have free access to run in our fields, consequently they are fit and are well muscled. Therefore, they have had the occasional accident when charging about, and whacking themselves and each other. However, we have never wrapped our dogs—or our children—in cotton wool.

We had a third litter from Carina, sired by *Westmount Xile Of Mochras*, and we kept a big wheaten bitch, *Ballyphelan Wild Cherry.* Cherry had a litter by Saxon, and initially was an amazing mother, who was so gentle and careful with her pups. She fed them well, and they were so fat they looked like Elephant Seals. However, after three weeks she decided that she had done her bit, and only under duress would agree to feed and clean them. We have often found that the intense, devoted 'over-the-top' mothers tire of their puppies much quicker than the slapdash ones. A dog puppy, *Ballyphelan Bold Pioneer*, went to Spain and became a Spanish Champion and the only bitch in the litter, *Ballyphelan Black Pearl of Shanimarle*, went to Chris and Janice Taylorson. Having three litters from a bitch is frowned upon now, but she was fit and healthy and we really needed to have offspring by different sires from this beautiful bitch.

In March 1990, the litter of *Ballyphelan Celtic Charm* x *Caredig Yankeedoodle* produced two puppies, *Ballyphelan Cascade Caredig* and *Ballyphelan Cassia*. We called them 'French and Saunders' in the nest, as one was a little roly-poly clown of a pup, and the other was much leaner and of a more serious disposition. Cassia, the tubby one, went as a much-loved pet and Cascade went to live at the Caredig Kennel, with Debbie and Roger Tebbutt, the owners of the sire. Cascade became UK & Irish *Ch. Ballyphelan Cascade Caredig.* She was B.I.S. at the Irish Wolfhound Club Show 1994, and was top wolfhound the same year.

In June 1991, the litter from *Ballyphelan Celtic Charm* x *Ainsea Rifleman* produced strong, powerful puppies with lovely confirmation, and we kept two who became *Ch. Ballyphelan Tarlach Dubh*, and *Ch. Ballyphelan Tiger Lily*. We had great success with these two in the show ring, as not only were they lovey to look at, but also were famous for their wonderful free and active movement.

Then in October 1993, *Ch. Ballyphelan Tiger Lily* x *Ch. Bokra George Caredig* produced an UK all-time record for the breed, with four champions in the same litter: *Ch. Ballyphelan Bran Beag* ('Strider'), owned by Jean and Dave Malley, won 37 CCs and 28 RCCs, and was the top winning wolfhound in 1995. The other three champions were *Ch. Ballyphelan Bara Brith* ('Lizzie'), owned by Chris and Janet Taylorson, *Ch. Ballyphelan Brown Brogue of Monarawn* ('TF'), owned by Malcom and Linda Lees, and *Ch. Ballyphelan Bryn Beran* ('Zac'), kept by us. All four siblings went on to produce outstanding stock of their own.

In March 1995, *Ch. Tiger Lily* x *Bleddyn Blewog O Caredig* produced a small litter of five, of which we kept two—*Ballyphelan Laura Bea* ('Biddy'), and *Ballyphelan Little Bear* ('Jacob'). Biddy won one CC and three RCC's. A bitch puppy, *Ballyphelan Loganberry of Gulgamech* ('Logan')—who I think won eleven RCCs—went to live with our friend Jean Timmins. We showed Jacob as a puppy, but he detested the show ring. He was not being stubborn like Carina, as he did everything John asked of him in the ring, and moved well. He just was not happy and did not enjoy his day at the show at all. If any of our dogs really dislike the show ring, then we stop taking them, whether they show well or not. He was very handsome, and it was such a shame he did not like the ring. However, our obsession for 'fame and glory' comes second to their comfort and wellbeing.

Heartbreakingly, we lost Tiger Lily at the early age of five to an overwhelming lung infection. Our vets fought for three days trying to save her, and cried with us when we made the decision to let her go. We were so utterly devastated at losing her, that we nearly gave up showing and breeding. It was only through the love and support of friends in the breed—talking some sense into us—that we kept the will to carry on. Bless you all, you know who you are. We are eternally grateful to you all.

Lily had been so very special. She was an amazing alpha bitch, who kept order in the pack and with her puppies. Although for the first few days with her first litter, she was a very lackadaisical mother, as she did not bother to clean up after them or keep them clean. They were the smelliest and stickiest pups we ever had, but eventually her brain clicked into caring mode and she became an exemplary mother. I can picture her now eating her food, with a semicircle of pups sitting around the bowl—not daring to go near it—giving little warning growls if they so much as blinked. I can also see her in my mind's eye walking across the field, with the pups walking behind her in a line. She was the only bitch we ever had who was willing to still play and interact with her puppies at twelve weeks of age, and actually teach them some manners.

We have had so many wonderful and much loved dogs over the years—Bravo, Bronty, Branwen, Blue Print, Moon Cloud, Butterfly, Red Admiral, Liquorice (another favourite of mine), Blackthorn, Boatswain (Bo'sun), Wave, Milly, Magic, Raven, Jeni Jones, Davy Jones—who became a German Champion—Black Adder and Black Cap to name but a few.

Ballyphelan Blue Print x *Ballyphelan Boatswain* produced *Ballyphelan The Raven*. She was not the biggest of bitches, but with her jet-black coat and wonderful confirmation, she was lovely. She had one CC, awarded by Mary McBryde, and five RCC's. Had she had a little more length of leg, she probably would have gained her title.

Raven produced a litter of five jet-black puppies in June 2009, sired by *Hazianne's Total Eclipse*. We kept three from that litter; *Ballyphelan Othello*, *Ballyphelan Damson* and *Ballyphelan Nightshade. Ballyphelan Panther Cornovi* went to live with Jean Timmins, and *Ballyphelan Bryony* ('Penguin') became the much-loved pet of Mr & Mrs Taylor. *Ch. Ballyphelan Othello* and *Ballyphelan Damson* were a joy to show. Othello has many winning offspring in the ring, plus two UK Champions at the Hydebeck Kennel, and one USA Champion bred from imported frozen semen by Ellen and Jim Kroll, of the August Kennel. We had a lovely puppy, *Killoughery Braela of Ballyphelan,* ('Sophie'), back as a stud fee from Othello's litter with *Killoughery Teagan* in 2012. Damson was veteran of the year in 2016, and was still winning as a veteran in 2017, as was her litter brother Panther.

Damson produced a lovely litter to *Ch. Rainster Rory*. We kept a bitch, *Ballyphelan Rosy Ryan*, who mated to the American import *Berwyck Arcangelo For Witchesbroom* ('Archie'). She produced an excellent litter in March 2017. Archie was something of an out-cross for us, but had sired excellent puppies to different types of bitches, and his litter with Rosy Ryan did not disappoint.

Our choice of stud dog, over the years, very often depended on what needed improving in the bitch. Although sometimes we would see a dog and just have a gut feeling that that was the one to use. We never went for the latest big winner, unless he had what we needed.

Although we are still both reasonably healthy and active today, we have to be sensible now, as we are now 77 years old. Consequently, this will be our last litter. We decided to keep three puppies from Rosy Ryan's litter—*Ballyphelan Anna Lisa*, *Ballyphelan Anemone* and *Ballyphelan Amadeus*—so we can carry on in the show ring for a few more years yet.

The Dog puppy, Amadeus, was Best Puppy in breed at Manchester Championship Show 2018.

By September 2018, as yearlings, Anna Lisa had won four RCC's and Amadeus one RCC. We did not show them again until Crufts 2019, as they needed to mature a little before going into the Post Graduate Class.

Anna Lisa has really done us proud. To date her achievements are:

- Best Puppy in Show, IW Society Championship Show, Sept 2017
- Best Puppy in Class, IW Society Open Show, Jan 2018
- Best Puppy in Breed, Crufts, 2018 under Chris Amoo
- Best Bitch (82 entered) and her 1st CC, Crufts, 2019, under Roger Tebutt
- 2nd CC, Blackpool Championship Show, June 2019, under Jean Timmins
- Best of Breed and 3rd CC (making her Champion), Paignton Championship Show, August 2019, under Diane Redfern

So there you have The Ballyphelan Story, if just a little condensed. All those years ago, we only wanted one nice wolfhound to show. Never in our wildest dreams did we think it would lead to us having our own Kennel Club prefix, and very successful kennel, and actually judging the breed at home and abroad. We are both so happy to have loved and owned this amazing breed, and we are proud that Ballyphelan has contributed just a little to the breed worldwide.

Fig. IV-1 John with Erindale Phelan ('Casey'), 1979

Fig. IV-2 Brooksborne McShaunessy ('Fergus'), Aston, 1980

Fig. IV-3 Ballyphelan Celtic Legend ('Saxon'), Hafod, 1990

Fig. IV-4 Ballyphelan Celtic Charm ('Ginty'), with her litter by Ainsea Rifleman, Hafod, 1991

Fig. IV-5 John and the Author, with Ch. Tarlach Dubh ('Tarlach'), as an adolescent, at Hafod after winning BIS at the IWC Show, 1991

Fig. IV-6 The Author sleeping with Ch. Ballyphelan Tiger Lily and her litter by Ch. Bokra George Caredig, Hafod, October 1993

Fig. IV-7 Tiger Lily with her pups, now 1 week old, Hafod, October, 1993

Fig. IV-8 John, with Ch. Ballyphelan Bryn Beran ('Zac'), winning BoB at Bournemouth Championship Show, 1995

Fig. IV-9 From left: Zac, Nelly (our rescue Greyhound) and Indy, Hafod, 1996

Fig. IV-10 Zac in the mountains, 1997

Fig. IV-11 Ballyphelan The Raven ('Raven'), Hafod, 2008

Fig. IV-12 Ballyphelan The Raven ('Raven'), Hafod, 2008

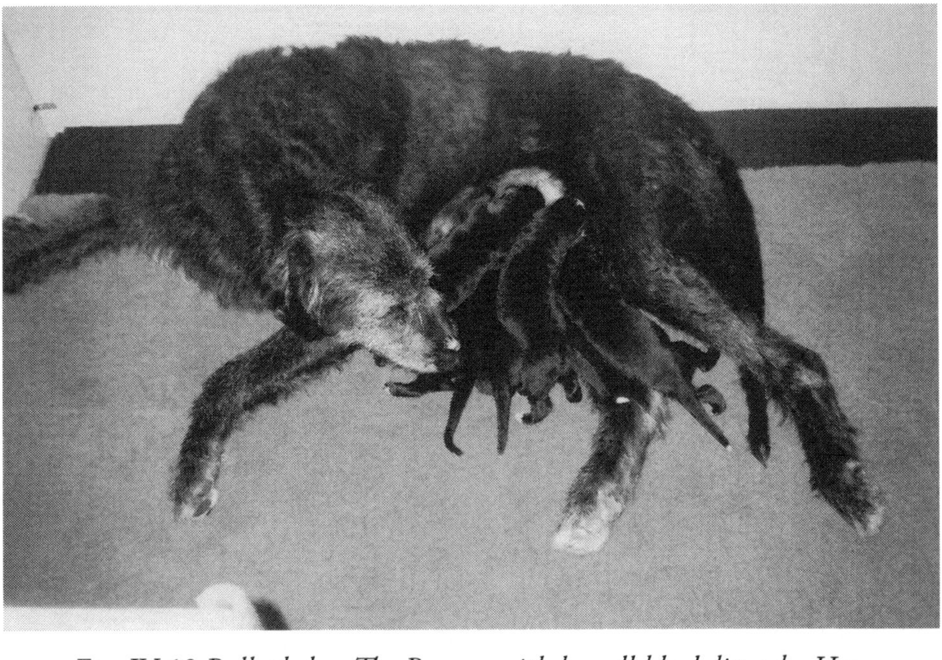

Fig. IV-13 Ballyphelan The Raven, with her all black litter by Hazianne's Total Eclipse, Hafod, 2009

Fig. IV-14 The Black Crew, 10 Weeks Old, Hafod, 2009

Fig. IV-15 Five of the Gang, Hafod

Fig. IV-16 Ballyphelan Bronze Pirate, Hafod, November 1993

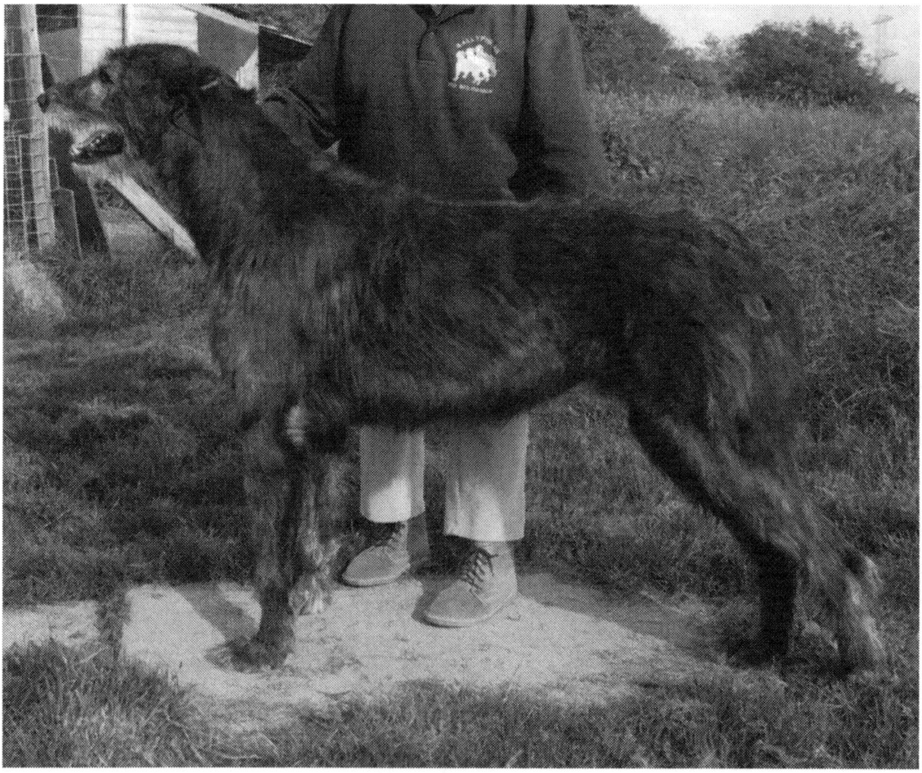

Fig. IV-17 Ch. Ballyphelan Othello, Hafod

Fig. IV-18 Best Pals, Doris and 'Magic' (Ballyphelan Night Magic), Hafod

Fig. IV-19 The troops gathering for their evening walk, Hafod

Fig. IV-20 Treacle's pups in Buttercups, Hafod

Fig. IV-21 Eight dogs in the yard, Hafod

Fig. IV-22 The Author, with Woflhouse Kennels, forest walk, Denmark, 2014

Fig. IV-23 The Author, with Woflhouse Kennels, forest walk, Denmark, 2014

Fig. IV-24 John, with Bo'sun, Hafod

Fig. IV-25 John, with Damson, Hafod

Fig. IV-26 John, with Jack, Hafod

Fig. IV-27 John, with Joseph, Hafod

Fig. IV-28 John, with Magic, Hafod

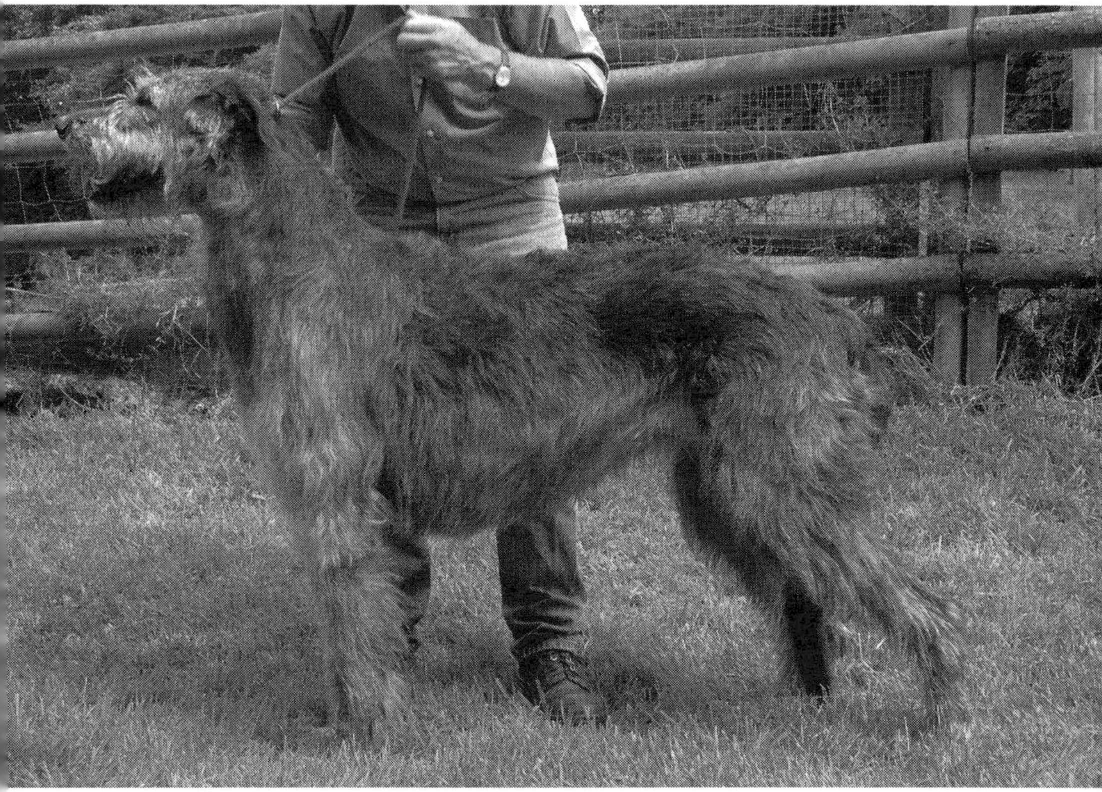

Fig. IV-29 John, with Milly, Hafod

Fig. IV-30 John, with Nightshade, Hafod

Fig. IV-31 John, with Panther, Hafod

Fig. IV-32 John, with Raven, Hafod

Fig. IV-33 John, with Starfish, Hafod

Fig. IV-34 Awards, Hafod